Muslim Minorities in Modern States

Muslim Minorities in Modern States

The Challenge of Assimilation

Raphael Israeli

Routledge
Taylor & Francis Group

LONDON AND NEW YORK

First published 2009 by Transaction Publishers

2 Park Square, Milton Park, Abingdon, Oxfordshire OX14 4RN
711 Third Avenue, New York, NY 10017

Routledge is an imprint of the Taylor & Francis Group, an informa business

First issued in paperback 2017

Library of Congress Catalog Number: 2008031101

Library of Congress Cataloging-in-Publication Data

Israeli, Raphael.
   Muslim minorities in modern states : the challenge of assimilation / Raphael Israeli.
        p. cm.
   Includes bibliographical references and index.
   ISBN 978-1-4128-0875-0 (acid-free paper)
      1. Muslims--Non-Muslim countries. 2. Muslims--Non-Muslim countries--Social conditions. 3. Terrorism--Religious aspects--Islam. 4. Muslims--Cultural assimilation. 5. Culture conflict. I. Title.

BP52.5.I87 2008
305.6'97--dc22

                                                          2008031101

ISBN 13: 978-1-4128-0875-0 (hbk)
ISBN 13: 978-1-138-51243-6 (pbk)

Dedicated to Anat Mishali
The Ultimate Secretary
A Model of diligence, promptness and responsibility
On leaving her position
At the Truman Institute, Hebrew University, Jerusalem
After a quarter century of exemplary service.

Contents

Preface and Acknowledgments

This volume is part of a larger research project on the extraordinary venture of Islam in modern Europe, which can be tackled as a study into the acculturation of an alien minority culture in Christian Europe, but can also be seen as part of the large wave of immigration since World War II whereby the less fortunate, but demographically affluent developing world of the south, has been inexorably attracted towards the prosperous and manpower-hungry countries of the North and the West. It can also be seen, from a historical perspective, as the third Muslim invasion of Europe. The first was that of the Iberian Peninsula in the eighth century, where Islam established a splendid culture and Caliphate until it was repulsed by the Christian *Reconquista* in the fifteenth century, while the second was into the Balkans, up to the gates of Vienna at the end of the fifteenth century, lasting until the end of the Ottoman Empire during World War I.

Granted that the approach to this study also conditions its method of research and its findings, it is important to note that while the mainstay of Islam in Europe will be dealt with other books[*], this volume is concerned with the migration of Islam into the periphery of the Western world, Canada, Australia and Asia, both as extensions of Europe and as a control group to gauge by comparison the fate of the main body of migratory Islam into the West. The chapters that accompany the detailed analysis of the periphery of Islam are but intended to provide a general background in order to acquaint the reader with the *problematique* of Muslim acculturation into European culture and political system.

I am indebted to my home institution, the Harry Truman Research Institute at the Hebrew University in Jerusalem, for all the facilities and services which enabled me to work in full tranquility to complete this book. It was during a sabbatical semester at the Shalom College, the University of New South Wales in Sydney, Australia in early 2006, that this volume took its shape. I thank its director Dr Hilton Immerman and his staff for all their assistance and staunch support.

[*] *The Spread of Islamikaze Terrorism in Europe*, Vallentine Mitchell & Co Ltd., London, 2008. *The Islamic Challenge in Europe*, Transaction Publishers, New Brunswick, NJ, 2008.

As usual, though I vastly benefited from the help and advice of many colleagues, the responsibility for all errors of fact and interpretation rests solely and squarely on my own shoulders.

Jerusalem, Summer 2007

Introduction:
The European and British Perspectives

Europe, like the rest of the world, was stunned by the horrors of September 11. Western delegations and leaders poured into Washington D.C. to present their condolences and sympathies to the United States. But as soon as the US began to react to terrorism by fighting it actively, first in Afghanistan and then in Iraq, it found itself almost alone but for the loyalty of Tony Blair and John Howard, who harnessed the resources of their countries to that battle. Moreover, many Europeans elected their narrow and immediate national interests over the eradication of Saddam's regime, and instead of instilling into their citizenry the need to stand up to the new terrorist barbarians, they behaved like "soft" states that had lost the will to stand up for their values and future. It is worthwhile recalling that in past millennia the rich, powerful, self-assured Empires of Rome, Persia, Byzantium and China had much to lose yet were unwilling to fight anymore. These empires subsequently lost their battles with Vandals, Arabs, Turks, and Mongols (and then the Manchu), respectively, because these had nothing to lose, looked with contempt upon life, but coveted the wealth of their neighbors and concluded that it behoove them to seize it, rather than let it languish in the hands of those declining empires which they ultimately attacked and destroyed.

People should learn, if not from others' experience, then at the very least from their own, from the antecedents that have tormented their own cultures when not heeded by their peers, forebears and cultural equivalents. As we shall see in the chapters that follow, disturbing warning signs developing in Western countries were unnoticed or denied, only to hit also the peripheral areas of the Muslim world. Canada and Australia, and to some extent the countries of Asia, fell into a syndrome of denial until they were shaken up and forced to listen, often at a price. At the core of the Muslim presence in Europe are countries like Britain, France and Germany, for example, which were lacking in law-enforcement against terrorists since the executive and judiciary systematically preferred hu-

1

man rights, and apparent safety by appeasement, over defensive measures to protect their citizens and way of life. Muslim immigrants, many of whom were accustomed to the often abusive law of their countries of origin, flooded by the millions to the heart of Europe; but even as clear threats of *Jihad* were heard in London and Paris, these threats were for the most part ignored by European governments.

The writing was on the wall, but the Britsh Home Secretary Jack Straw, for example, failed to read, see and hear it. His liberal policy, for which he was to repent only too late, was more convenient to embrace, rather than to heed the menace of terror. In so doing, he acted irresponsibly, and that is the only yardstick to judge a government: not by its liberal intentions, good-hearted policies or idealistic values, but by its failure to defend its citizens, by allowing terrorists to abuse Britain by wreaking havoc on its citizens, and by its myopic understanding of the growing Muslim threat permitted through his ideological blinders. It is a fact that too little and too late the same British government has had to reverse its policies and to seek even harsher measures than public opinion or Parliament would allow, which is an indication of its inability to foresee what was coming and to prepare its citizenry before terror struck.[1]

The United States was no different, for in spite of the documentary evidence gathered on film by Steven Emerson in the early 1990s under the threatening heading of *Jihad in America,* the US approach to potential terrorists was very human and liberal: Muslim associations were allowed to collect money under the cover of "charitable" institutions, and even to conduct military training with live ammunition, which Emerson documented in New Jersey, partly under the doctrinal supervision of the blind Sheikh Abdul Rahman, a fugitive from Egyptian law. While these goings-on were not sufficient to awaken the FBI to its responsibilities of internal security, the first attempted sabotage of one of the Twin Towers in 1993 brought about the arrest of Sheikh Abdul Rahman who had masterminded it.

Both models of Western democracy, the United States and Great Britain, needed a traumatic jolt before they moved to act. In the US, it would be the watershed event of September 11, 2001; in London, the July 7, 2005 bombings. And in other countries: in Spain, the March 2004 Madrid train bombings; in France, the violent riots of 2005; in Amsterdam, the van Gogh murder; in Asia, the Bali horror; and finally in Scandinavia, the Cartoon Affair. In all these instances, the jolt would be brutal for it would shatter the *naivete* of European populations who had believed in peaceful coexistence with their Muslim immigrant populations and in the feasibility of their integration into the European cultural and societal tissue.

Take, for example, the case of Abu Hamza al-Masri who took refuge in Britain in 1994. He never hid his destructive intentions and his subversive plans, but was not heeded until convicted in early 2006, for the very same crimes that he committed throughout the previous decade. That means that what has changed is not the man or his deeds, but the permissive attitude of Jack Straw and his likes, which was reversed by the London terror of July 2005. Abu Hamza, of Egyptian origin, arrived in London and became the Imam of the Finsbury Park Mosque. He headed the *Ansar al-Shari'a* (supporters of the *Shari'a),* a movement which would have surely been outlawed in Cairo, and wherein he promulgated the cause of the violent Algerian Armed Islamic Groups (GIA). Both his native Egypt and the Yemen demanded his extradition. He emerged from a background of moral corruption, something that is sure to have made him more radical than others, as if he wished to catch up on his "lost" years.[2] Thereafter he moved to Afghanistan with his family prior to the *Taliban* regime at a time when the *Islamikaze*[3] camps were disseminated throughout the various domains of the regional warlords.[4] He fought against withdrawing Soviet forces and was severely injured by a landmine which removed both his hands and destroyed one of his eyes.

In 1994, Abu Hamza, a civil engineer by training, found refuge in London at a time when the entire West was off guard with respect to the international Islamic terrorist networks that were being erected in its midst. And there he founded his *Ansar al-Shari'a* organization. Reminiscing about that period, he complained that while he had never lived off his hosts' money, those British "Infidels" levied heavy taxes on him when he worked for them as an engineer, and therefore, that justified his latter attacks against the West which "had plundered the lands of Islam". He never explained why he chose to live in the land of his alleged "robbers", unless we take his words at face value: "I am a cripple and I use their country to spread good, to counter the British authorities who use it to spread corruption". In spite of his continuous complaints that he was persecuted by the authorities, his Muslim activities went unhindered, until he was briefly arrested in May 1999 and then released, and finally arrested again in May 2004, and indicted and convicted in 2005-6 in the aftermath of the London bombings. On his Internet site he claimed that Yemen was the best launching pad after Afghanistan for the Islamic Revolution which was to spread worldwide.[5] And it was from Yemen that he directed his attention in 1998 after having left his London mosque to take care of his "Aden Abyan Muslim Army". He apparently masterminded an abortive attempt against the life of the Yemeni President and the kidnapping of foreign tourists. In a press conference which he conducted in London in January 2000, he called for the overthrow of the Yemeni regime and urged foreign visitors to leave Yemeni soil. And in a letter to the London-based Arabic daily *al-Hayat,* he warned the Ambassadors of Britain and the US that they should leave the Yemen, lest a painful strike against "the enemies of Islam" might be carried out against them. He also attacked Arab monarchs and depicted the deceased King Hussein of Jordan as "roasting in Hell".[6]

Al-Masri has also shown aggressive concern for Muslim communities under pressure or threat. In 1999 he convened a conference on Chechnian Muslims, and incited his audience against a group of Russian reporters who were on hand to cover the debates. On the same occasion he voiced support for the Chechnian attacks in Moscow in the summer of that year.[7] All this took place under the open eyes of the British authorities who saw not and cared not, foolishly believing that words did not hurt and deeds would not follow that incitement, contrary to all known precedents of hate-literature, anti-Semitism and terrorism, where defining and de-humanizing the enemy is a precursor to de-legitimizing and ultimately using violence against him. Somehow, Jack Straw assumed that Britain was immune to that law. Abu-Hamza's choice of the Yemen as the ideal place to launch the Muslim Revolution emanated from the fact that it was the only country in the Arabian Peninsula that had not yet "surrendered to the United Snakes [*sic*] of America", and he was certain that after the take-over of that country by the Islamists, other countries would fall as the domino effect unfolded. He denied in one of his interviews that he had called upon his followers to kill foreigners in the Yemen, specifying that he meant Infidels, unless they converted to Islam, paid the poll tax (*jizya*) that *dhimmis* (protected non-Muslims) were obliged to under the rules of the *dhimma,* or entered into a pact that guaranteed their safety in *Shari'a* country. Otherwise, he asserted, "their blood and wealth are not protected". He admitted that he had also operated from Algeria and Egypt, but because reform there was impossible from within due to the corrupt regimes in place, he came to the conclusion that only a Muslim invasion from outside would trigger the Islamic Revolution and the war-ranted change. And that invasion he envisaged as stemming from the Yemen, and then fanning out worldwide.[8]

Abu-Hamza's work consisted not only of promoting Muslim terror-ism, recruiting volunteers, indoctrinating others and collecting funds for Muslim organizations, but he also launched a campaign to recruit, convert and train British Muslims, which he was sure British suicidal liberalism would swallow and ignore. For that purpose he held "Islamic camps", usually in the grounds of his mosque, offering "military training for brothers, self-development skills, martial arts, map-reading etc." aimed at distracting the 30 young men in attendance from "television and the obscenity of Christmas". Incidentally, the website that carried this announcement was decorated with a picture of a hand grenade.[9] Some of those trainees found their way to Afghanistan and were killed there, but this did not come to the media attention until after the horrors of September 11.[10] During the Second Conference of the Islamic Movements held in London in February 1999, Abu-Hamza told the gathering of 500 Muslims of a plan to "blow up civil and military aircraft, so as to challenge Western monopoly of the skies". He even gave details of "new flying mines connected to balloons, currently being experimented on in Afghanistan" and hinted that sometime in the future such an operation would be carried out against Britain or the US.[11] But the British authorities, it seems, "thought" that he was "hallucinating" and elected to look the other way. There are indications that Abu Hamza knew of the upcoming September 11 plan; that he was involved in masterminding a scheme to kill President Bush during the G-8 meeting in Genoa two days before the New York attack so that an America in disarray over the death of its President would be less able to respond to September 11; and that he held a meeting in his mosque in London on 29 June 2001, where the idea of attacks using aircraft was raised.[12]

The most relevant aspect of Abu-Hamza from the western point of view is his encouragement of violence, which he cultivated and elevated into an ideology in its own right. His advocated use of violence had a two-pronged purpose: to topple existing regimes in the Arab and Islamic worlds in order to replace them with Islamist governments—that is, militant, extremist Islamic regimes which apply *Shari'a* Law, unlike the "godless" regimes which Abu-Hamza accused of "having sold out to the West" - and to boost the diffusion of Islam in the world. At a gathering in early 1999 commemorating the removal of the last Ottoman Caliph by Kemal Attaturk, the father of modern Turkey, he openly urged Muslims to resort to the sword in order to achieve his blueprint for domestic and international upheaval. One of his supporters, Muhammed Yussuf, seconded his mentor's ideas by urging his followers not only to fight back against the West in the Balkans and the Middle East, but also to establish a "strong fifth column" within the western world,[13] something that would have explained his own self-imposed "exile" in London and his cultivation of violent Islam there. But Jack Straw was still deep in slumber, and he neither saw nor heard. In 2001 Abu-Hamza became involved in a press debate geared to "clear" his name from the "abominable accusation" that he had relinquished the use of violence, something that would have been antithetical to the nature of his struggle. Indeed, according to the London-based *al-Quds al-Arabi*, Abu-Hamza had been "accused" by Abdul-Hakim Dyab, another Egyptian fundamentalist ex-patriot who also found asylum in London, of having dismissed a *fatwa* (religious verdict) of the Palestinian radical cleric, Abu Qatada, that Muslims should kill the wives and children of Egyptian police and army officers as part of the struggle against the existing Arab regimes.[14] Naturally, Abu-Hamza denied this allegation and defied his accuser.

The accusation was too much of an affront for Abu-Hamza. In his rebuttal in the same paper, he said that he did not recognize the term "violence" because it had become a weapon used by the world media to designate anyone who defends his faith and honor against existing Arab regimes which rule through "legislative and oppressive measures". Therefore, the very term "violence" seemed deceptive in his eyes and incompatible with Islamic religious law and the struggle for the survival of Islam. He asserted that *mujahideen* had never recognized that term because it was the ruling regimes who utilized it to sustain their own monopoly in their own use of terrorism while conversely using it to eliminate the Muslim religious precept of "doing good and avoiding evil" (this, as interpreted by the terrorists themselves whereby their own Muslim "terrorist" behaviour was considered as "good", while consequently, any attempt to fight it was inherently "evil"). This thinking also helps explain why, for the Muslim radicals, the western definition of terrorism is unacceptable inasmuch as it addresses itself to a means of combat or struggle (namely acting against innocent civilians to attain a political goal), instead of addressing the core issue of the struggle, that is, Islamic "good" against Western or anti-Islamic "evil". It is instructive to heed Abu-Hamza's own words:

> As a rule, Islam teaches that those holding opinions different from one's own should be treated gently and with flexibility, provided they are willing to listen and comply, and provided that one's tolerant efforts do not lead to a blurring of rights and borders.... Treating gently anyone who blocks his ears and forces perversion, heresy, abomination and humiliation upon Muslims in their own countries by the use of force, is a kind of idiocy and loss of rights and of religious precepts.... What can be said of Arab regimes which have enacted abominable laws, implemented them, and used tax moneys to finance military personnel for the protection of such abominations,

instead of protecting Jerusalem and its people? . . . This is the mark of Cain, which is unprecedented in the history of Egypt.[15]

According to such analysis, Islam is thus tolerant only as long as the challenger to its rules ultimately accepts it and complies with it. For Islam alone can define right and wrong, holy and profane, acceptable and abominable, and anyone opposing it is no longer to be subject to the "gentle treatment and flexibility" suggested in al-Masri's definition of "tolerance". Getting to the point of the use of violence, that he had been "outrageously accused" of having abandoned, he stated:

> My position is as clear as the sun, praised be Allah, and it will not change... I do not recognize the term "violence" and will not agree to abandon jihad or to sign a truce with the regimes of the tyrants. As Allah said: "Fight them so there will be no internal strife (fitna) and so that their religion will be Allah's religion". The Muslim nation to which I belong cannot come to terms with anyone who does not have mercy on and respect for the people.... Physical exile, far from my homeland, is much easier for me and for many like me than the exile of our souls, the slaughter of our faith and of our values, and the amputation of our tongues as the price for returning to our homeland.….. [16]

And finally, in defense of Islamic violence *(jihad)* against the West, he had this to say to the *Christian Science Monitor*:

> It was when the Americans took the knife out of the Russians [in Afghanistan] and stabbed us in the back.... In the meantime they were bombing Iraq and occupying the Arabian Peninsula, and then with their witch-hunt against mujahideen, everything became clear: it was a full-scale war.... The Americans wanted to fight the Russians with Muslim blood and they could justify that only by invoking the word jihad. Unfortunately for everyone, except Muslims, when the button of jihad is pushed it is not eradicated that easily. It continues and continues until the Muslim Empire swallows every other existing Empire.... I do not condone what happened [on September I I] nor do I condemn it. If somebody has done that just for mundane gain and political advancement, then obviously it is a cheap cause. But if it was done because people are desperate and their lives have been threatened, then it is a respectable cause.... Then those people who carried out the attacks would be martyrs. Martyrdom is the highest form of Jihad, and if you do things for the cause of Allah, losing your life for it is the most sublime expression of faith. This is in the Qur'an. America thinks it [life] comes first, but Muslims believe that Believers come first. When you damage a people and they have no home and no hope, and their babies and children are killed, then they retaliate. America took decisions to give arms to certain people and take arms away from others. What happened yesterday would be self-defense.... I have sympathy for the victims, but also for Bin Laden who is the victim of an American witch-hunt, but who is unable to commit an act like this, though he probably has millions of sympathizers [who could have done it].[17]

Abu-Hamza al-Masri's was not the only writing on the wall that was ignored by the British authorities who in their blindness elected to regard as mere rhetoric his ominous deeds that amounted to warnings of what was to come. Sheikh Umar al Bakri, of Syrian origin, who also sought and obtained asylum in Britain, was no less dangerous nor less unclear in his designs. He too, in flight from the oppression in his own country, fled to the freedom of Europe with the plan to undermine it from within, without arousing the suspicions of the complacent West. In London, he founded a local branch of the Palestinian-based *Hizb al-Tahrir* (Liberation Party) and also *Jama'at al-Muhajirun* (Association of Immigrants).[18] He has occasionally introduced himself to interlocutors as a spokesman for Osama Bin Laden's *International Islamic Front for Jihad against Jews and Crusaders,* dubbed al-Qa'ida, which is known to have raised funds for the Hamas, Islamic Jihad and Hizbullah, and recruited volunteers to train for *Islamikaze* attacks. He left Syria for Beirut following the bloodbath of the Muslim Brotherhood uprising in Hama in 1982. Then, under the name of Umar Fistuk he established his *Muhajirun* group in Jeddah, Saudi Arabia, as a front for the Liberation Party which spread thereafter to Europe, especially among the large concentrations of Muslims in Lille, France and Hannover, Germany, with headquarters in Hamburg. In all, some 47 Muslim organizations in Western Europe come under the heading of the Liberation party.[19] In 1985 he was evicted by the Saudis, landing in London where he fell into disagreement with his fellow Party members who wished to focus on the revival of the Caliphate, while he meddled in all manner of Muslim organizations.

In 1996 Bakri applied for British citizenship having become a legal resident three years previously. Since that time he has preached in London mosques and delivered fiery sermons to Muslim assemblies, the largest of which convened in Trafalgar Square and the Wembley Stadium. He founded the *Khilafa* (Caliphate) Publishing House and claims service in the *Shari'a* Court of the United Kingdom. In an interview with the *Daily Mirror he* admitted that he lived on a weekly state allowance of 300 pounds sterling to provide for his family of eight, rationalizing that "Islam permits me to take the benefits the system offers. I am fully eligible. It is very difficult for me to find a job. Anyway, most of the leadership of the Islamic Movement [in Britain] is on state benefit".[20] But after seven radical terrorists, some of them Egyptians, were arrested in Britain in September 1998, Bakri began attacking his benefactors unabashedly, denouncing Great Britain as the "spearhead of blasphemy that seeks to overthrow the Muslims and the Islamic Caliphate". He explained that the arrested Egyptians were political refugees who were not involved in terrorist activities and that the Muslims in Great Britain "condemned the barbaric acts of the British government against innocent Muslims who... were lulled and betrayed into believing they could seek sanctuary in Britain from their corrupt regime."[21]

This reversal of allegiance characterizes the behavior of Muslim terrorists who sought refuge in the detested West which they endeavour to undermine, even though mostly on the run from their own home regimes that they had unsuccessfully tried to topple. Since they are persuaded that they fight for the Path of Allah, they certainly do not regard themselves as terrorists, and when they are arrested for terrorist activities within their host countries which had generously, naively and self-defeatingly given them shelter and provided for their needs, they accuse their benefactors and condemn their "barbaric behavior". This mechanism of denial, which posits Western democracy as just a cow to be milked, owing them sustenance while they owe it nothing, allows them to deny the good and the protection they receive and to even create subversive cells that are liable to act in the heart of their countries of refuge, this all taken as a right to wreak havoc and cause terror in the nations that took them in, despite their repeated commitments to refrain from political or subversive activity as a condition for being accorded the status of refugees.[22] Denial was exhibited by Western chanceries as well, with the belief that if they were benevolent towards Muslim refugees, they would encounter exemplary behavior on their part in return. Even the al-Qai'da entrenchment in the US and Europe, with their illicit activities committed under various guises, was not enough to stir suspicions and to instigate the slumbering Western governments to take measures of self-defense, until the Muslim radicals struck, first in America then in Europe. The new Muslim terrorists put on the West the blame for rescuing them from their own corrupt regimes; so, the host countries which have tried to fight terrorism after their belated awakening, stand accused of racism, of an "anti-Islamic" drive, and of inhumanity and the like. The democratic countries sheltering , and then absorbing these streams of "refugees" now became the "oppressors" of the poor and peaceful Muslims, in kind with the oppressive countries of Saudi Arabia, Egypt and others.[23]

Building tensions between Bakri and his peers on the one hand, and the British authorities on the other, did not begin with the September 11 events nor with the awakening of Europe to the danger of international terror that was being posed by the growing, and increasingly radicalized, foreign Muslim population. Already during the Gulf War of the early 1990s the British MI5 had interrogated Bakri for his alleged call to assassinate British Prime Minister John Major. Indeed, Bakri was cited by the British press as declaring that Major was a "legitimate target. If one gets the opportunity to assassinate him ... it is our Islamic duty and we will celebrate his death."[24] Bakri declared that he had been misquoted, specifying that Major would have been a legitimate target only if he "set foot in a Muslim country", and that applied to Tony Blair his successor as well, confirming that, in such a case, he would not condemn the killers.[25] The lenient British, instead of making it clear that they rejected the Muslim way of assassinating rivals as a legitimate comment on current politics, let things go and forgivingly dismissed that threat to the British political system and way of life. But similar Islamic patterns of behavior were not slow in coming to the surface and ultimately, but belatedly, subsequent events convinced even the most diehard liberals to tighten the rules and supervision of these potentially subversive elements. Indeed, a spokesman for the *Muhajirun* in England, Salim abd al-Rahman, also announced after September 11 that Tony Blair had become a legitimate target for Muslims because of the British attacks on Afghanistan. In his words:

> Now that the Americans, the British and probably the French, have begun to bomb Muslims in Afghanistan, henceforth government buildings and military installations in Britain, even 10 Downing St, have become legitimate targets. If any Muslim wants to kill him [the PM] or get rid of him, I would not shed a tear for him. In the Islamic view, such a man would not be punished for his deeds but would be praised.[26]

In December 2000 Bakri went to Birmingham, under the open eye of the British security apparatus, to preach his brand of Islamic radicalism. He was so sure of himself, and of the numbing British indolence at the time, that he gave an interview to the local newspaper explaining that he had come to Birmingham to recruit volunteers not only for his *Muhajirun* group, but also to fight for the Muslim cause in such foreign countries as Kashmir, Afghanistan and Chechnia. He emphasized that in Britain there were only "physical training camps", but that volunteers were sent out from Britain for military training in South Africa, Nigeria, Afghanistan, Kashmir and the US.[27] This cleric, who depended for his living on the generosity of the British government's welfare system, admitted in another interview that he was involved in financing the training of volunteers for his *jihad* network; these were then dispatched to the US, taking advantage of the fact that training with firearms and live ammunition was more readily available there than in Britain. The rationale was simple: "As they [the British] started to label us as terrorists when we went to Afghanistan, we now go on to the US." He gave details of that training: the use of firearms and explosives, surveillance and other skills, in order to join *jihad* fighting in countries such as Chechnia, Palestine, Kashmir, and South Lebanon. He emphasized that the choice of the battle arena depended on each individual fighter. He stressed that the US training camps were run by private firms in states like Michigan and Missouri, and that the Muslim recruits came from various countries but held European or American citizenship and therefore did not need visas. Recruits stayed for periods ranging from one week to three months.[28]

With the *nonchalance* impossible in an Arab or Muslim setting, and borne out of the absolute certainty of the Muslims in the West that their western nationality gave them immunity, they felt it incumbent upon themselves to assert their *(jihadist)* duty to subvert their countries of asylum, Bakri made explicit his military activities:

> It is not illegal. We are not hiding anything. It should be looked at with an open mind. We are talking purely about helping people who would like to train. The skills they learn are part of the religious obligations every Muslim has. A Muslim must have military training at least once in his lifetime.[29]

But lest the reader think that only military training *per se* was imperative for Muslims in their lands of dwelling and citizenship, a clarification followed: "In Muslim countries we can fulfill this obligation by joining the national armies. But some Muslims would not want to join British or American troops and would rather go to an independent training camp. Why call this terrorist training? All Americans can learn how to shoot, so what happens when this American happens to be a Muslim? Unless, of course, you consider us second- or third class citizens."[30] The answer to those questions came 15 months later, on September 11, 2001. In other press interviews Bakri admitted that the International Islamic Front Against Jews and Crusaders (IIP), created by Bin Laden, and with which he was himself connected, supported Hamas and Islamic Jihad, the acknowledged masters of *Islamikaze* in Palestine. The Front collected funds for them, recruited "militiamen" and took care of their propaganda needs in Europe. Bakri related that in October 2000 alone, the month the al-Aqsa *Intifadah* was picking up steam against Israel, British "volunteers" were recruited and sent to Jordan where they awaited "opportunities to infiltrate the West Bank" and join the Palestinian outburst of violence. He said that more recruits were sent to Lebanon, training in Palestinian refugee camps with a view to opening up a new front against Israel in the southern part of the country. He confirmed that his group, the IIP, maintained connections with Hizbullah and other Islamic movements such as *Usbat al-Ansar (The Faction of Supporters* [of Islam]) which are committed to fight for the "liberation of Jerusalem".[31] Bakri was also active on the Asian front. He claimed that it was he who recruited Muhammed Bilal to carry out the *Islamikaze* attack in Srinagar in Indian Kashmir in December 2000, where a number of Indian soldiers were killed, that he also trained Bila's brothers and cousins for similar operations, and that Bilal's parents were "proud of their son's sacrifice". According to him, he additionally recruited 600 British Muslims in universities and mosques to fight in Kashmir, and some media attributed to him the financing (again he, who lived off British unemployment and social welfare benefits) of *al-Madad* (literally "assistance" or "supplies") organization which, together with other groups, has recruited 2000 other young men across Britain.[32]

Bakri's activities in Asia also encompassed the Malay Muslim rebel minority in southern Thailand, where reports surfaced about foreign supporters who "provided money and training to southern separatists", and about a training farm 20 kilometers from the Malay border linked with "the Middle East and with radical Muslims based in London", one of whose foreign supporters was Bakri.[33] He voiced his support for aircraft hijackings and in an interview gave his harrowing judgment on the worth of Muslim blood compared to that of others:

> The Islamic Movement has the right to sacrifice whomever it sees fit. The rule is that children, women and the weak should not be targeted, except in one situation: if it is difficult to win without sacrificing them. So, if hijackers find [Muslim] women, children and elderly people on the [hijacked] plane, they should set them free except if the goal of the hijackers is to free other [Muslim] women, children or elderly people held prisoners in other countries. In this case they can be kept because the blood of Muslims is equal, but they can sacrifice foreigners on the plane... If you study Shari'a, you will know that. The ransom of a Muslim is 12,000 dirham while that of a dhimmi (Christian or Jew) is 4000 dirham.[34]

Bakri's renown as the "leader of the Islamic movements" is widespread in the Islamic world.[35] Although he denied any organizational or hierarchical link to Bin Laden, he has repeatedly declared that they were both committed to the same ideology, but he objected to defining Bin Laden as a terrorist, explaining that "if one supports Muslims against the occupying forces in Somalia or Arabia I will never call him a terrorist. I will call him a freedom fighter. I will call him a hero".[36] After the bombing of US embassies in Saudi Arabia and East Africa in 1998, Bakri insisted that even if it were proven that Bin Laden was responsible, "those still remained legitimate acts" because the US troops in the Gulf were there to fight against Muslims and Islam, and it was therefore the duty of every Muslim to fight them. He cited the US bombing of Sudan and Afghanistan, the war against Iraq, and the US "blind support" for Israel, as "acts of war against Allah and his Prophet".[37] Following the US missile attack on Sudan and Afghanistan as a result of the 1998 destruction of the American Embassies in Tanzania and Kenya, Bakri read a statement to the Italian press, allegedly coming directly from Bin Laden:

> The war has begun. Our response to the barbaric bombardment against Muslims of Afghanistan and Sudan will be ruthless and violent.... Our response could happen in any corner of the world. Retaliation for the US attacks will end only when the last American soldier has left Saudi Arabia and the Gulf, and when the embargo against Iraq is over.... We will not accord a truce to America . . . [38]

In July 1999 Bakri published a letter to Bin Laden on his *Muhajirun* website, calling upon him to act against the West. And though the letter was removed from the site following a US protest, it was read out in mosques in London, Bradford, Sheffield and Leicester. Bakri warned in his letter that the Islamic movements had not used the "real weapon" yet, and addressed Bin Laden thus:

> Oh Osama!.... You and your brothers are now breathing new life and dignity into the body of the umma.... Our main mission as Muslims is to carry the Islamic message to the entire world.... We are an umma of jihad, and beyond doubt we have been chosen by Allah to lead the whole world if we hold to His command . .. The opportunity is here and we must not miss it.... Our Muslim brothers are firm in their jihad so we must not lose time aimlessly and act now..... Oh, Osama! Let us hear the good news from you and your brothers, for a new dawn is near at hand.[39]

Allegedly, that letter was heeded by Bin Laden and answered in a circular read out in mosques in London and Pakistan. Another letter by Bin Laden to Bakri was faxed in the summer of 1998 and later published in the *Los Angeles Times*. It allegedly contained the four specific objectives of *jihad* against the US: "bring down their airlines, prevent the safe passage of their ships, occupy their embassies and force the closure of their companies and banks".[40] Had the West heeded those threats and arrested those dangerous Muslim operatives, instead of sheltering them in its cities and letting them foment incitement and hatred in their midst, the events of September 11 might never have taken place. Journalists like Steve Emerson in the US and a handful of academic writers who were warning during those years against the impending explosion of Muslim radical rage, were dismissed as alarmist, hysterical, racist and Islamophobic. Even when, on occasion, a security apparatus in the West learned about the facts, it misinterpreted them and rejected them in disbelief, thus allowing one of the greatest strategic surprise attacks in modern times to come to pass, while the prosperous, complacent, hypocritical, shortsighted and sycophantic West, with the exception of the US, looked on indolently and helplessly, although it had itself unwittingly bred the catastrophe by naively allowing in the Trojan horse, leaving itself open and vulnerable when the hidden fighters surged forth and attacked.

Bakri, being at the time perhaps the most virulent and dangerous western-based spokesman of the world war that radical Islam has declared against the West, made no effort to hide his program. Not only did he side openly with Bin Laden, and recruit and indoctrinate would-be *Islamikaze* in the heart of the West and in Islamic countries further afield, but he did not relent from his open campaign of hatred against Jews, and then the West in general, when the latter did not react decisively in response to this threat. His posters "Kill the Jews!" were plastered on the walls around him, and to escape punishment he claimed that those were the words of the "Holy Scriptures", not his own.[41] He accused Jews of exploiting the Holocaust to achieve "hegemony over Muslims" and insisted that far worse war crimes had been perpetrated by others against Muslims in Chechnia, Kashmir, Palestine than those of which Muslims were accused in other parts of the globe.[42] He also said that he had no problems with Jewish communities as such, only against Israel, which was a "cancer in the heart of the Islamic world", and which therefore had to be "eradicated and removed". He told his followers demonstrating in front of the Regent's Park Mosque upon the outbreak of the al-Aqsa *Intifadah,* that "all Israeli targets are legitimate for you. All Israelis must be destroyed".[43] His campaign of incitement extended to the suggestion that all homosexuals ought to throw themselves down from the top of London's Big Ben.[44]

The most relevant aspect of Bakri's teachings, however, as far as use of violence is concerned, is his reliance on *jihad.* In a document entitled *"Jihad"* which he posted on the *Muhajirun* website, he offered a lengthy analysis of what he meant:

> Jihad, as a term, cannot be translated as "Holy War", nor can it be translated as "struggle" .... At best, its legal meaning can be understood as "using military force where diplomacy fails, to remove the obstacles the Islamic state faces in carrying its ideology to mankind.... The aim of jihad, unlike the Crusades, past and present, is not forcibly to convert to Islam the inhabitants of other lands.

> Rather, it is to provide them with the security that comes from the application of Islam, leaving them the choice of adopting Islam or keeping their own religions.... History confirms that this is, and always has been, the role of jihad, for it was in Muslim Spain that the Muslims, Christians and Jews could live peacefully under an Islamic authority.... The difference between the use of force by the West and Islam is that the capitalist West uses violence covertly and overtly for the benefit of a few, such as corporations, while Islam uses force openly and justly to carry its mercy to

others.... Jihad is one of the Pillars of Islam after tawhid (the assertion of the unity of Allah) and da'wa (proselytizing)![45] In fact jihad is daw'a by the Islamic state and its foreign policy.[46]

Unlike his fellow expatriate, Abu-Hamza, who posited the Yemen as the launching pad for the impending Islamic revolution, or al-Qa'ida leaders who relied on the *Taliban* regime to kindle the world fire, Bakri thought it must all start in London, thus lending *ex post facto* rationale to his exile there. He aspired to establish a world Islamic Caliphate, starting in the United Kingdom, as the first Islamic state in a new world order. Thus, he conveniently called British law and democracy that had allowed him to take up refuge there in the first place, "phony rules" made up by the "monkeys in Parliament".[47] Indeed, he stated unequivocally to *Le Monde* his intention to "make the flag of Islam fly high at 10 Downing St and at the Elysee". In his view, "Islam is the supreme ideology facing an immoral West. . . and all contemporary leaders of the Islamic world, with no exception, are pawns of the West".[48] In interviews and public lectures by Bakri, he made his doctrine clear and explicit:

> With thanks to Allah, we bring peace to all, and we help the world realize that Islam is the only way of life.... Terrorism according to the West is defined as "the systematic use of violence to achieve political or religious goals", but al-Muhajirun define terrorism as "an attack without the divine right".... Clinton is a target of jihad, and American forces are a target of jihad wherever they are.... The American people must reconsider their foreign policy, or their children will be sent back to them in coffins.... Clinton is responsible and he will pay.... The existence of Israel is a crime and must be removed.... Our duty is to work to establish a Muslim state anywhere in the world, even in Britain.... Life is protected under us. There will be no minorities or majorities as in America. Anti-Semitism in America is disgraceful. Synagogues and Churches will flourish in the Islamic Caliphate, as long as they yield to Islamic Law.... We restored life for the Jews after the Crusades, and we plan to do so again.... What President Clinton and Prime Minister Barak are doing [that is, negotiating peace] is putting themselves in the position of Allah, therefore they are now in a direct war with the people who believe in Allah.... [49]

The horrors of September 11 neither surprised Bakri, who had been consistently preaching for action of this sort, nor generated any remorse in him. Quite the contrary, he regarded them as "compensation for the atrocities the United States committed against Islam",[50] and warned that should the US attack the *Taliban* in reprisal the "verdict of Allah" would descend on American installations which would become legitimate targets. He exhorted all Muslims to unite in the fight, sacrifice themselves and their wealth in order to enter Paradise, and to "make clear the difference between truth and falsehood, belief and heresy, oppressors and oppressed, the Alliance of Satan and that of Allah".[51] After the beginning of the US attack on Afghanistan, Bakri issued a *fatwa* against Pakistani President Musharraf and other Muslim leaders who permitted their territories to be used by the Americans against a fellow Muslim state. The verdict stated:

> There is no doubt that America has attacked, and is still attacking, the Muslims in every place and is carrying out massacres against them.... It is the obligation of all Muslims to be in a state or war against it. The minimal obligation is a total boycott, by means of annulling diplomatic relations.... The only ones who claim that diplomatic relations are permitted are the clerics and the treacherous sultans; most of them are donkeys bearing books, and some behave like dogs. They have renounced the verses of Allah and have become like dogs that should be left to pant, as a place is already reserved for them, surely on the lowest level of the fires of hell.... Those people are heretics *(murtaddun)*, if they were Muslims at all in the first place. They are all involved in the war against Islam and Muslims, and therefore the sentence of *murtadd harbi* (a heretic who should be fought) applies to them.[52]

Viewed against this background of blatant intolerance and aggression, the soothing, even sycophantic declarations made by the Prince of Wales *vis-a-vis* Islam not only sound hollow, naive and offensive to intelligence, but especially counter-productive, because when words of provocation and utter rejection of the other are countered with benevolent acceptance, appeasement and ignorance, they can only invite more friction, aggression and conflict. Remember Munich? In fact, sitting on a divan inside a Bedouin tent, the Prince of Wales called for greater respect between religions and gave warning that too much literal interpretation of religious tenets could lead to fundamentalist extremism, as if current interpretations of Islam were not yet already contaminated by extremism. How does he know and under what authority does he speak? His plea for "understanding and tolerance" was familiar, an echo of his recent calls to senior Muslims in Egypt and Saudi Arabia, but set against the statements of intolerance that he hears from Muslim clerics and politicians in his own country and worldwide, his speech sounded absurdly *naive*. The tent from which he spoke was tucked among skyscrapers on a bombsite at the back of St Ethelburga's, the oldest medieval church in London, destroyed in 1993 by the IRA Bishopsgate bomb and rebuilt as a centre for reconciliation and peace. It must have been the only Arab tent pitched in London, not exactly an adequate site for tolerance in the heart of a Western city. Flanked by the Bishop of London, the Chief Rabbi and leaders of seven other world faiths, Prince Charles inaugurated the exotic new centre for interfaith dialogue which is adorned by sacred geometric and astrological rather than religious symbols. It will be used by people of all religions for meditation, worship, storytelling and discussion of religious conflicts, social issues, spiritual authority, women in faith, suffering and other issues. This was Prince Charles' second visit to the centre, which he opened officially in 2002. He also unveiled a plaque to the Rev. John Rodwell, the Rector of St Ethelburga's from 1843 to 1900, an orientalist who published the first reliable translation of the Qur'an in English. While laudable as an idea, the whole ceremony did not address specifically the issue of Islamic militancy, it being known that none of the other faiths represented has ever used violence or threatened the public order in the United Kingdom. Indeed, no members of any faith other than Islam have killed, wounded, maimed, threatened violence or promised the takeover of Britain, not necessarily by gentle means, and have incontrovertibly demonstrated that they intend to deliver on their promises.

Representatives in Britain of the Baha'is, Buddhists, Jains, Zoroastrians, Hindus, Sikhs, Muslims and Jews recited prayers, read passages extolling tolerance and ceremonially laid copies of their scriptures on a table at the centre of the tent. President Clinton, Archbishop Desmond Tutu, the U2 singer Bono and the President of the World Jewish Congress sent messages saluting the centre's use of religion to underpin dialogue and replace conflict with understanding. It only remained to clarify what Muslims meant by dialogue and tolerance. Richard Chartres, the Bishop of London, who has been the driving force behind the rebuilding of St Ethelburga's, noted that the three Abrahamic religions of Christianity, Judaism and Islam began in desert tents. Sir Jonathan Sacks, the Chief Rabbi, spoke of the significance of the tabernacle - a form of tent - in the Old Testament. The St Ethelburga's Bedouin tent, paid for by an anonymous benefactor and with windows inscribed with motifs and messages in Chinese, Sanskrit, Arabic, Japanese, Hebrew, English and Inuit, is a far cry from the desert, however: it will be heated in winter, is able to withstand the London rain and will be pitched permanently in one of the world's most densely populated cities. Prince Charles told the faith leaders: "We are all trying to explain the nature of mystery and, in a sense, it is almost impossible to explain. If only we could understand each other's gropings to understand the mystery, not try to overdo the way in which we decide that we know everything, we might, perhaps, reduce the level of conflict and violence and misunderstanding."[53] The problem is that dialogue has been treated in the West as if it were a real policy, whereas it is in fact a non-policy, designed only to fill an awkward vacuum and to make royal princes and legislators feel virtuous for "doing something". But while Europeans have regularly entered a "dialogue" in good faith, fully intending to find common ground with their unruly

Muslim interlocutors - for the Muslims, "dialogue" means something else entirely. For them, it signifies the submission of a lesser culture and religion to their own superior one.

Muslims hope to inspire in the Europeans a "Damascene conversion" to an Islamist view of the world. This means radical Muslims who want to implement *Shari'a* law here and now, violently if necessary, unlike ordinary Muslims who strive to do the same, but more gently and gradually. Anything short of that is regarded by them as an abject "failure of dialogue", and a signal to resort to threats of violence or acts of terrorism. They are well practiced at both, while the Europeans have literally become pushovers at this stage in their history. They don't believe anything to be worth fighting for. Nor do they have a stomach for a fight of unlimited duration. They would rather capitulate than investigate in depth the meanings of tolerance, understanding, dialogue and peace to Islamists. The problem today lies in the juxtaposition of a resurgent Islam on the one hand, and a self-deprecating Europe on the other, unsure of itself, its values or even what it stands for. Its people have made a virtue of instant self-gratification, and therefore invest next to nothing in the future - even to the extent of having few or no children. Their preferred way of life amounts to a "credit card culture", wanting everything, and wanting it instantly. Never mind that their governments no longer raise sufficient funds from taxation to cover exorbitant welfare entitlements, or that a bleak financial future awaits tomorrow's pensioners. In short, Europe has become a disgrace to its own heritage in sharp reversal of its fortunes when at the turn of the twentieth century the Muslim Ottoman Empire was considered the 'sick man of Europe', and was therefore no match for a confident West. US Defense Secretary Donald Rumsfeld perceived something other than the obvious when he distinguished between 'old' and 'new' Europe - except that in their eagerness to grab some, necessarily short-term, economic benefits after emerging from Soviet control, that headlong rush of "new" Europe to join the EU will inevitably contaminate it with this prevalent Western disease.

There is another drawback to the constant resort to "dialogue". It lulls Western populations into believing that their governments are acting constructively to avert violence or threats of violence in the future. In reality, nothing could be further from the truth, for this non-policy simply serves to embolden and concomitantly empower those Muslims whom Western governments have chosen to act as intermediaries with the wider Muslim community. Invariably, the government has elected such Muslims largely because they are the activists and therefore prominent in their communities, while the government comforts itself with the in-judicious belief that these figures represent "moderate" Islam. However, these Muslims have been living in Europe long enough to have learned to tailor their vocabulary precisely according to whom they are facing across the table. They speak the language of peace, reconciliation and goodwill to Westerners, and reserve their true thoughts and beliefs for fellow Muslims. In other words, they have learned to "work the system", admirably so. In effect, these "moderate" Muslim leaders gradually ex-tract one concession after another from Western policymakers, rendering "dialogue" a one-way street. They enter each session with the full inten-tion of testing the limits of the concessions they can extract, and it is a rare government minister who would risk disappointing them - or else the headlines in the papers the following day would be sure to inflame the Muslim community. Herein lies the value of the worldwide Muslim penchant for overreacting to every perceived slight, real or imagined, by demonstrating loudly and violently their "rage". Temperament comes into play here too, for unlike other peoples who experience anger or humiliation, many Muslims are either unable or unwilling to contain those sentiments. One has only to recall the Arafat-orchestrated "days of rage" in the early days of the *Intifadah* against Israel to understand that, in sharp contrast to Westerners, Muslims make a fetish of celebrating their anger. Such an uncontrolled behavior is unthinkable in the West, but not because of lack of provocation, particularly since September 11. Funerals too are manipulated to vent wrath and fury, emotion, general mayhem and impromptu rifle-shooting. The total and shameless lack of dignity, even at what should be a somber occasion, is jarring to western eyes. Bodies are held aloft and bounced along the route, in a manner that would be regarded as disrespectful to the deceased in other cultures. Bodies have been known to fall off the stretcher amid the *melee,* as was recorded for posterity in the case of Iran's Ayatollah Khomeini funeral.

Iran's ambassador to Copenhagen, Ahmad Danialy, making his first public appearance back in Denmark after being recalled by the Iranian Foreign Ministry in January 2006 following the Cartoon affair, addressed a public gathering and noted that the crisis had "hurt the feelings of the Muslim world and caused a great deal of concern. Now after the lapse of this period of unpleasant and bitter experience, I am very pleased to witness a beautiful and jovial gathering of the erudite and learned here in Copenhagen…. The conference is a step in the right direction for improving relations. The truth of the matter is that the world needs to direct new attention to one fundamental principle and that is: respect for the sanctity of religions in all places and at all political, cultural and social levels...."[54] And this, when the Ambassador is fully aware of how his President speaks about Jews and Israel, and how his clerics deprecate Christianity and other faiths, and how the Iranian regime supports the burning down of Jewish synagogues in the West Bank and in European cities. But if the purpose of the conference was "to introduce the Prophet (the Muslim one, not all others) the proper way", then why should we expect any care or concern for any faith except the Islamic one? The conference in the United Arab Emirates, organized by the Tabah Foundation, brought 60 young people from Denmark and the Arab world together under the banner "The Search for Mutual Understanding", namely that the Danes should learn to respect Islam, never mind their own beliefs and culture. The delegates discussed a range of issues which the cartoon crisis had revealed as sore points between religious Muslims and secular Western culture, for example freedom of expression and the role the media can play in hindering or facilitating global understanding. The four-day conference held in Abu Dhabi "exceeded the expectations of Jeppe Bruus Christensen", chairman of the Danish Youth Council, who naively and prematurely declared: "I don't think we should underestimate how important this is in the Arab world. It has gathered a great deal of attention." What he did not realize was that his statements were interpreted throughout the Arab world as a desperate attempt by Denmark to apologize for its "horrible" deed as a capitulation to Muslim demands. It did not earn Denmark any credit, but only scorn and contempt. Christensen felt the two groups managed to "understand" each other, and "accepted" mutual criticism, but he failed to comprehend that the Muslim goal was to assert its victory, and not to compromise, since the Muslim system cannot recognize itself as ever at fault, unlike other (lesser) faiths. Thus, his feeling that the whole exercise "has been very constructive and positive" and that "we have been able to agree upon common values, such as having the right to criticize each other", would have been in vain had he read the Arab reports of the conference. Other participants from Denmark and the Middle East were more sober and realistic when they merely agreed that the conference "underscored the need for bridging the gaps that the conflict had revealed", and that "We have to accept that there are areas where we remain distant from each other". Moreover, to illustrate the depth of that gap, some Muslims continued to consider Denmark, one of the most open, tolerant and hospitable countries of the world, to be "a racist and closed country".[55]

Much closer to the reality was the evaluation by some Danish participants who heard their country deprecated, albeit that it could be the model
of tolerance for the entire Islamic world, when they said: "we have to
acknowledge that that's the way it's going to be for some time". The
conference also gave young Muslims the chance to meet their Danish
counterparts and test the images presented by the media in their countries.
"It's been very important for me to obtain the human aspect. To meet
people and hear their opinion instead of seeing it in the media," said a
19-year-old Egyptian who admitted that preconceived notions, such as
"the Danes hate us", were difficult to reject, but the conference's people-
to-people approach helped. Another Arab youth, from Saudi Arabia,
where Danish goods were initially boycotted, said that he was surprised
in a positive way about the Danish young people, for "They were much
more open and understanding about our culture than I had expected."
But was this attitude in fact reciprocated? He did acknowledge that while
dialogue and respect had been established at the conference, transferring
the experience to his home country could prove difficult. He explained:
"We'll be challenged when we come back to our countries, because some
people have different attitudes. They use a different approach than dialogue, but we still need to work to spread the message that it is possible
to live in this world together."[56] One wishes he were right.

The Danish Queen, Margrethe, more reflective than the British Royal
House, stated that Islam poses a challenge both globally and locally, and
is a challenge to be taken seriously. In her biography, based on interviews
between the Queen and the book's author, journalist Annelise Bistrup, the
Queen affirmed that "There is something impressive about people whose
existence is immersed in religion from dawn to dusk, from the cradle
to the grave . . . , but it is a challenge, which we need to take seriously.
We have admittedly ignored it for too long. Because we are tolerant and
a little lazy, I don't find it easy at all. Nor especially pleasant". Unlike
other royals and politicians who make gratuitous declarations just to
please their Muslim citizens or to placate their wrath, Queen Margrethe
has studied Islam through her archaeological pursuits, and says she does
not feel entirely unprepared to enter the debate. "There is something
fascinating about people who go to such lengths to surrender themselves
to a religion. But there is also something frightening about the all-encompassing side of Islam", she said, and then courageously added, "The
challenge must be met, at the risk of getting some less flattering labels
attached, for there are some things we should not meet with tolerance.
When we are tolerant, we should be careful to note whether it stems

from convenience or conviction". Queen Margrethe explained that her nation and the West stand at a crossroads, but it needs to be recognized that crossroads often only reveal themselves when they are crossed. She warned that "one doesn't always turn out to have taken the right road. But we have at least realized that we cannot let ourselves be shooed off by things that frighten us. We cannot compromise our notions of justice and legitimacy". Queen Margrethe pointed out that her interviews with her biographer Bistrup brought up forgotten memories that could be worthwhile for others, especially young people, to hear.[57] She was most certainly referring to the seeming *nonchalance* with which the complacent younger generation looks upon the muti-cultural states that exact an ever increasing price from present-day European societies.

This European mood allows converts to Islam to take up the vocation of the likes of Abu-Hamza and Bakri, with the help of foreign financing, thus lending to Islam the aura of a "native" religion, no longer introduced by foreigners into Britain and the rest of Europe, but followed by Britons and other Europeans and thus completely legitimate. Indeed, a British Muslim convert has emerged as successor to Omar Bakri as the leader of a radical group which wants Britain ruled by Islamic law. *The Times* has obtained transcripts of Omar Brooks, now known as Abu Izzadeen, preaching holy war *(jihad)* and discussing killing Tony Blair in a recent sermon in London. Abu Izzadeen had previously described the July 7 bombings as "completely praiseworthy" and organized demonstrations in support of the September 11 hijackers. His organization, the Saved Sect, of which he became head, was formed from the remnants of the disbanded extremist group *al-Muhajirun,* which the government intended to proscribe. However, it was not on the Home Office's list of 40 banned terrorist organisations, and a spokeswoman refused to comment on whether it could be outlawed. The Crown Prosecution Service did not rule out charges against Abu Izzadeen, which may include solicitation to murder and withholding information about acts of terrorism. Abu Izzadeen, 31 (in 2006), was born into a Christian family of Jamaican origin, in Hackney, East London, and was known as Trevor to some acquaintances. He converted to Islam at the age of 17 and is believed to have become involved with Bakri at Finsbury Park mosque in the late 1990s. Before he was fully radicalized, Abu Izzadeen trained and worked as an electrician. He eventually chose a new name, which means "Might of the Faith" in Arabic, and immersed himself in his new religion. He married and was living in Leyton, East London, with his wife and three young children. Vitriolic lectures for his website were recorded - until recently - by Bakri, who is now in exile in Lebanon. But Abu Izzadeen has started preaching sermons and posting them on the website, suggesting that he has taken over as *"emir"* of the Saved Sect. He is one of a generation of young British-born radical converts to step into the shoes of notorious clerics such as Bakri, Abu Qatada and Abu Hamza al-Masri. Abu-Hamza is in jail, as of Summer 2007 and Abu Qatada is held without charge under anti-terrorism laws, trying to escape deportation to his native Jordan. The Saved Sect, also known as the Saviour Sect, rejects democracy and wants Britain to adopt *Shari'a,* or Islamic law. It believes that it is the only group representing the true Islamic path, but has links with another *al-Muhajirun* successor, *al-Ghuraba'* (the Strangers), whose leader was arrested during extremist protests against the publication of cartoons depicting the Prophet Muhammad in early 2006.[58]

In lectures given at a London location, Abu Izzadeen expounded that a war was being fought to make Islamic law "completely dominant" in Britain, and that "all Jews and Christians are going to hell-fire". He also praised Mullah Omar, the *Taliban* leader, saying: "This man is a winner." His lectures, entitled "The Christian Crusades" - parts 1 and 2 describe conflict in the Middle East and Britain as a present-day crusade. Abu Izzadeen proclaimed:

> There is a war here [in Britain]. Maybe you don't have weapons, but there are arrests against the Muslim community, there is brutality by the police. It is a form of war against the Muslims here as well.... If I said to you we're going to conquer Rome, or if I said to you, we're going to kill George Bush and we're going to kill Tony Blair, you would say to me: 'Which come first bro?' . . . Muslims do not need to stand by the British flag .... There is without doubt a war taking place between the Muslims and the non-Muslims ... you must take part in the struggle.... Tony Blair is a *taghoot* [believer of false religions]. The British forces in Iraq and Afghanistan, the police in the UK , they are all fighting for the sake of taghoot.[59]

When Mr Blair announced after the London bombings that he would ban the successor organization of *al-Muhajirun,* the group praised the September 11 terrorists, describing them as the "Magnificent 19". Legislation tightening the Terrorism Act came into force some months later, when it became illegal to glorify or incite terrorism. A Home Office spokeswoman stated: "The list of proscribed organizations is kept under constant review. The Terrorism Act 2006 widens the criteria of proscription to include those groups which glorify terrorism. All possible candidates for proscription will be considered against these criteria." The website of the Saved Sect also carried a statement from Abu Mus'ab al-Zarqawi, the commander of al-Qa'ida in Iraq who was killed in the summer of 2006. On the BBC programme *Newsnight* in 2005, Abu Izzadeen said that the July 7 bombings would make people "wake up and smell the coffee". He added that he would never denounce "suicide bombings", "even if my own family was to suffer, because we always stand with the Muslims regardless of the consequences". He then elaborated on his group's program:

> We can envisage that, if alive in the UK today, Jesus would undoubtedly have supported *jihad* in Afghanistan and Iraq, as opposed to the capitalist-driven US-led alliance ... and would also have been no doubt interned under the Home Secretary Mr Clarke's new terrorism laws, thereby languishing in Belmarsh Prison.... The call of moderate and apostate 'Muslims' [of the Muslim Council of Britain] upon the Metropolitan Police to take action and arrest the 'extremists' behind the peaceful protests in central London (against the cartoons of Prophet Muhammad), was indeed a call of apostasy and betrayal. They have repeatedly called for the arrest and deportation of a vast number of Islamic activists, including scholars such as Sheikh Abu Hamza, Sheikh Faisal and Sheikh Abu Qatada - may Allah assist them and release them from captivity.... Since the majority of Muslims living in the West are on the brink of committing apostasy (e.g. by voting for man-made law and allying with the disbelievers), it is important for us to identify the ways in which they are leaving the fold of Islam and tackle these problems directly.... If we look to the reality of the so-called mosques in Britain today, hardly any are built by Muslims ... therefore, they cannot be considered to be mosques. These halls have become places of corruption, calling Muslims to vote, inviting *kuffar* (Unbelievers) MPs and prime ministers, as well as lying about Allah, His Messenger and the religion of Islam. It is even considered to be a form of heresy to call these places Houses of Allah.... Sodomy, bestiality and incest are all crimes that are acceptable in un-Islamic societies. Recently the British government legalized homosexual marriages. It was not enough that they allowed homosexuals to practice their vile filth openly, but they felt the need to take a step further into the pits of humanity.[60]

All this causes much less outrage in Britain than if it occurred in Muslim lands, where citizens are executed for homosexuality and apostasy. A comparative story of two converts in Britain, who then became more fanatical than the most extremist Muslims, was reported by the *Times*.[61] One of these, David Copeland, a Neo-Nazi whose ideas were said to be the inspiration for the man who let off a nail bomb in Central London in 1999, had converted to an extremist form of Islam. Another, David Myatt, a founder of the hardline British National Socialist Movement (NSM) who has been jailed for racist attacks, changed his name to Abdul Aziz ibn Myatt. Copeland, who is serving six life sentences after three people died in his Soho bomb attacks, was a member of the NSM. Myatt is reportedly the author of a fascist terrorist handbook and a former leader of the violent far-right group Combat 18. But he now subscribes to radical Islamist views. In an internet essay entitled From Neo-Nazi to Muslim, Myatt asks:

> How was it that I, a Westerner with a history of over 25 years of political involvement in extreme right-wing organizations, a former leader of the political wing of the neo-

Nazi group Combat 18, came to be standing outside a mosque with a sincere desire to go inside and convert to Islam? These were the people who I had been fighting on the streets, I had sworn at and had used violence against - indeed, one of my terms of imprisonment was a result of me leading a gang of skinheads in a fight against "Pakis". [I support] the killing of any Muslim who breaks his oath of loyalty to Islam, and the setting up of a Muslim super state. I had been staunchly opposed to non-white immigration into Britain and twice jailed for violence in pursuit of my political aims. I spent several decades of my life fighting for what I regarded as my people, my race and my nation, and endured two terms of imprisonment arising out of my political activities.... But the pure authentic Islam of the revival, which recognizes practical *jihad* (holy war) as a duty, is the only force that is capable of fighting and destroying the dishonour, the arrogance, the materialism of the West.... For the West, nothing is sacred, except perhaps Zionists, Zionism, the hoax of the so-called Holocaust, and the idols which the West and its lackeys worship, or pretend to worship, such as democracy. They want, and demand, that we abandon the purity of authentic Islam and either bow down before them and their idols, or accept the tame, secularized, so-called Islam which they and their apostate lackeys have created. This may well be a long war, of decades or more - and we Muslims have to plan accordingly. We must affirm practical *jihad* - to take part in the fight to free our lands from the *kuffar* (Unbelievers). Jihad is our duty.[62]

Myatt, who briefly became a monk after his second spell in prison, said that he became a Muslim while working long hours alone on a farm. He grew up in Africa, moved to Britain in 1967 and lived for a time in Worcestershire. In July 2000 *Searchlight,* an anti-fascist magazine, described him as "the most ideologically-driven Nazi in Britain, preaching race war and terrorism". Myatt issued a statement in response to the Soho nail bombings saying: "Neither myself nor anyone else connected to the NSM can be held responsible for these bombs in any way. That responsibility lies with the person who constructed them, planted them and caused them to explode. Only that person, and God, know the motive behind the attacks." Myatt said that "all bombs are terrible and barbaric", whether detonated by lone bombers, Western governments in Iraq or Zionists in Palestine. He continued: "the NSM considered the creation of a revolutionary situation in this country as necessary since it wished to build an entirely new society, based upon personal honour, and believed this could only be done by destroying its present dishonourable and corrupt society. However, the NSM neither preached, nor sought to incite, what is called "racial hatred". Instead, it strove to propagate the warrior values of honour, loyalty and duty, and make the British people aware of, and come to value, their ancestral warrior culture and warrior heritage." Myatt also said that he had given up hope of a breakthrough by the far Right and believed that Muslims were the best hope for combating Zionism and the West. Echoing the current reality in Britain and elsewhere in Europe, where prisons have become fertile grounds for converts to Islam, Myatt appealed to other dysfunctional people like himself to rally to his new religion:

> There will not be an uprising, a revolution, in any Western nation, by nationalists, racial nationalists, or National Socialists - because these people lack the desire, the motivation, the ethos, to do this and because they do not have the support of even a large minority of their own folk.... If these nationalists, or some of them, desire to aid us, to help us ... they can do the right thing, the honourable thing, and convert, revert to Islam - accepting the superiority of Islam over and above each and every way of the West.[63]

Despite these voices, which openly called for conversion to Islam and were quite widespread in Britain and elsewhere in Europe before the July 7 bombings, few were ready for the terrorist onslaught, although there was a keen awareness in security and political circles that a major terrorist attack might take place. The British authorities were slow to recognize the growing threat of terrorism by angry British Muslims before the deadly bombings in London of July 7, although there is no evidence that the attack could have been prevented, according to a report issued in May 2006. "If more resources had been in place sooner, the chances of preventing the July attacks could have increased," stated the report by Parliament's Intelligence and Security Committee. Acknowledging that its determinations were reached "largely by hindsight," the committee also concluded that no matter how extensive the government's anti-terrorism efforts, "it seems highly unlikely that it will be possible to stop all attacks". The parliamentary report on the deadliest attack in Britain since World War II, and a separate report issued by the Home Office, concluded that two of the July 7 bombers probably had contact with al-Qa'ida during visits to Pakistan in 2003, and from late 2004 into early 2005. But they said there was no solid evidence to suggest that al-Qa'ida directly planned or directed the London attacks in which 52 commuters were killed on the three subway trains and a bus. The bombers, all young British Muslims who mixed chemicals for their crude bombs in a bathtub, were likely inspired by al-Qa'ida but acted on their own, motivated by "fierce antagonism to perceived injustices by the West against Muslims," the Home Office report stated. The long-awaited reports did not end the speculation about the July 7 attack and another failed attack in which five men were charged with getting onto London subways and a bus with bombs that failed to explode. Although British officials for years had warned of the likelihood of an attack by Islamic extremists, many Britons were shocked to learn that three of the four July 7 bombers were British-born. Had the authorities and the public heeded the press reports and interviews by Bakri and Abu-Hamza, they would have certainly not been surprised. David Davis, Shadow Home Secretary of the opposition Conservative Party, noted that the reports "raised more questions than answers" about what he called "a major failure of our intelligence services" to develop concerns earlier, regarding a homegrown extremist threat. But this was not precise, since the information was indeed there; it was simply not taken seriously. He also questioned the reports' independence from Prime Minister Tony Blair's government and security services, which, despite being the focus of key aspects of the probes, provided much of the information used to compile those reports. "It is the government's view, not an independent view," Davis told the House of Commons.[64]

Davis reiterated calls for a "fully resourced, independent inquiry" involving public hearings and witness testimony, similar to the 9/11 Commission that studied the September 11, 2001 attacks in the United States. Families of some of the bombing victims have made similar demands, but Blair insisted that the incidents could be fully explored by the parliamentary committee investigation and the Home Office, which is in charge of domestic security. Home Secretary John Reid, also appearing before the House of Commons, stated that there was no need for a further inquiry into the bombings, although investigations by security services continue. The reports noted that some data were withheld because British law limited the release of information during criminal trials; the two reports also found no connection between the July 7 and July 21 attacks. The parliamentary panel generally painted a picture of British security services as slow to recognize "the speed and scale" of the growing threat from home-grown radicals. Despite evidence that some British citizens might attempt "suicide" attacks - most notably the botched 2001 attempt to blow up an airliner by "shoe bomber" Richard Reid - British security services predicted that such attacks would "not become the norm in Europe," the report stated. "We are concerned that this judgment could have had an impact on the alertness of the authorities to the kind of threat they were facing and their ability to respond," the report continued, adding: "The chances of identifying attack planning and of preventing the 7 July attacks might have been greater had different investigative decisions been taken by the Security Service in 2003-2005."

Perhaps the most intriguing sections of the two reports are those dealing with the July 7 bombers themselves, particularly Mohammed Sidique Khan, aged 30, the group's presumed ringleader, and Shehzad Tanweer, aged 22. The parliamentary report noted that Khan and Tanweer had been spotted, in 2004, as unidentified men "on the peripheries of other surveillance and investigative operations". Security services did not investigate them further and focused instead on "higher investigative priorities," including attempts to disrupt "known plans to attack the UK". "In light of the other priority investigations being conducted and the limitations on Security Service resources, the decisions not to give greater investigative priority to these two individuals were understandable," the report pointed out.

Khan, Tanweer and bomber Hasib Hussain, aged 18, were all British-born children of Pakistani immigrants who conducted middle-class lives in Beeston, on the outskirts of the English city of Leeds.[65] Khan was a well-respected special-needs teacher and youth worker. Tanweer and Hussain were still living with their parents when they died; Tanweer played cricket and drove a red Mercedes given to him by his parents. While all were known for their strict religious observance and each was seen to become more religious in the months leading up to the attack, none was regarded by friends as a potential extremist. The fourth bomber, Jermaine Lindsay, aged 19, was born in Jamaica and moved to Britain with his mother in 1986. He converted to Islam in 2000 and took the name "Jamal". The report stated that Lindsay had handed out leaflets supporting al-Qa'ida and had been "strongly influenced" by Abdallah al-Faisal, an extremist preacher who is serving a prison sentence for incitement to murder and incitement to racial hatred. Khan visited Pakistan in 2003 and then spent time there with Tanweer between November 2004 and February 2005. The report emphasized that it is unclear who they met there, although it is "likely that they had some contact with al-Qa'ida figures". Security officials believe that both men had undergone "some form of operational training" in terrorist activity during their time in Pakistan, or possibly over the border in Afghanistan. While planning for the July bombings seems to have started just after Khan and Tanweer returned to Britain, the Home Office report notes, "The extent to which the 7 July attacks were externally planned, directed or controlled by contacts in Pakistan or elsewhere remains unclear." The report goes on to explain that the men had contact with someone in Pakistan before the attacks, but it does not elaborate. Further, the men likely had received some assistance in handling the chemicals they used to make their bombs. While the chemicals were cheap and readily available, they were volatile and required careful handling. The men's hair apparently lightened in color from handling the chemicals so closely, and the tops of plants just outside their bathroom died from exposure to fumes. The Home Office report concludes that "the best indications of the group's motivation" are contained in a video left by Khan which was aired on the Arabic television channel *al-Jazeera* on September 1 (2005), and which security agents believe he may have recorded during his trip to Pakistan. On the tape, Khan focused on "perceived injustices carried out by the West against Muslims" and justified violence through his own interpretation of Islam. "We are at war and I am a soldier," Khan says on the video, speaking in an emphatically British accent. Shortly after the tape aired, al-Qa'ida's number two official, Ayman Zawahiri, praised the bombers and implied that al-Qa'ida had been behind the attacks. The report stated that there is no evidence to support that claim, but emphasized that the July 7 bombing was "typical of al-Qa'ida and those inspired by its ideologies".[66]

As if all this incriminating evidence of the brewing Islamic subversion in Britain and elsewhere was not sufficient to stop terrorism before it erupted, it was accompanied by the distancing of Europe, except for Britain, from the furious American reprisals after September 11, which indicated to the Islamists that they can pursue their anti-Western activities in the heart of the West almost undisturbed. Granted that September 11 traumatized the entire West, which began to awaken to the new dangers Islam posed to its security, yet the sense of urgency and immediacy of the issues was late in coming. Until September 11, the Islamic world was considered friendly to the West, and the essentially Islamic struggles taking place in Bosnia, Kosovo, Palestine, Kashmir or the Philippines were regarded as so remote, incomprehensible and irrelevant to Western culture that few bothered to deepen their knowledge about them. But as of September 11, not only did these names begin to resound clearly in the minds of ordinary people in the West who had been unaware of them, but many rushed to read the Qur'an and works about Islam, or to visit Islamic centers in the West in a quest to comprehend the Islamic faith. More than a few individuals even asked to join the ranks of the Believers. So, in a small measure, the "Islam Rush" was due not to an "invading" foreign Islam that one needed to know and understand, but to the shocking realization that the "enemy" emerged from within. After all, the 19 *Islamikaze* who committed the Twin Tower horror were apparent asylum seekers in the US who were educated there or in Europe, became acquainted with Western openness and democracy, and were expected to demonstrate loyalty to their countries of refuge. The fact that they did not, and that their common denominator was their Islamic faith, took the Americans, as well as the Europeans, by surprise, especially due to the Saudi and Egyptian identity of the perpetrators. There was a gnawing sense that a fifth column was growing in their midst, especially when it turned out that their operators, in this case al-Qai'da, had organized, financed, indoctrinated and dispatched them from the outside.

In Western Europe, Australia and Canada - the main targets of legal and illegal immigration from Muslim countries - the first thoughts of putting strictures on those immigrants began to rise, as these countries realized that some Muslim immigrants did not move to the Western democracies just to improve their lot, or to work and provide for their families who stayed behind, but that an entire scheme lay behind their move which would revolutionize the status of entire Muslim communities in the US and Europe namely from being asylum seekers, political refugees and foreign workers, to becoming a real social and security liability. For, while many Muslims are grateful for their new home and go about their legitimate and everyday business, the political and religious activists among them pressure others to take a stand on current affairs which they claim to be of concern to all Muslims, encourage them to demonstrate, even violently, against their new countries and in favor of their original ones, and strive to increase their numbers and make an impact on local demography and politics. The difficulty of distinguishing the activists apart from the others makes all of them suspicious in the eye of the unsuspecting citizens of the host countries, who while for the most part escaping the label of "racism" by not voicing in public their concern and fear of Islam, do venture to complain privately, as they begin to feel like strangers in certain neighborhoods of their country, where even police do not dare to enter and impose order and safety. As we shall see in the following chapters, and as has already become known in the satellite *cites* around Paris and in certain neighborhoods in all major European cities, this state of affairs has become the rule rather than the exception. Every wave of new immigrants, legal or illegal, is aided by the previous one, which under the humanitarian excuse of "family reunion" brings entire clans in their wake. As long as the Muslim immigrants constituted negligible minorities, no one would have been overly concerned about their impact, political or cultural, on their host countries; but as their greatly increasing numbers lower the median age of the general popula- tion significantly - due to a high childbirth rate and an ever increasing percentage of children and young people - their demographic "threat" becomes increasingly apparent.

Had these minorities aspired to assimilate into their host societies and just become French, Swedes or Spaniards, peacefully and individu- ally following their cult of Islam as a personal endeavor, no one would even notice. But as the Muslim communities grow larger they also grow more vociferous, with increasing violence, and are no longer content to be absorbed into the host societies as individuals. Instead they begin to claim group rights and to justify their often violent behavior by their right to differ from the overwhelming majority, as has been evident in most European countries, especially those, like Holland, France and southern Sweden, where the high proportion of immigrants on the one hand and the liberal attitudes of those societies towards the newcomers on the other, have permitted such phenomena. Many minorities had been absorbed by these countries over the centuries, especially the immigration-oriented among them, such as Canada, the US and Australia, but seldom has a minority clung to its original roots in an effort to force the host majority to yield to its will. For example, the Poles, Irish, Germans, Japanese and Jews who flocked to the US or Australia since the nineteenth century, have willingly and wholeheartedly hoisted their new national colors and participated in the fighting forces of their adopted countries in times of war. Now, some Arab youths in France (as in Israel), like other Muslims in other European countries, refuse to sing the anthems of their adopted countries and demand that their ethnic and religious heritage be recognized in their school curricula, even if it contradicts the local national ethos. Evidence of this occurs in French schools and football stadiums, not to mention the refusal of British and other European Muslims to participate in official national commemorations of the Holocaust. Again, were it not for Muslim spokesmen who proclaim their blueprint for infiltrating Western societies in order to subvert them from within and take them over, as we have seen above, one would have tended to believe that these manifestations of recalcitrance among Muslim youth in Europe were merely pangs of assimilation and demonstrations of passing displeasure with their lower living standards or with the prevailing discrimination against them.

Worst of all are the violent methods some groups of Muslim immigrants often resort to beyond the expected levels in any migrant and less affluent society. In Western Europe the native populations in some places are terrified by the high rate of crime which is linked, according to some statistics[67] with the immigrant Muslim population. In fact, it's not only that everyone reads about the arrested suspects of terrorism throughout the world who happen to be Muslim for the most part, and about the "out of bounds" Muslim neighborhoods throughout Europe, but the perception of high Muslim criminality is expressed by local populations in any field contact with them. The police departments of Malmo (Sweden), Marseille

(France), Antwerp (Belgium), or Birmingham (England), provide ample evidence of that. There are recurrent, and increasingly also public, complaints by Europeans in this regard, who no longer fear being branded "racist" if they share their thoughts with others, once the level of risk to their national identity has grown so perceptible and pressing. Many are dismayed by the changing character of their cities and towns where Muslim immigrants live and bring their religious rituals to the public square, altering forever the cultural ambience that the local population had been accustomed to. Many Europeans now shun the use of public transportation in certain areas and at certain hours. Entire urban areas have introduced the Muslim market place into Western cities, with the attendant voices, sights and smells, much to the distress of many, though also to the delight of some who would laud cultural diversity if it were not for the accompanying atmosphere of violence and fear.

Right-wing political parties in European countries have learned to tap cultural change concerns and to strengthen themselves politically, because they dare to voice in public what liberals and left-wingers consider taboo. And so, paradoxically, the liberal and socialist parties, generally lenient towards immigration, with increased size of their constituencies when newcomers became naturalized citizens and began voting, now find themselves politically impoverished when their original European constituents turn their backs on them. This has happened in France, the Netherlands, Australia and Italy, and is likely to spread to Germany and the United Kingdom if these countries do not tighten their restrictions on immigration into their respective territories. In the meantime, those who have immigrated - including Muslim radicals who admit in public their aspirations to subvert their benefactor states—have no qualms about milking the generous welfare systems which have absorbed them, nor of using taxpayers' money, earned by the hard work of the local populations, to cultivate a whole sub-culture of dependence on state allowances while building up hatred against their naive and well-meaning hosts. Thus, rapid breeding—in order for their community to grow demographically and strengthen its electoral influence, and thus allow it to demand more funds and allocations - has become a way for these immigrants to exert political pressure and achieve political goals. Their children are taken care of by the host states, as is their housing, education, healthcare, unemployment benefits, pensions and minimum wages, thus freeing from work the troublemakers among them and enabling them to sustain their unpublicized goals, such as sabotage and terrorism, the building up of caches of weapons, increasing Muslim proselytization, and demonstrating, at times violently, for their fellow Arabs and Muslims around the world.

Muslim diasporas in the West, having acquired political power through sheer numbers, have also been attempting to dislodge from their advantageous positions the older and more established, though far less numerous, Jewish communities. By doing so they wish to eliminate the "Jewish influence" on the local governments and thereby shift traditional political sympathies of the West from Israel to the Arabs. That is the reason why Islamic protests in western societies almost invariably go hand in hand with anti-Semitic eruptions of violence and rampage. Note, for example, that during the vast Muslim demonstrations in Europe, in support of the Palestinian *Intifadah* in the years 2000-2, hundreds of attacks against Jewish institutions, synagogues and cemeteries were registered in all major cities of the continent: London and Manchester, Paris and Marseille, Antwerp and Amsterdam, Hamburg and Munich, Moscow and St Petersburg. Such activity contravenes any acceptable and legitimate way of political action in an open and liberal political system. But Muslim populations do not, for the most part, fulfill the two conditions that go hand in hand with political protest: they do not act in the interest of their host countries; nor do they refrain from violence. Muslim immigrants do not seem to have internalized and digested these restrictions and values at the same pace as they have mastered the list of benefits they can extract from their countries of shelter. On the first count, many naturalized Muslims - for example some of the perpetrators of September 11 and then the London attacks of July 2005, have not hesitated to act against the hosts who have showered them with benefits, while many other Muslims, who have sought shelter in Europe, Canada and Australia, devote their time not to assimilating into the new environment by implementing its rules, but instead cultivate their separate identities and build enclaves of Islam in, and to the detriment of, their host countries. For example, far from accepting their countries' Middle Eastern policies, or their anti-terrorist struggles, they protest against them, often violently.[68]

The second count of using violence, which is usually shunned in western societies, raises even more concern because it ultimately harms public order and the core of their value systems. Since the outbreak of the Palestinian *al-Aqsa Intifadah* in late 2000, thousands of violent demonstrations by Muslim immigrant populations have unfolded from Montreal to Sydney, from Sao Paolo to Durban (South Africa), from Oslo to Rome.[69] Anti-Israel demonstrations are certainly legitimate, but when they involve bouts of rage, the burning down of foreign embassies and flags, (as during the Danish cartoon crisis), and the pelting of rocks against foreign missions and houses of prayer (for example against the Israeli Consulate in Sydney Australia, and Jewish synagogues in Paris in October 2000), sometimes ending up in the murder of innocent civilians, like in the Halimi case in Paris (2006); or when effigies of American and Israeli leaders are burnt and abuses hurled at them, this reaches the outer limit of permissibility of the rule of law of which the Muslim immigrants seem to be unaware or oblivious. Indeed, few local Westerners participate in these acts of violence and rampage. Conversely, no Jews have responded by committing the same acts against the interests of Muslim countries with which the host society maintains relations. What is more, although Jewish communities worldwide have rallied around Israel, they have done so with dignity and full respect for the law, and have not allowed harm to be committed against their country of citizenship, or against the violent crowds of Muslims and their supporters.

The most distressing aspects of these outbursts of violence have been that western countries have been turned, by their Muslim communities, into violent arenas where the Middle Eastern conflict has been exported and replayed. Not content with attacking American and Israeli symbols in most western capitals and large cities, those hooligans who terrorize the downtown areas of their countries of residence, have on occasion turned to cruel and brutal onslaughts on the local Jewish communities in France, Britain, Germany, Belgium and elsewhere, thus signaling to the world that the notions of "Jews" and "Israel" are interchangeable, and that anti-Zionism means also anti-Semitism. The worst hit were the Jewish communities of France, Britain, Germany and Belgium where hundreds of Jewish synagogues, cemeteries, schools and other institutions were torched or otherwise desecrated, Jewish adults were attacked on their way to and from prayer, and children on their way to and from school;[70] all under the eye of the local police who apparently did not dare to intervene forcefully for fear of politically correct politicians on the eve of elections. One can only imagine what would have happened if a mosque or a church were likewise burned, or non-Jewish worshippers or children attacked and harmed. Other places too have experienced the full extent of this pogrom which in many Jewish circles was reminiscent of the infamous *Kristallnacht* of 1938. In most, though not all cases, these horrific anti-Semitic attacks were orchestrated by the Muslim communities of Europe, at times in conjunction with local inveterate anti-Semites.

The outcome of all this is that Muslim communities in western democracies have shown that they can act in unison to undermine public order, to pose a real threat to national security, and to harm their fellow citizens, Jewish and otherwise; this means that they can organize and demonstrate in the same fashion in their host countries whenever they judge an issue sufficiently important to them, or when the local authorities are too lenient or reluctant to confront them. However, polls conducted in the US after September 11 found that Americans overwhelmingly tied Islam and Muslims to those horrific events; 68% of them approved of randomly stopping people who might fit the profile of suspected terrorists; 83% of Americans favored stricter controls on Muslims entering the country; 58% wanted tighter controls on Muslims traveling on planes and trains; 35% of New Yorkers favored establishing internment camps for individuals who the authorities identified as sympathetic to terrorist causes; and 31% of all Americans favored detention camps for the Arab Americans as a way of preventing terrorist attacks in the US.[71] One concludes that the threatened host populations fully appreciated their situation and, in this, were ahead of their governmental administrations; the latter were far more cautious regarding drastically limiting civil rights, and predominantly unprepared to replay the unfortunate experience of the internment during World War II of the Japanese-Americans population in the USA. It is to be expected then that if and when more major acts of terror unfold in the West, the authorities would be compelled by public reaction to curtail civil liberties and take radical measures against the Muslim minorities in its midst.

So, after September 11 we could observe two contradictory trends in the West: on the one hand, Muslim minorities decried their "persecution and humiliation" for being lumped together with the terrorists of September 11; but on the other hand, they themselves and other Muslims who were stunned by the outcome of those events, defied their countries of refuge and some of them boasted of those feats, threatening a takeover of their host societies. For example, some Arab-French of North African origin, including the second and third generation of *beurre,* as they call themselves, recently whistled in contempt on several occasions when they heard the *Marseillaise* sung or saw the French colors hoisted in international football matches. Some began to congregate around Muslim fundamentalist leaders and to associate with various shady Muslim organizations, some of which operated under the cover of "charitable" institutions mostly financed by Saudi Arabia or by violent groups bent on underground activity. Others resorted to collecting weapons for a rainy day and training their fellow Muslims for acts of terrorism. The same trends were identifiable on the morning after September 11 in other parts of Europe: England, France, Germany, Benelux and the Balkans. It is significant that a columnist for the *Wall Street Journal* (European edition), Jonathan Stevenson, had to remind his readers after September 11 that as the subversive statements of Sheikh al-Bakri and his likes went ignored and unpunished in the United Kingdom, 11 out of the 19 *Islamikaze* hijackers had stayed in Britain a few months prior to that day of horror. He emphasized that Abu-Hamza, who acted from his Finsbury Park Mosque and was wanted in the Yemen for terrorism, had called for *jihad* against Western Infidels, but his call remained ignored by the British authorities. He gave a detailed account of several of the hijackers, of their training and shelter in Britain; and, as British law did not permit their extradition, the authorities permitted them to thrive instead of closing the ring around them and amending legislation to allow their preventive arrest and expulsion. These troublemakers continued to raise funds, purchase property, publish their propaganda and escape scrutiny. He confirmed that since the 1970s Britain had concentrated on the terrorist threat of the IRA, thinking it could wean Sinn Fein from terrorism by allowing them full expression of their agenda. The British authorities believed they could carry this non-confrontational policy over to al-Qa'ida and other Islamic groups who subscribe to its grand strategy. But Jonathan Stevenson concluded that since Bin Laden's objectives were non-negotiable and did not fit that strategy, and since Bin Laden simply wanted to "debilitate the US and its allies through violence", those counter-terrorism measures would not work. Only after September 11 did London wake up and outlaw 21 terrorist front organizations, 16 of them Islamic, but it still remained, all the same, a staging and logistics center for al-Qa'ida. Over 100 British Muslims have joined the *Taliban* in Afghanistan, and at least 55 British Muslims have received military training at terrorist bases in Afghanistan since 1996.[72]

The US adopted stiff measures of screening its Muslim population and Muslim immigrants together with other supervisory measures for curtailing prospective terrorist activities. But the squeamish, hesitant and disunited Europeans, not only did not follow immediately in US footsteps, but were quick to disparage America's "hysteria" and castigate Washington for its "disproportionate" reactions. In their June 2002 Conference in Spain, where they discussed clamping down on Muslim illegal immigration with a view to blocking entrance to fundamentalist elements, their disunity, when it became apparent, was disappointing. But it was also becoming clear that the emergency measures adopted by the US, Britain (and Israel for that matter), could not be sustained in the long run, because not only were they untenable in terms of accepted civil liberties, but they also demanded a long-term state of alert that could wear out innocent civilians who would have to pay the collective price for their leaders' incompetence, irresponsibility and lack of foresight and courage in tackling a dangerous situation that had been in the making for years but which they had chosen not to confront. Hence the need to draw up a new policy, not a stop-gap, of re-educating the public; the re-organizing of state institutions to deal with the enemy from within, but without imposing new immigration limitations; the surveillance of potentially subversive groups; the repatriation to their countries of origin of inciters and promoters of violence; institution of new legal systems to deal firmly and swiftly with subversive elements; constant testing of the allegiance of troublemakers to their host countries; and evincing of resoluteness in battling terrorists, their supporters, and assistants in Western Europe. However, while President Bush had singled out the candidate targets for Western retaliation, Europe continued to avoid confrontation, hoping to continue to buy the "goodwill" of terrorist organizations by allowing them to operate on its soil with impunity.

These soft policies were bound to fail, however, because unlike the "carrot and stick" policy of the US, which rewarded allies and came down harshly on terrorists and their supporters, European governments naively thought that not using the stick was the biggest carrot they could offer, not realizing that the terrified public in their cities, towns and neighborhoods had understood that the permissive policies of the past, which had allowed hundreds of thousands of potential terrorists to flock in unchecked, could no longer be pursued. They began to clamor for security in their homes and environments, that their cities be re-Westernized, and that the grounds lost to the hordes of terrorists, by domestic oversight and blind "liberalism", or by oblivious "multi-culturalism" (which have hitherto served the purposes of politicians to whom the immigrants felt obligated on election day), must be reclaimed. The public in Western Europe, Canada and Australia has indeed rewarded its tougher politicians, who have spoken out against unbridled immigration by electing right-wing parties and foregoing socialists, this becoming a trend which seems to have taken hold and forced some politicians to change course, while a rear-guard of them and their dependents, like Cherie Blair and Jack Straw, were still expressing "compassion for the bombers" and "understanding" for their "despair".[73] Just imagine that if everyone who feels despair in this world be shown compassion for mass-murdering others, then the world population would rapidly diminish. Bernard Lewis, the great luminary of Middle Eastern studies, presciently wrote, in the 1990s, about the quandary of modern Islam, where "traditional dignity and courtesy towards others turned into an explosive mixture of rage and hatred", impelling their governments to "espouse kidnapping and assassination and try to find in the life of their Prophet, approval and indeed precedent for such an action".[74] Now, the most urgent question has become how to tame that rage, which promotes Muslim groups to blow up restaurants and buses, Buddha statues and Churches, to desecrate others' holy sites and call them names, to kidnap people and behead them live on video, and then to claim that they are the "victims" of others. This behaviour was reinforced by Western liberals, who instead of castigating terrorists, urged their compatriots to "understand" them, and instead of helping to uproot them, elected to look at the "root causes" of terrorism, whatever they are, and to call upon their governments to alter their policies.

For their part, Muslims have quickly grasped that by wrapping themselves in the cloak of victimhood, they have achieved the earthly vision of *nirvana*. It licenses them to kill and sow mayhem wherever they go, in the certainty that they will not be held accountable for their misdeeds. It is always indicated as the fault of others, the occupation, the aggression, the humiliation, the political degradation, the economic deprivation, the sanctions, the "fence of apartheid", and so on, inflicted on "defenseless" Muslims by America, Israel, Britain, and latterly Denmark. A visitor from another planet could be forgiven for thinking that Muslims have been passive actors throughout their 1,400-year history, rather than occupiers, expansionists, founders of empires, eliminators of other nations and cultures, aggressors and conquerors. Western liberals have not done the Muslims a favor by infantilizing them to such an extent in this way. That the Muslims continue to live down to the low expectations of those who are volubly sympathetic to them, has actually had the perverse effect of contributing to the arrest of their development. A cursory look at the UN Arab Human Development Report, for instance, will attest to a staggering level of backwardness for a part of the Muslim world which has benefited from enormous inflows of cash from oil sales and foreign aid over the past decades.

In Britain, immediately after September 11, people were gripped by fear and began to prepare for the next terrorist attack, which many thought might occur in London, as did indeed take place on 7 July, 2005. Shops began to sell gas masks and protective suits for biological, chemical and even nuclear attacks. Iran's insistence on developing nuclear weapons, and its possession of systems of delivery to the heart of Europe, only make that fear more concrete. The authorities in London have updated the procedures for mass evacuation, at the same time that Mayor Livingstone continues to embrace the top ideologue of the *Islamikaze,* Sheikh Yussuf al-Qaradawi. At the same time as the London Underground Railway system is preparing once again to fulfill the function of a mass shelter as did the Tube Stations in World War II, July 7 has demonstrated that the subway tunnels are the least safe place for Londoners, against *Islamikaze* bombers. While Tony Blair warned against "fanatics who are totally indifferent to the sanctity of life, and have few compunctions about how many people they kill",[75] his determination was in disarray when those feared terrorists hit on 7 July, he describing them as "criminals" and voicing his "astonishment" that homegrown Britons should commit these horrors. Criminals are people who break the law for their own gain, while the young Britons who committed the July 7 horrendous acts did not seek gain. On the contrary, they were prepared to risk their lives for their ideas and beliefs. They were certainly fanatics, as he had appropriately dubbed them before. The writing was on the wall since September 11, when John Stevens, the Metropolitan Police Commissioner of London, proclaimed that his city was next in line.[76] On the face of it, Bin Laden had attained his goal: to sow panic in the West and to force it not only to squander its resources and energies on defensive measures, but also to be passive and wait for the next strike which the *Islamikaze* might deliver at any time and any place of their choice. Truly, the London Police have been on terrorist alert ever since, and many more officers have been patrolling the streets, more than ever before in peace time. More security guards were posted in strategic areas such as the Stock Exchange, telephone switchboards, water pumps and electric power stations; passenger airplanes were prohibited from over-flying the center of London, and emergency legislation to compel everyone in Britain to carry an ID card was proposed. But all of that was not sufficient, because terrorists always seek the vulnerable points in the defense system and hit wherever alertness leaves something to be desired. ID cards were proposed but not yet distributed to the population, entrances to subways, movie theaters, shopping malls, buses and restaurants remained unguarded, and it is there that the terrorists struck on 7 July.

It is certainly a heavy burden to take these kinds of security measures, but it is not impossible. In other countries like Israel those precautions are taken with some measure of success. However, it is too late to simply impose such costly safeguards after terrorists have succeeded. What is more important is that security experts have admitted that Britain has been a safe haven for terrorist networks for too many years due to its liberal immigration policies, the many breaches at border crossing stations, the rigorous consideration shown for individual rights, the legislation that made extradition difficult, and the large Muslim population (well in excess of the stated two million, but no precise data are available). Those experts also realized that the links between Arab *sheikhs* and businessmen and the Home and Foreign Offices had for years allowed liberal distribution of work permits, with a depleted police force rarely carrying out spot-checks in streets, trains and other surface transportation. London has also served as an international center for financial services, investment, and transactions of Muslim companies and organizations, these often using a straw man to launder money in the service of terrorist groups. No wonder, then that 11 of the 19 terrorists who carried out the attacks on September 11 had spent time in London before proceeding to their targets; the fear is rife that more cells of Bin Laden might still be operating clandestinely. The British distinguish between "mouths" and "brains" in these organizations, the former being extremist propaganda groups, such as the *Muhajirun* already mentioned above, headed by al-Bakri. These groups, though under surveillance, are active in recruiting Believers and disseminating hate literature, especially against Jews and homosexuals, Israel and the US. The "brains" are smaller (certainly in quantity if not in quality), compartmentalized underground groups who keep a low profile.[77] Now the British will have to adjust their categorization and add a third group, that of the "active terrorists", especially after the July 7, 2005 terrorist attacks in London.

Much of what was depicted above, regarding Britain, in terms of personalities, activities, ideologies, norms of behavior and the psychological attitude of denial of the general public, would be recognizable as equally true of Western public opinion everywhere else. Rosemary Righter was one of the few authors who criticized Europe for its lack of support of the American counter-attack in Afghanistan after September 11, and was full of praise for the US stand against terrorism on behalf of the entire West. She said that Saddam shared the goals of the fundamentalists in evicting the US from the Middle East and that Europe should be made aware that some of the killers in New York had spent time in Britain while others were plotting in Genoa, Hamburg, Milan and Paris, because "this conspiracy found in European cities and suburbs a general welcome, space, privacy and financial support that is completely chilling". She castigated the critics of the US and the triumphalists in Europe, whose view was shared by many Arabists there, who could not hide their pleasure at seeing "arrogant and bloody America finally getting it in the neck". She asked, "would there have been as many armchair fatalists if Piccadilly Circus or Montmartre had been leveled on a crowded Saturday night?", and answered, "my necessarily tentative answer is yes quite probably, for one reason: Britain and France, Europe's only credible military powers, could not have taken the war to the enemy unless NATO declared the attack on American soil to be an assault on all". Only Tony Blair understood the prevailing and future situation, and that is the reason he would not retreat from the position of unhesitating support for the US and its policies against Iraq. For the US power, and especially its will to project it, have exposed not only Europe's vulnerability and the hollowness of the EU pretensions of military self-sufficiency, but have also demonstrated how vital US power was for their security. Rosemary Righter concluded that the rise in anti-Americanism in Europe and its corollary - anti-Israel prejudice - tended to distort the political prism through which Britain's national interest was seen, and called upon the Conservatives in Britain to lend Bush their support.[78]

Even in the field of "regular", let alone ideological, criminality, there is a great concern among some European populations about the sharp rise of crime in their communities due to Muslim immigrants who do not always show respect for the rule of law. Particularly alarming has been a series of rapes of European women, which is claimed to be connected with the fact that they are not "properly veiled". *Front Page Magazine*[79] has recently brought to public attention a revealing debate between experts, headlined by an atrocious picture of a beaten and bleeding Swedish woman who was said to be a "victim of Muslim gang rape". The participants, all specialists of various aspects of Islamic martyrdom *(Islamikaze},* made some harrowing interpretations of the phenomenon. Peter Raddatz, a German scholar of Islam, advanced the thesis that in Orthodox Islam there is a deep division between sexes, with Allah licensing men to be the masters of females, to go to them whenever they like, to enjoy them however they like and to discipline them in case they develop their own ideas, like sexual self-determination. The woman is regarded as a "seed-field" that under strict male surveillance entails "Islamic correct" veiling for the continued survival and expansion of Islam.[80] Family "honor", which is the province of men to protect, installs male control over women, which sometimes can end in brutal rape. Since the man is the pure element who supervises the impure women, sexuality becomes the double-edged way of both fertilizing and punishing. Therefore, just as *Islamikaze* bombings are a "protest" against the "arrogance" of the West, Raddatz regards the rape wave under discussion as *a jihad* against women who, under Western influence, may drift out of male control. He cites as a corollary the sodomization of French officers by Algerian independence fighters, as a way to achieve the enemy's degradation, and he laments the Western mainstream propensity to accept these norms and to adjust itself to Muslim immigrant *shari'a* demands based on the growing Islamist influence in Europe.[81]

Another participant in that debate, journalist Gudrun Eussner from Berlin, thought that the attacks against European women by guest Muslims was related to the new definition of Western countries by fundamentalist *salafists,* such as Tariq Ramadan of Geneva, who viewed them no longer as *Dar-al-Harb,* or the space of war, but rather as *Dar al-Da'wa* (the Call, or mission, on Islam's behalf), or *Dar-al-Shahada* (the space of "testimony"), with its double meaning as "bearing witness that there is no God but Allah and Muhammed is His Messenger", and "to die as a *shahid* (Martyr) in the Path of Allah". This soft way of interpreting *Dar-al-Harb,* which otherwise obliges Muslims to fight the opponent until submission, calls upon the Muslims to wait and not challenge the enemy as long as they are not strong enough to defeat him, this not to be understood as resignation from converting that enemy to Islam, but as what the French call *"entrisme",* namely a patient and persistent long-term penetration that will gnaw at and exhaust the enemy from within. Eussner cited the case of the inauguration of a mosque in Granada, Spain, in July 2003, where a Turkish scholar, who is also a member of the Turkish Parliament, made the remark that Paris, Rome and Madrid had become part of *Dar al-Islam,* due to the erection of mosques there and the free spread of the Word of Allah ironically under the protective wings of the liberties established by unsuspecting and naive Europeans. But when *Dar al-Da'wa* fails to produce compliance with the laws of Allah, then *jihad* is required to punish those who refuse to submit, among them those women who do not obey the laws of Islam by accepting male supremacy and remaining unveiled. Non-Muslim women, who by the definition of Danish Mufti Shahid Mehdi in 2004, "are asking for rape" by their public conduct, are then punishable by Muslim men who cannot accept their "obstruction" of the expansion of Muslim territory and morality. Eussner rejects Norwegian Professor Unni Wikan's *dhimmi*-like[82] contention that Norwegian women have to take their part of the blame for these rapes, because they are not dressing and behaving according to Muslim rules.[83]

This very revealing debate, which from treating an issue of criminology grew to tackle intriguing problems of religion, theology, mass psychology and sociology, continued with Pierre Rehov, a French filmmaker of Palestinian films regarding the *Intifadah*. He contends that in Muslim society there is a great temptation to rape as a result of female "provocation", the latter including anything from smiling and singing, being alone in a room with the rapist, to wearing "inappropriate" clothes - all these fashions of "misconduct" justifying "revenge". In Muslim society where any pre-marital or extra-marital relationship is taboo, men are made in the image of God and woman is the closest thing to a devil to tempt them, thus re-enacting the role of the carrier of the original sin. When a Muslim male rapes the improper woman, then he is fighting the Devil, and what happens is not the result of his own will, but against it; and because of that he is sure to get absolution for his deed. The Muslim male must react to the temptation, and since he is permanently frustrated by the limitations on sexual behavior, his reaction is violent and may end up in rape. Rehov cites the case of a district in southern France where 80% of the rapes were committed by Muslim men (a manifold higher proportion than their numbers in the population), of which 30% involved gang-rape. The police frequently apprehended the rapists who were young Muslims, and when they complained, the parents not only backed up their children but could not understand the reason for their arrests in the first place. Those parents saw evil in the irresistible "temptation" that the non-Muslim victims posed to the rapists. They therefore viewed their children's behavior as a natural reaction to the "unacceptable" behavior of Western women.

Nancy Kobrin, an American psychoanalyst, who has conducted years of field work interviewing abused female Muslims in the US, generally agrees with the above, but adds that while female immigrant women in America would call the police when abused, they would turn around and defend the rapists as part of their mentality of identifying with the aggressors. Some of them justified wife-beating as "educational", since they were probably brutalized as young girls and cannot find any reason to exonerate from blame the unveiled Western woman. She says that every Muslim male or female she interviewed had witnessed their mother beaten and experienced brutality themselves. Therefore, rape and the acceptance of being raped becomes a learned behavior at home, implying male supremacy and the denigration of women, and the protection of the rapist within the family due to "family honor". There is nothing surprising, then, when those rapists move into European streets to commit their acts of violence. She also regards rape as an "additional weapon in the arsenal of *jihad"* in *Dar-al-Shahada.* She believes that Muslim rapists not only attack Western women but at the same time ambush the Western male. For example, when the Moroccan Bouyeri killed Van Gogh, it was not only because, as claimed, of his movie *Submission,* where he dubbed Muslims a "fifth column", but because he also accused them of being "goat f_ _ _ers", something that hurt the masculinity of Muslim men in more ways than one: a goat herder is the bottom of the social pile, the goat is slaughtered and eaten. Children are often treated as if they were goats. Kobrin attacks the Western women in academe who have "sold out to political correctness", and go to extreme lengths to defend "their" male rapists.[84]

Further evidence was produced during the debate about Muslim women who, once in the West, feel free to open their hearts and report the abuses they had been subjected to in childhood by their parents and brothers, or in adulthood with their husbands, but public discussion of these issues has remained muted for the most part. Conversely, male Muslim immigrants in the West often hate their countries of refuge because they are not totally free to live according to *shari'a* and dominate their women, since the latter often call the police when they are abused. Due to their totalitarian heritage, some Muslim men target the most vulnerable elements of their society, namely women. In Europe, the past decade has seen feminists, intellectuals and political parties submitting to Islamic laws and demands; in other words, the Islamization of Europe was in the making. The handling of the cartoon crisis by the Danish authorities was seen as a sure sign of Europe pulling back and submitting to Muslim claims. But the permissiveness towards things Islamic would certainly not put an end to the cases of rape, which are "understood", sometimes even "justified" in both "liberal" and Muslim women's circles which rush to the defense of their culture even though they are its first victims. Some saw in the raping of European women by Muslim males also a political act of racism, of "conquest" of the "oppressor's women", which additionally punished the perceived "oppressors". Furthermore, European society is hated because it creates equality between men and women, thus challenging male-dominated Muslim society, exposing its inadequacies in the modern world, while at the same time inciting Muslim women to emulate the West by shaking off the burden of male domination. Therefore, raping a woman from another culture is a statement of contempt for, hatred toward and fear from, that entire other culture.[85]

On the other hand, it was precisely the demonstration of power, violence and fear elicited among Westerners which attracted many to convert to Islam. In post-September 11 America, for example, we have the enthusiastic reports of Dr Fatihi, from the Harvard Medical School, who wrote that in the eleven days that elapsed after September 11, the Boston Muslim community achieved more success with proselytizing than in the previous 11 years.[86] Some of these cases of conversion came to the attention of journalists. Charles Vincent is an example to be heeded. His experience can be expected to be replicated throughout Europe, following the tens of thousands of Westerners who, for all sorts of reasons, have converted to Islam and are becoming some of its more devoted adepts and sometimes most dangerous activists. Five days before 9/11, Charles Vincent bought his first Qur'an. Six weeks later, while smoke was still billowing from the remains of the World Trade Center, he formally converted to Islam in the mosque attached to the Islamic Cultural Center on 96th Street and Third Avenue in New York City. A blond, blue-eyed 29-year-old from Torrance, California, he readily admits that he chose an unlikely moment to fall in love with the world's most newsworthy religion. But in the years since, his devotion to Islam has only deepened. Like a growing number of white Americans and Europeans, he has discovered that Islam is not just the religion of those "other" people. "Every day I'm more surprised than the day before," he told a journalist one evening in October 2001, breaking his Ramadan fast in a fast-food restaurant a few blocks from the 96th Street mosque. "The last religion I wanted to belong to was Islam. The last word that came out of my mouth was Allah. Islam pulled me out of the biggest hole I've ever been in." Dressed as he is in an Islamic-style tunic and a white cap, Vincent may look unusual, but he certainly isn't alienated, or for that matter, alone. In the United States, there are estimated to be roughly 80,000 white and Hispanic Muslims, along with a far greater number of African-American ones. In France, there are perhaps 50,000, according to a secret government intelligence report leaked to the French newspaper *Le Figaro*. (A Muslim resident of the racially mixed Belleville district of Paris said that out of every 100 Muslims one sees there, 30 are former French Catholics.) The report stated that conversion to Islam "has become a phenomenon [in France] that needs to be followed closely." A recent study commissioned by Jonathan ("Yahya") Birt, a Muslim convert and the son of a former director-general of the BBC, put the figure in Britain at a more modest 14,000, and there are similar estimates for Spain and Germany. More people are converting throughout the globe - from Australia and New

Zealand to Sweden and Denmark. The number of converts in steadily increasing, and thereby gathering power. Becoming a Muslim is surprisingly easy. All you need to do is take *shahada* - say, *La ilaha illa Allah, Muhammad rasulu Allah* ("There is no God but Allah, and Muhammed is the Messenger of Allah") in front of two Muslim witnesses and you're a Muslim.[87] For reasons of male dominance, there are more male than female converts to Islam, though no exact data exist.

Muslims are required to pray five times a day, donate a certain amount of money to charity, fast between sunrise and sunset during the month of Ramadan, and, health and finances permitting, make at least one *haj,* or pilgrimage, to Mecca during their lifetime. But why would a non-Muslim choose to convert to a religion increasingly associated with dictatorial governments, mass terrorism, videotaped beheadings and the oppression of women? One reason, according to author and journalist Brendan Bernhard, might be disillusionment with wall-to-wall entertainment, jaded sexuality, spiritual anomie and all the other ailments of the materialistic West. Another might be protest. He reports that he was present as Heriberto Silva, a Catholic teacher of Spanish literature at the City University of New York, took *shahada* and became Abdullah Silva, Muslim, during Friday prayers at the 96th Street mosque. A frail 60-year-old bundled into an old jacket, a thick volume titled *A History of the Arabs* tucked under his arm, he told Bernhard afterward that his conversion was due to three factors: a long-standing fascination with the Islamic world; the encouragement of his Muslim friends; and a desire to register a personal objection to the Iraq War. "We see a president who is preaching about freedom and democracy, and it is not true! It is all lies!" he said. "I am looking for something that is real truth, and I found in Islam that truth." Vincent's conversion appears to have been a more muddled, emotional affair, but also a more dramatic one, since it took place in New York against the backdrop of 9/11. Like many people who convert to Islam or any other religion, he did so after a particularly difficult period in his life in which he not only lost his "way" but also his job and his apartment, climaxing with a fight outside a nightclub in which he almost lost the sight in one eye. He had a good Moroccan friend who strongly encouraged him to convert, and may even have insisted that he do so as a price of friendship. Muslims are just as intrigued by Vincent's transformation as anyone else. "I was making prayer in this mosque during Ramadan in November 2001," he said, "and I could feel the brother next to me stare. After the prayers, the first thing out of his mouth was, 'How did you become a Muslim?'. That was very strange to me. I didn't know how to answer him. I said, 'What do you mean, how did I become a Muslim?' And he said, "How did you become a Muslim? You have to have a story of how you became a Muslim.' And I realized he was right. There was a process I went through. Muslims know that it's not by chance that you come into this religion. I know that now too."[88]

There is a point of view that maybe Bin Laden did the European Muslims a disservice by precipitating his attack on America. Had he waited another ten years or so, Muslims would have been far more firmly entrenched in the institutions and society of the various countries they inhabit, and may have also irreversibly infiltrated the security forces and apparatus. Then they would have been in a much more advantageous position to strike. But what happened, happened, and public opinion in Europe woke up following September 11 and began to wonder about what was taking place in their countries. A castigating article by George Weigel, which describes the caving in of Europe and its consequences, sums up the situation. He tells that at the height of the morning commute on March 11, 2004, when ten bombs exploded in and around four train stations in Madrid, almost 200 Spaniards were killed, and some 2,000 wounded. Spain seemed to be standing firm against terror, with demonstrators around the country wielding signs denouncing the "murderers" and "assassins." Yet this did not hold. Seventy-two hours after the bombs had strewn arms, legs, heads, and other body parts over three train stations and a marshaling yard, the Spanish government of Jose Maria Aznar, a staunch ally of the United States and Great Britain regarding Iraq, was soundly defeated in an election that the socialist opposition had long sought to turn into a referendum on Spain's role in the war on terror. A 54-page al-Qa'ida document, which came to light three months after the bombings, had speculated that the Aznar government would be unable to "suffer more than two or three strikes before pulling out [of Iraq] under pressure from its own people." In the event, it was one strike and out, as it was for the Spanish troops in Iraq who were withdrawn shortly thereafter, just as the newly elected prime minister, Jose Luis Zapatero, had promised on the day after Spanish voters chose appeasement.

What is more, sixty years after the end of World War II, the European instinct for appeasement is alive and well. French public swimming pools have been segregated by sex because of Muslim protests. "Piglet" mugs have disappeared from certain British retailers after Muslim complaints that the A.A. Milne character was offensive to Islamic sensibilities. So have Burger King chocolate ice-cream swirls, which reminded some

Muslims of Arabic script from the Qur'an. Then he referred to author Bruce Bawer's report that the British Red Cross banished Christmas trees and nativity scenes from its charity stores for fear of offending Muslims and that for similar reasons, the Dutch police in the wake of the van Gogh murder destroyed a piece of Amsterdam street art that proclaimed "Thou shalt not kill", and school-children were forbidden to display Dutch flags on their backpacks because immigrants might think them "provocative." He says that European media frequently censor themselves in matters relating to domestic Islamic radicalism and crimes committed by Muslims, and, with rare exceptions, their coverage of the war against terrorism makes, by contrast, the American mainstream media look balanced. When domestic problems relating to Muslim immigrants do come to light, the typical European reaction, according to Weigel's interpretation of Bawer, is usually one of self-criticism. In Malmo, Sweden, the country's third-largest city, rapes, robberies, school-burnings, "honor" killings, and anti-Semitic agitation became so out of hand that large numbers of native Swedes reportedly moved to other locations; the government blamed Malmo's problems instead on Swedish racism, and chastised those who had wrongly conceived of integration as "two hierarchically ordered categories, a 'we' who shall integrate and a 'they' who shall be integrated."[89] Belgium, for its part, has established a governmental Center for Equal Opportunities and Opposition to Racism (CEEOR) which recently sued a manufacturer of garage security gates since their Moroccan employees work only in the factory and are not sent out to install the gates in Belgian homes. By contrast, according to the Belgian journalist Paul Belien, whose online *"Brussels Journal"* (www. brusselsjournal.com) is an important source of information on Europe's culture wars, CEEOR declined to prosecute a Muslim who created an anti-Semitic cartoon series, on the grounds that doing so would "inflame the situation."[90]

Perhaps predictably, European Jews have frequently played the role of the canary in the mineshaft amid the trials of Islamic integration. In 2004, a Parisian disc jockey was brutally murdered, his assailant crying "I have killed my Jew. I will go to heaven." That same night, another Muslim murdered a Jewish woman while her daughter watched, horrified. Yet at the time, as the columnist Mark Steyn has written, "no major French newspaper carried the story" of these homicides. In February 2006, the French media did report on the gruesome murder of a twenty-three-year old Jewish man, Ilan Halimi, who had been tortured for three weeks by an Islamist gang; his screams under torture were heard by his family during phone calls demanding ransom while, Steyn reports, "the torturers read out verses from the Qur'an." He quotes one police detective shrugging off the *jihadist* dimension of the horror by saying that it was all rather simple: "Jews equal money."[91]

These patterns of sedition and appeasement finally came to global attention in early 2006 in the Danish-cartoons jihad. The cartoons themselves, depicting Muhammad, caused little comment in Denmark or anywhere else when they were originally published months earlier in the Copenhagen daily *Jyllands-Posten*. But after Islamist Danish imams began agitating throughout the Middle East (aided by three additional and far more offensive cartoons of their own devising), an international furor erupted, with dozens of people killed by rioting Muslims in Europe, Africa, and Asia. As Henrik Bering put it in the *Weekly Standard*, "the Danes were suddenly the most hated people on earth, with their embassies under attack, their flag being burned, and their consciousness being raised by lectures on religious tolerance from Iran, Saudi Arabia, and other beacons of enlightenment." The response from Europe, in the main, was to intensify appeasement. Thus the Italian "Reforms Minister," Roberto Calderoli, was forced to resign for having worn a T-shirt featuring one of the offending cartoons - a "thoughtless action" that, Prime Minister Silvio Berlusconi deduced, had caused a riot outside the Italian consulate in Benghazi, Libya, in which eleven people were killed. Newspapers that ran the cartoons were put under intense political pressure; some journalists faced criminal charges; websites were forced to close. The pan-European Carrefour supermarket chain, bowing to Islamist demands for a boycott of Danish goods, placed signs in its stores in both Arabic and English expressing "solidarity" with the "Islamic community" and noting, inelegantly if revealingly, "Carrefour don't carry Danish products." The Norwegian government forced the editor of a Christian publication to apologize publicly for printing the Danish cartoons; at his press conference, the hapless editor was surrounded by Norwegian cabinet ministers and imams. EU foreign minister Javier Solana groveled before one Arab nation after another, pleading that Europeans shared the "anguish" of Muslims "offended" by the Danish cartoons. Not to be outdone, the EU's justice minister, Franco Frattini, announced that the EU would establish a "media code" to encourage "prudence" - "prudence" being a synonym for "surrender," regardless of one's view of the artistic merits of, or the cultural sensitivity displayed by, the world's most notorious cartoons.[92]

For all the blindness of the politicians who in the 1930s attempted to appease totalitarian aggression, they at least thought that they were thereby preserving their way of life. Bruce Bawer (following the researcher and author Bat Ye'or) suggests that twenty-first century Europe's appeasement of Islamists amounts to a self-inflicted *dhimmitude:* in an attempt to slow the advance of a rising Islamist tide, many of Europe's national and transnational political leaders are surrendering core aspects of sovereignty and turning Europe's native populations into second- and third-class citizens in their own countries.[93] No one has so brilliantly extracted from these sets of data the most exhaustive conclusions as did George Weigel. He writes:

> Bawer blames Europe's appeasement mentality and its consequences on multi-culturalist political correctness run amok, and there is surely something to that. For, in a nice piece of intellectual irony, European multiculturalism, based on postmodern theories of the alleged incoherence of knowledge (and thus the relativity of all truth claims), has itself become utterly incoherent, not to say self-contradictory. Take, for example, the case of Iqbal Sacranie, general secretary of the Muslim Council of Britain, whom Prime Minister Tony Blair appointed as one of his advisers on Muslim affairs and for whom Blair procured a knighthood. In a series of episodes that indeed seem like something from beyond Lewis Carroll's looking glass, Sir Iqbal soon went on the BBC to announce that homosexuality "damages the very foundation of society"; following the protests of a British gay lobby, he was investigated by the "community safety unit" of Scotland Yard, whose mandate includes "hate crimes and homophobia"; then, when a Muslim lobby demanded that Blair scrap the "Holocaust Memorial Day" he had created several years earlier, Sir Iqbal backed the demand, informing the *Daily Telegraph* that "Muslims feel hurt and excluded that their lives are not equally valuable to those lives lost in the Holocaust time." Yet to blame "multi-culti" p.c. for Europe's paralysis is to remain on the surface of things…. The attempt to impose multiculturalism and "lifestyle" libertinism in Europe by limiting free speech, defining religious and moral conviction as bigotry, and using state power to enforce "inclusivity" and "sensitivity"-is a war over the very meaning of tolerance itself. What Bruce Bawer rightly deplores as out-of-control political correctness in Europe is rooted in a deeper malady: a rejection of the belief that human beings, however inadequately or incompletely, can grasp the truth - a belief that has, for almost two millennia, underwritten the European civilization that grew out of the interaction of Athens, Jerusalem, and Rome.[94]

1

Subversive Terminology and Lethal Rhetoric

Words have a meaning and are used to transmit messages, but they are also culture-bound, and when Muslims pronounce a word which we know in our western parlance to have a specific meaning - like democracy, tolerance, terrorism - they might comprehend it differently. Words that we consider abrasive and subversive might well be spoken where their understood meanings are softer and not subversive. Nonetheless, there are words, phrases and slogans which are not ambiguous: for killing is killing, be it to punish a criminal, to eliminate an innocent person for the sake of an ideology or otherwise. Thus, though we may disagree on the purposes and justifications for killing, or on the value of human life, yet the end result is death. These are the distinctions we shall be making if we are to entertain any significant discourse with the world of Islam, our interlocutor. We have also to bear in mind that abuse and de-humanization of the enemy is a prerequisite to justify the battle; it makes the enemy a free prey ("permissible" in their jargon) for any Muslim, under circumstances of their own choosing, with the right to go unpunished for spilling blood of an enemy. For example, if one battles Muslims, or insults them or their Prophet or their Scripture, or humiliates them, one becomes "permissible" for punishment, regardless of what Muslims did to provoke, to attack, to invade or mutilate the enemy. Muslims alone hold the yardstick to measure who humiliates whom, who provokes whom, and who committed injustice, aggression or invasion against whom. The abrasive rhetoric does not always have to be verbal, but can also be expressed by body image or scenes of massive massacres which, far from evoking human sympathy for the victims, on the contrary arouse a mad thirst for more blood, not only among the killers but also amidst the Muslim masses who watch these scenes. For example, when bodies of Western or Israeli troops or civilians are mutilated in public, or decapitated live on television or lynched in a mad orgy of murder, Muslim masses in general play and replay these horrors to remind their constituencies of the "heroism" of the Muslim killers or incite the crowds to demonstrate their jubilation at the sight of their enemy's suffering. Scenes of this sort took place after September 11, after acts of terror against Israeli buses and after executions of Westerners in Iraq and Afghanistan. This in itself in turn creates not only an *ambiance* of tolerance for such acts of bloodlust, but "educates" the Muslim younger generation to emulate these killings amidst blatant demonstrations of obtuseness, cruelty and inhumanity.

Brutalization of life under puritanical Islam, which in turn renders speech abusively vulgar and generates rhetorical excess, is expressed *inter alia* by the application of harsh, inhuman, physical punishment under *shar-i'a* Law. Public beheadings are commonplace in Saudi Arabia, as are hangings, even of minors, in Iran. Stonings are still administered to adulterers and crude amputation of thieves' limbs is still common practice. Moreover, people commonly seen on the streets with missing limbs, not necessarily as a result of war wounds, but of punitive amputations, debases human life and tends to brutalize it. For if fellow Muslims can be treated worse than animals, it is not surprising that beheading enemies or mutilating their bodies after they are dead, seems to come naturally. The most gruesome state-sanctioned punishments, known to be carried out in the Taliban's Afghanistan and more recently in Iran and Saudi Arabia, may even involve the surgical removal of eyes. An intrepid Canadian journalist, Jane Kokan, obtained a video filmed undercover of just such a procedure while on a trip to Iran, along with videos of botched attempts at finger amputations and the like. In her film a man was shown whimpering during the extraction of his eyes under local anesthetic, this, for viewing pornographic magazines. The film was put together by Kokan (and shown on British television's Channel 4 on December 2, 2003).[1] Raised in this atmosphere of worthlessness of human life and of the human body, Muslims grow to denigrate it and to use abusive language to dismiss it. Horrible scenes are described in detail in Islamic texts, about punishments meted out to transgressors of the law, corporal chastisement of the enemy, self-mutilation or even self-immolation, as in the case of the *Islamikaze,* coupled with the harsh, coarse language of threat and intimidation. As examples, it suffices to refer to mutilation of dead American GIs in Iraq in 2005-6, or to the beheading, alive, of western hostages in that same country together with the abusive language that accompanies such executions.

These abuses of what is generally considered basic human conduct are not only the fruit of "spontaneous" rage of uncontrollable crowds at the sight of "desecrations" of their Holy sites or their saintly leaders, but are routinely so often repeated in the Muslim streets and over the media that they become the acceptable norm of conduct, in which a new generation is brought up to despise human life, discard human rights, reject peace with their neighbors, show intolerance for different views, and actually seek confrontations. A leader of an Islamist movement in Iraq declared recently to a foreign correspondent: "We know that we have a bad reputation in the West due to the scenes of summary executions that are shown in the West about us. This is done not by village boys like us, but by foreigners coming from Syria, Saudi Arabia, Jordan and Afghanistan, who are the most extremist." Another said: "Slashing the throat of a hostage is not our style, but if he is a spy, we got to do it, but without filming the scene."[2] So, even this "moderate village boy" who decries "foreign extremists", uses his own discretion in determining who is a spy - and slashing this individual's throat without due investigation or legal procedure - is justified *ipso facto.* Those who hesitate to perform such an act are yet urged to do so by the ideology of al-Qa'ida which proclaims without inhibition that "Jews and Christians must be killed" - a proclamation that finds wide appeal amidst young Muslims, especially converts to Islam among them, with their passion to demonstrate new religious zeal. No less important is that Europeans are made aware of Muslim words of hatred. A French weekly, *Le Point,* for example, made an in-depth investigative study of the mounting threat of Islam in Europe, collecting in the process many disturbing pronouncements of Muslim leaders.

Yussuf al-Qaradawi, a Muslim radical Sheikh in exile from his native Egypt and now living in Qatar, regularly appears on *al-Jazeera* network to expound his ideas and deliver *fatwas* (new decrees which become law) in Muslim fundamentalist circles. He is also President of the European Fatwa Council, namely the recognized authority of all European Muslims, "Islamist" or not, to deliberate on their problems, religious and otherwise, and to deliver verdicts that are seen by many as authoritative and enforceable. His friendship with the Lord Mayor of London, Ken Livingstone, who has repeatedly hosted him in the British capital, against the protests of many Britons, naturally lends legitimacy to both his Islamic theories and verdicts which are widely respected and heeded by Muslims. The French investigative report cited above recounts one of those pronouncements: "You must continue to battle the Jews. They will try to defend themselves, but you will get them ultimately. For the Jews will hide behind trees and rocks, who will announce out-loud : 'a Jew is hiding behind me, come and kill him!'; this will be a prerequisite for the coming of the Resurrection."[3] This commandment is an oft-repeated tradition of the Prophet of Islam *(hadith),* recurring *ad nauseam* in Islamist writings, and cited in full in the Charter of the Hamas. But hardly anyone wonders how it is that the followers of this Prophet of Islam, who feel insulted every step of the way for whatever is said of him, are not incensed by his appeal to wanton and indiscriminate murder of the followers of another faith, by those who claim to represent a "religion of peace and tolerance". Consequently, French Muslims manifest their hatred by attacking individual Jews on their way to synagogues, Jewish children on their way to school, or set fire to Jewish places of worship and cemeteries, and burn Israeli flags and effigies of Jewish leaders.[4] In this culture of hatred and vengeance, fantasy is prolific and the spoken word or symbolic act go a long way to substitute for the real thing.

Sheikh Yusuf Al-Qaradawi, whom Lord Mayor, Ken Livingstone, has termed "moderate", and whose influence extends also to the most radical groups in contemporary Islam, has made some stunning disclosures that are true to Islam but hardly qualify the man or any of his followers (and there are many) as moderate.[5] He said, *inter alia,* that:

> [John] Kerry, who ran against Bush in the 2004 elections, was supported by homosexuals and nudists. But it was Bush who won, because he is Christian, right-wing, tenacious, and unyielding. In other words, the religious overcame the perverted. So we cannot blame all Americans and Westerners. But unfortunately, because the Westerners - Americans and others - want to flatter these people on account of the elections, a disaster occurs. In order to succeed and win the elections, he flatters these people, rather than saying to them: No, you are sinning against yourselves, against society, and against humanity. This is forbidden. Instead of leveling with them, people flatter them to win their votes. This is the disaster that has befallen humanity.... Lesbians and homosexuals should be punished the same punishment as any sexual pervert - the same as the fornicator. The schools of thought disagree about the punishment [disagreement is not between moderate and radical but between bad and worse]. Some say they should be punished like fornicators, and then we distinguish between married and unmarried men, and between married and unmarried women. Some say both should be punished the same way. Some say we should throw them from a high place, like God did with the people of Sodom. Some say we should burn them, and so on. There is disagreement. The important thing is to treat this act as a crime.... Lesbianism is not as bad as homosexuality, in practical terms.[6]

Such abrasive statements were finally picked up, monitored and heeded by French police when they realized that words led to deeds. The French *Le Point* indeed reported that the General Intelligence Directorate

(DCRG - Direction Centrale des Renseignements Generaux) collected extracts from the Friday sermons in radical mosques and, acting upon this intelligence 19 activists were expelled from France in 2005 alone, and more thereafter, including one imam and one preacher. The other expellees were "ideological operators" who led groups whose potential for subversion was detected by the authorities and whose rhetoric against Jews and Americans was among their chief targets. One of these expelled imams protested incessantly against the "West that was ruled under the boot of Zionists and their mercenaries" and vowed that "the land must burn from New York to Jerusalem". He preached that "*jihad* must be waged everywhere on Allah's land", so that the "Holy Places should be cleansed from Jews, Christians and heretic Muslims". Europe in general, and the French Republic in particular, also come under this all-encompassing definition of the enemies of Islam, for *jihad* ought to be launched against "the Great Americano-Zionist Satan and its undistinguishable petty allies of all sorts". The rationale is chillingly simple: "secularism is a diabolical concept, a Zionist invention", and Islam cannot accept democracy because "democracy means rule by the people while in Islam it is exclusively the domain of Allah". One of those Muslim radical imams, who follows the Turkish *Kaplan* stream of worship, has called on his adepts to "never submit to French demands" and dubbed in 1994 the then Minister of the Interior, Charles Pasqua, "a poisonous snake who aspires for the death of Islam so that he can enslave the Muslims". In 1997, this imam attacked France on account of its "corrupt politicians and its decadent society, which have to be brought back to reason one of these days". He also voiced his opposition to the "Catholic idolaters" and to the "criminal and perfidious French language". All of this amounted to a Muslim refusal "to acculturate into any society that is not Islamic". He further castigated Believers who let their wives dress like "loose western women" and specifically attacked a young Muslim Turkish woman who in 2005 married a French man, for having "infected the blood of the True Faith".[7]

Even though some of the provocative and inflamed rhetoric was toned down among Islamists in the West, who were desirous to lower their profile after 11 September, some, like the *Kaplan* Turkish radical movement in Europe, whose declared goal is to restore the Caliphate to their home country, did not relent. The above-mentioned hate-citations from the *kaplangi* Imam who was expelled from France have been repeated by others of the same conviction and indeed their preachers are regularly also expelled back to Turkey. But those who escape expulsion continue to propagate their horrific ideology. One of them declared on April 1, 2005 that "Jews are at the root cause of all problems of the Muslims", and that "all media are controlled by Jews". On May 27 thereafter, he entreated his followers to "be patient, for Allah, Islam and Muslims will emerge victorious ultimately". When such public pronouncements are heard or monitored, the Paris Criminal Police *(Brigade Criminelle)* "reminds" them of the stringencies of the law. But these measures cannot prevent the incendiary discourse from spreading via the internet or private meetings of small groups of radicals. For example, the *salafi* movement in France, which aspires to return Islam to the days of the Prophet, and counts about 5,000 amongst its membership according to the General Intelligence Directorate, also controls some 40 mosques throughout the country. A French sociologist of Persian descent, Farhad Kosrokhavar, who prepared a report for General Intelligence on that group, came to the conclusion that those young Muslims who cultivate "social rancor" in their midst are preparing "to cross sabres with the Republic." The young radical Muslim generation in France views negatively the large Muslim organizations in France which negotiated with the state the Constitution of the CFCM (the state-sponsored umbrella organization of the Muslims in France). For them, that constitution drawn up through the initiative of Nicholas Sarkozy, then Home Secretary but since elected President in May 2007, was a " sell out" to the French, as also believed the militant *tablighis* and fiery Tariq Ramadan.[8]

The hero of those diehard *salafists* is Abdelkader Bouziane, former imam of the mosque in Venissieux, who was expelled in 2004 for suggesting in public that "beating one's wife was part of his marital duties". When interrogated about this, he said that while the French penal code prohibited wife beating, the Qur'an allowed it. The Court of Law in Lyon convicted him to six months in prison. But *salafists* are not alone in their pursuit of applying literally the rules of their Qur'an. Yussuf Qaradawi, mentioned above as Head of the European *Fatwa* Council, is also the spiritual guide of the Union of the Islamic Organizations of France (UOIF -Union des Organizations Islamiques de France), and his *fatwas* are much heeded. A booklet containing a selection of such verdicts, prefaced by Tariq Ramadan, was published with a blue cover and yellow stars sprinkled on it so as to give it the appearance of an official European publication. In it Qaradawi specifies that a woman can cut her hair without her husband's permission only if the cut is unnoticeable, but any change in appearance as a result requires the "agreement between the spouses prior to its implementation"; in other words the husband reserves the right of veto.

Another preacher of the Muslim Brothers confirmed that "the husband has the right to proscribe to his wife the visit of any other woman, Muslim or otherwise, when he has reason to fear that the visit might hurt his wife, his children or their marital life". This example of "equality" between the genders was sure to arouse the negative sentiment of the French regarding the application of *shari'a* in their own country. Much more alarming to the French, however, beyond the petty details that concern relations between men and women, were the diatribes against France itself, often uttered by Muslim radicals. For example, when France is accused by those fundamentalists of being "neither democratic nor the country of human rights" because "Truth does not reside in human rights but in Islam", and they claim that "never was a church closed down in Turkey", contrary to some mosques that were closed down in Europe, no history-conscious Frenchman can remain indifferent. For in fact, not only do the churches in Turkey and the rest of the Islamic world not incite against their countries and governments, unlike some mosques in Europe, but in a blatant denial of history, Muslims want to conveniently forget that they converted many churches (and synagogues) to mosques, the most famous of them being the Aya Sophia in Christian Constantinople, which became Istanbul under Muslim occupation since 1453.[9]

A *salafi* imam of the Paris region was cited as declaring that "France is an impious state that wishes the principles of Islam to dissipate gradually", and that "western liberalism is the origin of all perversions". Like the proponents of the radical Islamist theme of "*al-Takfir wal-Hijra*" (which declares others as *Unbelievers* and demands *migration* away from their midst), some of those Muslim preachers in Europe do indeed hint at the possibility of migrating from the corrupt and unjust societies where they live and failing that, at the very least, to cut themselves off from their sinful environment, into Muslim enclaves where they can apply their laws and customs, clear from the infections of western society, to which they have to resort only when it is absolutely necessary. In other words, while they "migrated" from their countries of origin, which had persecuted them due to their radicalism, in order to find freedom of worship and of political activity in the West, now that they realize that the West is not to their liking either, due to its "corruption", "injustice" and "perversion", where can they go? Since there are no signs that they wish to return *en masse* to their home countries, one can surmise that they would rather attempt to change their lands of asylum to fit their convictions. On September 9, 2005, a French radical imam was heard to enjoin his followers to confine their social contacts to "good relationships with people who fear Allah". On the previous February 11, another imam called upon his congregation to "avoid contacts with Unbelievers *(kuffar),* be they Muslims who misbehave or non-Muslims, and shy from visiting them even in hospital". That was the only way for him to evade the impurities of French and Western societies in general. Hassan Iquioussen, a popular preacher who presents himself as the *alter-ego* of the intellectual Tariq Ramadan, has also attacked the Jews in the past as "Misers and interest-loaners" and added that Zionists had plotted together with Hitler, a contention often heard in Arab circles, including from the "moderate" President of the Palestinian Authority, Mahmoud Abbas, who won a "doctorate" in Moscow on that "merit".[10]

The incendiary statements of Abu Hamza and al-Bakri in England, discussed above, provide a straightforward exposition of their goals. Likewise, does Yacine Kassab, who publishes in French. Kassab has published at Editions Lanterne, a name which exactly translates as *al-Manar,* the mouthpiece of one of the celebrated founders of Muslim activism in the twentieth century, Rashid Rida. *Al-Manar* is also the information organ of Hizbullah as well as the name of its TV station. In his book *Muslim Divisions in the Face of Western Hegemony*[11] Kassab laments the "depraved western society where money has been raised to the rank of a universal deity" and proceeds to claim that the *Taliban* were nothing more than "Students of Theology", which is indeed the literal meaning of the word, "who possessed a sense of humanity much superior to that of their [American] persecutors". For him, the "Western Hell is a place where criminal practices are permitted, including incest and paedophilia, which are favorably regarded and practiced in secrecy by a growing number of those who pretend to incarnate the morality of human kind". In this scheme, Muslims represent the good and the Unbelievers the evil, and he specifies that "exactly as there can be no atheist-, Communist- or liberal-Muslim, there cannot exist a Muslim who kills children, who slashes throats, who rapes women or who murders innocent people". For Kassab, "all Muslims are innocent, and all the culprits are Christian or Jewish". In his view, Islam in France is subjected to an attempt by the immoral West to modify it in order to make it fashionable, to accord with the French vogue and push Muslims to drift without purpose.[12]

There are, of course, apparent voices of moderation as well, such as the Sufi Sheikh Muhammed Hisham Kabbani, the central figure in the Islamic Supreme Council of America (ISCA). On the one hand, he launched attacks on the Saudis in no uncertain terms, probably because of their suppression of the Sufis. He says that the Saudi agenda is to impose their policies on the world, using Muslims who live in foreign lands - particularly the West - as their propaganda tool. He emphasized in a public lecture in London (in 2006) the manner and method by which the Saudis throw hate in every direction, stating that the "*jihad* of hate" is disseminated by brainwashing as a prelude to the anticipated fight with the West. He expounded on some of the obtuse language used by Bin Laden, e.g. "diamonds scratch diamonds", eliciting bewilderment in the audience. (He was apparently referring to Bin Laden's statement in one of his video-cassettes, where he hinted that his operations are financed by his worldwide diamond trade.) He also pointed out how Muslim radicals have been hacking into computer systems in the sub-continent of India to track people and funds for their own nefarious purposes. Kabbani was scathing about the way Westerners unthinkingly misapply the word "moderate" in relation to some Muslim figures who reside in the West. Much of his criticism was also directed against the *ikhwan* (Muslim Brothers), and their infiltration of the Indonesian parliament (where the current speaker of the house is a member). Egypt's destruction of their infrastructure, he said, has only hastened their re-grouping into myriad cells, which are much harder for western security services to locate. He emphasized that only Morocco has made some headway in reversing the gains of *salafis* in recent years via the expedient of encouraging Sufi grass-roots among Moroccans. At the conclusion of that lecture he answered all questions adequately, but discredited himself when a questioner asked why he insisted that Islam respected Jews and Christians despite the contents of some Qur'anic verses. Kabbani replied that the unpleasant verses were abrogated by the more respectful ones. However, while it is true that the Law of Abrogation *(al-Nasekh wal-mansukh)* exists in Islam, it does not apply to "bad verses" that are replaced by "good ones". The contrary seems to have prevailed, as a result of Islamist theology's choice to prefer the later-revealed verses in the Qur'an over the earlier ones, whenever there is contradiction between them. It so happens that the latest "revelations" (as the verses of the Book are dubbed), condemn the Jews to "eternal misery" and demean and incite hatred towards the People of the Book, while it is the laudatory verses promising to the Jews the Holy Land which are considered abrogated.

On the other hand, in his writings which are disseminated by ISCA, Kabbani seems to "understand" some moves of the fundamentalists, though on the surface he condemns them. In his *Globalization of Jihad*[13] for example, he writes that after the collapse of the Soviet Union, a loose Islamic coalition has become the only power to challenge the power of the US, in conjunction with America haters in South America. For this purpose, Muslim movements are adopting an increasingly Marxist and anti-imperialistic rhetoric, such as class struggle and anti-capitalism, to appeal to their new allies in countering America. He contends that al-Qa'ida has not been destroyed, though it was organizationally shattered into myriad pieces which are able to act independently and penetrate even deeper than before into western targets, and that the western war on terrorism has spawned new dispersed organizations which receive financing and assistance from Bin Laden but operate independently of him. Other noteworthy points in Kabbani's essay include:

1. Al-Qa'ida and its affiliates have moved their operations to more vulnerable areas of the world like Asia and Africa, where defenses are less sophisticated and less alert than in the West. At the same time, al-Qa'ida continues to infiltrate the West through student visas which they obtain for their membership through expending "charitable" monies, and through recruitment of Caucasians for terrorist attacks, hoping to take advantage of their lesser visibility in Western societies.

2. To increase their recruits and lessen their conspicuousness in the environment, al-Qa'ida operatives hack into medical records of individuals and spot the more mentally disturbed who are likely to be talked into joining their ranks in order to commit *Islamikaze* operations or to use chemical or biological weapons against large concentrations of civilians.

3. Kabbani calls the indoctrination that is imparted to those recruits a "twisted version of Islam" and warns the US against falling into the trap of heeding insurgent misinformation in Iraq which inveigles innocent people into collaborating with the insurgents, so that retaliation be mounted against them by the Americans. Thereafter coalition forces are accused of injustice towards the innocent, so as to boost hatred against them.

4. The *jihadists* use the Internet to compile targets and coordinate operations between the diffuse groups of terrorists. According to Kabbani, Italian authorities have identified thousands of potential targets in their territory and deployed thousands of security forces and computer experts to scuttle acts of terrorism against their citizens. They monitor more than 13,000 suspicious websites of incitement, information for recruits, and

instructions for rioting. Among others, those websites resulted in the riots in France of late 2005.

5. He warns against Western attempts to impose democracy on an unprepared Muslim world, that is, a world not prepared for democracy to override Muslim values. It is the leaders of the Islamist movements who profess these ideas, who spread resentment against the West, not the heads of states who are themselves threatened by their own fundamentalists. The rioters against the cartoons did not want to condemn the cartoons as much as they wished to demonstrate Muslim power. Only in Muslim countries where the official rulers lead an anti-American policy did the riots turn violent; elsewhere there were demonstrations without recourse to violence.

Less ambiguous were the voices among moderate Muslims in Europe who saw their gains in European society jeopardized by the Cartoon Affair and the ensuing riots. Even before the Cartoon Affair, some Danish Muslims made an effort to bridge the gap with their host society. Though Denmark's moderate Muslims have shied away from speaking out critically against Islamic radicalism out of fear of reprisals and social isolation, threats and violence, several immigrant pundits and politicians stated their concerns to the daily newspaper *Jyllands-Posten* (the same paper which was to trigger the cartoon controversy a year later), following the murder of Dutch filmmaker Theo van Gogh in November 2004. Danish-Pakistani author and political adviser Mohammad Rafiq published a book in which he openly criticized the practice of forced marriages. Following the book's release, Rafiq was the target of threats from Muslim extremists. He has so far refused to withdraw from the public arena, but says he knows people who are deliberately keeping quiet out of fear of reprisals. "I've nearly been assaulted, and I've gotten threats. Not many people dare to speak out -they're just keeping quiet," said Rafiq. Iranian-born social worker and Socialist People's Party City Council candidate for Svendborg, Masoun Moradi, also received death threats for writings perceived as critical of Islam. Moradi likewise says he has no plans to censor himself, but says the reaction to his criticism from fellow Muslims is proof that others have given up. "I've received three calls so far from other Danes of foreign descent who've become involved in the debate. They say they've also received death threats, but they haven't gone public. It's horrible that this kind of thing is allowed to happen. People born in Denmark regard freedom of speech as something quite natural, but for me it's a gift that must be safeguarded," said Moradi. Lebanese-born Rabhi Azad-Ahmad agrees. Azad-Ahmad chairs a multicultural association in the Arhus suburb of Gellerup. The group arranges regular debates, and as chairman, Rabhi Azad-Ahmad is active in local media. "There are still extremists out there making life miserable for their own, and completely robbing some people of the desire to discuss anything. I myself have received threatening letters and heard rumours going around that I was anti-Islam," he said, noting that his own mother once asked him to refrain from speaking publicly. "But I fled another country because I did not have freedom of speech," he explained.[14]

MP Naser Khader was born in Syria, and since moving to Denmark has become a well-known pundit and unapologetic critic of some aspects of Islam. "I know several people who've become involved in the debate and subsequently pulled out of it altogether. One woman called me, quite shaken, and said she'd been threatened. Maybe the rest of us are tougher, but the fact remains that freedom of speech is the breath of democracy -and if you take that away, then democracy dies," said Khader. Tanwir Ahmad is a member of Copenhagen's City Council for the Radical Liberal party. Ahmad has called for equal protection under free speech laws in Denmark. "Free speech has a pretty long leash in this country. But it's a question of how far it leads when free speech is abused - or in cases of diverging viewpoints. Many people assume that free speech is absolute, but there are clear limits. The problem is that it's rarely enforced. Every time a critic of Islam shows up, then it's free speech - but if anyone dares to defend Islam, their freedoms are limited," said Ahmad.[15]

As the most heated rhetoric in the conflict over the Mohammed cartoons began to cool, moderate Muslims offered advice to Prime Minister Anders Fogh Rasmussen. He had invited a score of representatives from the newly founded "Democratic Muslims" to a meeting at his official residence to discuss how to improve the integration of Muslims. "The conflict shows that something is wrong, so let's use this situation to find out how we can do things better," said Naser Khader, group founder and opposition MP. Khader also stated that the meeting with the prime minister was intended as a signal to Muslims in Denmark and abroad: "We don't like what's happening out in the world. Our message to the Islamic world is that what's happening is not in the interest of Islam or Muslims." He thus unwittingly revealed another trait, this time of egocentrism, in many Islamic quarters, which believe that the entire universe revolves around them. All too often, when their leaders "apologize" for wrongdoing, they rarely criticize the intrinsic immorality of their act, or the travesty it might have caused to others, but only whether or not it serves the interest of Islam and Muslims, never of the country or the people they have hurt. When a horrific act of Islamic terror is perpetrated, the first criticism one hears from Islamic leaders is not of condemnation of the terrorists or identification with their victims, but that "it does not serve the interests of Muslims". Watch, for example, the recurrent "condemna- tions" of terrorism by "moderate" Muslims like the Presidents of Egypt and the Palestinian Authority, who reserve harsh words for the "act", not for its Palestinian perpetrators, with the perennial rationale that terrorism does "not serve Palestinian interests". For that reason, seldom does the public learn that the terrorists or their organizations are taken to task, even if they announced their authorship of the horror and boasted of it. Instead, the public is inundated by statements that condemn the act itself, as if it were a natural calamity, and the leaders of the world, including the UN secretariat, follow suit in order not to disturb the world consensus or raise resentment against themselves in the Muslim world.

This inability to properly condemn terrorist acts is particularly true of Palestinian (Hamas or Islamic Jihad, Tanzim or Al-Aqsa Brigades) acts of terror, where Palestinian leaders "condemn" the act itself but not its perpetrators, even though they know who carried out the deed, is founded on the principle that "it does not serve the interests of the Palestinian people". And so Israelis are murdered without the Palestinian authorities prosecuting or punishing the murderers, who then see themselves free to repeat their acts. This manipulative standard is in sharp contrast with that of US, western and Israeli policy by which, when unintentionally and accidentally, innocent civilians are killed or injured by them in the pursuit of their military targets, those responsible accept that responsi- bility, a part of which may extend to the offering of compensation. It is never declared that it was not in "their interest". This inability to condemn terrorists and not only their acts illustrates the difference between states which are compelled to accept responsibility and act to redress wrongs, and terrorists who have no obligations to acknowledge their acts, let alone to compensate the victims.

In Denmark, a group of moderate Muslims stated that it was vital that young immigrants be able to find on-the-job training positions as part of their education. The group also said that a special effort had to be made to integrate immigrant women. "We need to get hold of young immigrant women whose only contact with Danish society is their family. We need to get them out of the house and into Danish courses and courses about democracy," explained group member Rushy Rashid. Khader, whose role in finding common ground in the debate ensuing from the Mohammed cartoons has made him the man of the hour in Danish politics, said the group found it unacceptable that a handful of Muslims 'stole Islam' from the entire group. "The prime minister was moved when we told him that Denmark is not a racist country, and that we would fight for Denmark and to spread knowledge of democracy," Khader said. Both sides in the debate, according to the group, had a role to play in contributing to an improved dialogue. They said extremist anti-Muslim voices were just as harmful as extremist Islamicists in the search for dialogue and reconciliation.[16]

Later, Naser Khader became more explicit, as his patience with what he considered "extremist" Muslims ran out. "The time has come for moderate Muslims to confront extremist groups", the Syrian-born MP told the weekly newspaper *Sondagsavisen.* "To be a practicing Muslim is not the same as being an extremist. I'll fight the people who think they can tell me and others how to be a good Muslim. That is a matter between Allah and individual Muslims," he pronounced. Together with 120 other Muslims, Khader recently announced the creation of the *Alternative Muslim Network*, a group that seeks to provide a voice for moderate Muslims. Khader considered imams and fundamentalists as "self-appointed police officers of Allah". According to the 42-year-old MP, they are responsible for deepening the gaps between Muslims and Danes. "Imams and fundamentalists have secured too much influence in Denmark. We need to show that the opinions they represent are not shared by the majority of Muslims," he said. "I don't think the end of the world is right around the corner. But if we don't do something about this development, I think the future looks grim." He hoped the group could provide a historic turning point for a tolerant form of Islam that demonstrated that it is possible to be Muslim, democratic, and Danish. "The Danish society should know that we support democracy and freedom of expression one hundred percent. That we don't support *shari'a* law - not even in a Muslim country", said Khader.

As one of the country's most prominent Muslims, Khader has found himself in the line of fire from many sides since being elected to parliament in 2001. He is often asked by journalists to act as a spokesperson for the country's 200,000 Muslims, but fundamentalist Muslims have also turned on Khader for what they consider his secular ways. Despite their criticism, Khader maintains that it is possible to be both modern and Muslim. "The difference between me and the fundamentalists is that

I am a Muslim in a dynamic way. Islam should be interpreted based on the contemporary times we live in," explained Khader. "Fundamentalists say that what is written in the Qur'an is the Truth for all time. That is an opinion we moderate Muslims want to challenge."[17] Genuine moderate and open-minded Muslims of Khader's type could revolutionize the relations between Europe and its Muslim minority. But the problem is that there are too few of them and they are by far overwhelmed, in numbers and influence, by the virulent radical imams who not only battle them, threaten them and boycott them, but also push their flocks towards a collision course with their host societies. As long as this situation persists, and no alternative organized Islam emerges that reforms the *shari'a* or distances itself from it, it will not be possible to speak of a genuinely "moderate Islam" as a trend and a viable option.

Any discussion of Europe's future in light (or rather obscurity) of what is to come cannot ignore the wake-up words - of published views that demonstrate how this *jihadi* war is panning out.One of the world's most respected Deobandi scholars believes that aggressive military *jihad* should be waged by Muslims "to establish the supremacy of Islam" worldwide. Justice Muhammad Taqi Usmani argues that Muslims should live peacefully in countries such as Britain, where they have the freedom to practice Islam, only until they gain enough power to engage in battle. His views explode the myth that the creed of offensive, expansionist *jihad* represents a distortion of traditional Islamic thinking. Mr Usmani, 64 (in 2007), sat for 20 years as a *shari'a* judge in Pakistan's Supreme Court. He is an adviser to several global financial institutions and a regular visitor to Britain. Polite and soft-spoken, he revealed to *The Times* a detailed knowledge of world events and his words, for the most part, were balanced and considered. He agreed that it was wrong to suggest that the entire non-Muslim world was intent on destroying Islam. Yet this is a man who, in his published work, argues the case for Muslims to wage an expansionist war against non-Muslim lands. Mr Usmani's justification for aggressive military *jihad* as a means of establishing global Islamic supremacy is revealed at the climax of his book, *Islam and Modernism*. The work is a polemic against Islamic modernists who seek to convert the entire Qur'an into "a poetic and metaphorical book" because, he says, they have been bewitched by Western culture and ideology. The final chapter delivers a rebuke to those who believe that only defensive *jihad* (fighting to defend a Muslim land that is under attack or occupation) is permissible in Islam. He refutes the suggestion that *jihad is* unlawful against a non-Muslim state that freely permits the preaching of Islam. For Usmani, "the question is whether aggressive battle is by itself commendable or not". "If it is, why should the Muslims stop simply because territorial expansion in these days is regarded as bad? And if it is not commendable, but deplorable, why did Islam not stop it in the past?" He answers his own question thus: "Even in those days ... aggressive *jihads* were waged . . . because it was truly commendable for establishing the grandeur of the religion of Allah." These words are not the product of a radical extremist. They come from the pen of one of the most acclaimed scholars in the Deobandi tradition. Mr Usmani told *The Times* that *Islam and Modernism* was an English translation of his original Urdu book, "which at times gives a connotation different from the original".[18]

When one reads what Islamists have been up to, one can appreciate all the more the invidious role broadcasters such as CNN and the BBC have played in giving them a platform, in the name of freedom of expression, which at times is exercised to death. From secret hideouts in South Asia, a Spanish-Syrian al-Qa'ida strategist published thousands of pages of Internet tracts on how small teams of Islamic extremists could wage a decentralized global war against the United States and its allies. With the Afghanistan base lost, he argued, radicals would need to shift their approach and work primarily on their own, though sometimes with guidance from roving operatives acting on behalf of the broader movement. In October 2005, the writing career of Mustafa Setmariam Nasar both became known in public and came to an abrupt end when Pakistani agents seized him at a friend's house in the border city of Quetta and turned him over to US intelligence operatives, according to two senior Pakistani intelligence officials. With Spanish, British and Syrian interrogators lining up with requests to question him, he has turned out to be a prize catch, a man who is neither a bomb-maker nor an operational planner but one of the *jihad* movement's prime theorists for the post-September 11, 2001 world. Counter-terrorism officials and analysts have seen Nasar's theories in action in major terrorist attacks in Casablanca in 2003, Madrid in 2004 and London in 2005. In each case, the perpetrators organized themselves into local, self-sustaining cells that acted on their own but also likely accepted guidance from visiting emissaries of the global movement. Nasar's masterwork, a 1,600-page volume titled *The Call for a Global Islamic Resistance* has been circulating on websites since the end of 2004. The treatise, written under the pen name Abu Mus'ab al-Suri ("the Syrian"), draws heavily on lessons from past conflicts. Nasar, 47 (in 2006), outlined a strategy for a truly global conflict on as many fronts as possible and in the form of resistance by small cells or individuals, rather than by traditional guerrilla warfare. To avoid penetration and defeat by security services, he insists that organizational links should be kept to an absolute minimum. "The enemy is strong and powerful, we are weak and poor; the war duration is going to be long and the best way to fight it is in a revolutionary *jihad* way for the sake of Allah," he wrote in one paper. "The preparations better be deliberate, comprehensive and properly planned, taking into account past experiences and lessons." Intelligence officials stated that Nasar's doctrine has made ripples in radical Islamist chat rooms and on websites about *jihad* - holy war or struggle - over the past years. His capture, they said, has only added to his mystique. "He is probably the first to spell out a doctrine for a decentralized global *jihad*" explained Brynjar Lia, a senior counter-terrorism researcher at the Norwegian Defense Research Establishment, who is writing a book on Nasar. "In my humble opinion, he is the best theoretician among the *jihadi* ideologues and strategists out there. Nobody is as systematic and comprehensive in their analysis as he is. His brutal honesty and self-criticism is unique in *jihadi* circles."[19]

After the bombings in Madrid and London, investigators fingered Nasar as the possible hands-on organizer of those attacks, because he had lived in both cities in the 1990s. But so far, investigators have unearthed no hard evidence of his direct involvement in those attacks or any others, although they suspect he established sleeper cells in Spain and other European countries. Nasar was born in Aleppo, Syria, in 1958 and studied engineering (as did, in Hamburg, some of the perpetrators of September 11). In the early 1980s he took part in a failed revolt by the fundamentalist Muslim Brotherhood against Syrian strongman Hafez al-Assad. According to his own written accounts, he fled the country after that, then trained in camps in Jordan and Egypt. Later, he moved to Europe when it became clear that Assad was firmly entrenched in power. He arrived in Spain in 1985, married a Spanish woman who had converted to Islam, and through that connection became a dual Spanish-Syrian citizen. He also made contacts with other Syrian *emigres* who belonged to the Muslim Brotherhood. His neighbor in a small town in the province of Granada was Tayssir Alouni, a journalist for the *al-Jazeera* satellite television network who would later interview Osama bin Laden. Another friend was Imad Eddin Barakat Yarkas, who was convicted in 2005 on charges of running an al-Qa'ida cell in Spain. In 1987, Nasar journeyed to Pakistan and Afghanistan to help Muslim fighters in their rebellion against Soviet forces in Afghanistan. He trained at camps, met bin Laden and joined the ruling council of al-Qa'ida, according to a Spanish indictment filed against him. When he returned to Spain in 1992, he concentrated on building his own cell there and also traveled widely in Europe to set up other al-Qa'ida groups in Italy and France, according to the Spanish. "He's pretty much designed the structure of the cells that have operated in Europe," stated Rogelio Alonso, a terrorism expert and professor at King Juan Carlos University in Madrid. "He was the one with the prominent role as the individual who had the links with the higher echelons of al-Qa'ida". Although Nasar attracted the notice of Spanish police, investigators did not classify him as a serious threat. According to Spanish court papers, detectives had Nasar under surveillance in 1995. But when he moved to London in 2005, they stopped paying attention. In London, Nasar led an above-ground life as a writer and voice of Islamic extremism. He did publicity work for al-Qa'ida, helping to arrange interviews with bin Laden in Afghanistan for CNN and the BBC. He edited an Arabic-language newsletter called *al-Ansar,* (the Supporters, the title given to the Prophet's supporters in Medina after he moved there from his native Mecca in AD 622), which was devoted primarily to the cause of fundamentalists fighting a long and bloody civil war in Algeria. Even in London's sizable community of Arab exiles and radical Muslims, Nasar stood out for his strong views and unwillingness to compromise.[20]

In his newsletter, he defended the Armed Islamic Group, the Algerian rebel force known by its French acronym, GIA, for targeting Algerian civilians in a series of massacres that destroyed entire villages. When other Arab dissidents decried the tactics, Nasar turned on them as well, denouncing his critics in letters and in person. "In Algeria, he pushed people to violence," said one Arab exile living in Britain who tangled with Nasar in the mid-1990s. "He was not just an editor. He served as a strategist for those people and played a very bad role in what happened in Algeria," said the exile, who spoke on condition of anonymity, explaining that he feared harassment from al-Qa'ida supporters. British intelligence officials also took note of Nasar's activities in their country and questioned him on at least two occasions, according to people who knew him. But he was never placed under formal investigation, they inferred. "He's very intelligent and powerful in making his arguments," said an Arab dissident who knew Nasar well and also spoke on condition of anonymity. "But he is also a very difficult man. His tough attitude created many, many enemies for him, even in *jihadi* circles." With his

pale white skin and red hair, Nasar physically blended into British society more easily than many Islamic fundamentalists. But he sometimes
struggled to reconcile his beliefs with his surroundings. For instance,
friends said, he was well educated on the finer points of Western classi-
cal music and enjoyed talking at dinner parties about composers. But he
refused to actually listen to the music, for religious reasons. And while
he rejected the authority of secular institutions, he once filed a libel lawsuit in a British court against the Arabic-language newspaper *al-Hayat.*
Unlike many of his acquaintances who favored arranged marriages, the
unsmiling Nasar possessed a romantic streak and surprised friends by
doting on his Spanish-born spouse. "I was in his house once and he was
putting out all these romantic touches for his wife," said one of the Arab
dissidents. "I asked him, 'Where did you learn how to do that?' He said,
'We Syrians, we know these things.'" Nasar departed London in 1998
to return to Afghanistan, according to intelligence sources. There, he
forged close ties with the new *Taliban* government and swore an oath of
allegiance to Mullah Mohammad Omar, the *Taliban* leader. He was given
a position in the *Taliban* Defense Ministry. He also resumed his contacts
with al-Qa'ida, but frequently clashed with bin Laden, according to Arab
dissidents and Nasar's own writings.[21]

In an e-mail to bin Laden in 1999, recovered from a computer hard
drive in Kabul by the *Wall Street Journal,* Nasar complained that bin
Laden was getting a 'big head' from his frequent media appearances.
"I think our brother has caught the disease of screens, flashes, fans, and
applause," Nasar wrote. In public statements and in interviews with Arab
media, Nasar said he was happy to work with al-Qa'ida but emphasized
that he was an independent operator. His theories of decentralization
had already taken shape: It would be a mistake, he said, for the global
movement to pin its hopes on a single group or set of leaders. "My guess
is that he saw bin Laden as a narrow-minded thinker," explained Jarret
Brachman, research director for the Combating Terrorism Center at the
US Military Academy at West Point. "He clearly says that al-Qa'ida
was an important step but it's not the end step and it's not sufficient."
Nasar's theories of war also called for the most deadly weapons possible.
In Afghanistan, he worked with al-Qa'ida leaders to train fighters in the
use of "poisons and chemicals" at two camps near Jalalabad and Kabul,
according to the State Department. After the September 11 hijackings,
Nasar praised the attacks. But he said a better plan would have been to
load the hijacked airplanes with weapons of mass destruction. "Let the
American people - those who voted for killing, destruction, the looting of

other nations' wealth, megalomania and the desire to control others - be contaminated with radiation," he wrote. "We apologize for the radioactive fallout," he declared sarcastically.

After the US-led invasion of Afghanistan in late 2001, Nasar went into hiding, moving to Iran, northern Iraq and Pakistan, according to intelligence officials. In November 2004, the State Department posted a $5 million reward for his capture. Within a few weeks, Nasar responded by posting a lengthy statement on the Internet. He denied reports that he was involved in the September 11 attacks or the Madrid bombings, but issued warnings of his own. "As a result of the US government's declaration about me, the lies it contained and the new security requirements forced upon us, I have taken the decision to end my period of isolation," he wrote. "I will also resume my ideological, media-related and operational activities. I wish to God that America will regret bitterly that she provoked me and others to combat her with pen and sword." Around the same time, Nasar posted his 1,600-page book on the Internet. In it, he critiqued failed insurgencies in Syria, Egypt and Afghanistan and offered a new model aimed at drawing individuals and small groups into a global *jihad*. Reuven Paz, director of the Project for the Research of Islamist Movements, in Herzliya, Israel, called Nasar's book "brilliant - from their point of view." He said researchers fear that it was already serving as a how-to manual for uniting isolated groups of radical Muslims for a common cause. "We are witnessing a new generation of *jihadists* who were not trained in the camps in Afghanistan," Paz said. "Unfortunately, this book has operational sections that may be more appealing to this new generation."[22]

Much of the Muslim resentment against the West emanates from the seemingly inexorable process by which young Muslims are sucked into Western culture and forget about their Islam. A web-based debate (May 2006) reveals a rare glimpse into the outlook of Muslim scholars who are concerned about Christianity's growth, exactly as Christianity is concerned the other way round. The invited guest is Sheikh Ahmad Al Katani, the president of *The Companions Lighthouse* for the Science of Islamic Law in Libya, an institution specializing in graduating imams and Islamic preachers. Katani started off by describing the overall problem:

> Islam used to represent, as previously mentioned, Africa's main religion and there were 30 African languages that used to be written in Arabic script. The number of Muslims in Africa has diminished to 316 million, half of whom are Arabs in North Africa. So in the section of Africa that we are talking about, the non Arab section, the number of Muslims does not exceed 150 million people. When we realize that the entire population of Africa is one billion people, we see that the number of Muslims

has diminished greatly from what it was in the beginning of the last century. On the other hand, the number of Catholics has increased from one million in 1902 to 329,882,000. Let us round off that number to 330 million in the year 2000. As to how that happened, well there are now 1.5 million churches whose congregations account for 46 million people. In every hour, 667 Muslims convert to Christianity. Everyday, 16,000 Muslims convert to Christianity. Every year, 6 million Muslims convert to Christianity. These numbers are very large indeed.... From what I have heard from reliable sources, six million may be too low. Reliable accounts say that one hundred thousand Africans convert to Christianity per day, though not all of them come from Islam. Muslims should build schools before mosques, in order to build the worshipper (Muslim) before the building. Why? To stop the dangerous "Christian missionary octopus". This happens often! The wealthy Arab builds a mosque for himself or for one of his parents or his friend, but my dear sir, building a mosque comes as a second stage. In America, the price of building an Islamic school is 5 million dollars. In Africa, 50 thousand dollars are enough to build a very reasonably sized school. I say this and I take full responsibility for it; building a school comes before building a mosque. Build the worshiper before you build the mosque. Take for example yourself; you go to the mosque five times a day and if you added all that time it would equal an hour or maybe two hours if you include the Friday prayer. However, if I ask you how long you stayed at school, you will reply that you spent years in middle school and years in high school. Likewise the African goes to the mosque, but if we built him a school where he could spend most of his time, and provided specialized educators we could at least stop this dangerous Christian missionary octopus.[23]

Katani states the purpose of his school:

The truth is, the institution that I administer is considered pre-college. As for the issue of attracting and preparing specialized missionaries to bring them from their countries to Libya in order to train them and return them back to their countries, that is done through the Islamic Propagation Organization. This organization has graduated a number of classes, some of whose students had masters and doctoral degrees. These efforts were fruitful in that these graduates were able to attract people from their lands and countries because they spoke the language and understood the customs of the people they were proselytizing. This way, the missionary is not a foreigner to the community he is working with, contrast that to what would happen if I went to the Philippines for example. I can't speak a single Filipino [i.e. Tagalo] word; much less invite people to the faith.[24]

Now let other Muslim leaders join the discussion. Abbas Hamid lives in Holland, and he deplores the un-Islamic way of life: "My brother, may Allah reward you. We Muslims in Holland suffer a lot when we see issues like this and we really suffer when we see a Muslim, as the *sheikh* said, who spends millions in bars and entertainment while other Muslims are lost and cannot find a translation of the Qur'an. Even their children who are able to learn cannot memorize the Qur'an, they can't find a translated Qur'an or even any translated book. The first thing we must do is mend our selves; Islamic countries must fix themselves first and then they can look at Africa. May Allah reward you and this issue is interesting". Later, on the same web program, an Arabic-speaking

Christian discussed how Islam must preach peace and love: "No one denies, as none of the Muslim scholars do, that a religion has the right to spread his faith (except in hard line Islamic countries), but these leaders seem panicky. They express frustration at Islam's disorganized efforts to maintain Africa. But this one idea eludes them: Islam itself is the problem because it is a burdensome and harsh religion. This is apparent when one Muslim scholar talks about implementing *shari'a* as if it is self-evident that it benefits society."[25]

Laurent Murawiec (from the Hudson Institute) gave a talk entitled "Deterring Those Who Are Already Dead?", which points out to a flaw in terminology in the communication between the West and Islam, where reform does not mean reform, tolerance means the reverse of tolerance and bigotry and hatred dominate the scene of Muslim so-called "revised" schoolbooks. He said, *inter alia:*

> If our enemy was merely "terrorism," we could defang it, admittedly at great cost: by destroying the Saudi-Wahhabi nexus and their grip on power, by wiping out the Iranian Ayatollahs' strength, and by squeezing hard the noxious Pakistani military-intelligence establishment-all in all, the linchpins of Muslim terrorism. Once this infrastructure of terror collapsed, much of terror would. But terror itself is nothing but the principal para-military instrument of jihad: the operative concept is jihad, not terror. The jihadis' purpose, (the Clausewitzian Zweck) in the very words of the Qur'an, is to "strike terror in the hearts of Unbelievers", it is a quasi-military objective: once terrorized, the Unbelievers, the schismatics and the polytheists will convert, submit or die. The strategic aim (Ziel) of jihad is the Gnostic takeover of the world. To some extent, we may be able to lessen, hinder or hamper the Zweck. But the Ziel is unconditional and cannot be altered. Can we de-fang jihad by pulling its terrorist teeth?[26]

Murawiec offered a review of a sample of official Saudi textbooks for Islamic studies used currently which reveal that, despite the Saudi government's statements to the contrary, there remains in this area of the public school system an ideology of hatred toward Christians, Jews, and Muslim so-called "schismatics" who do not follow *Wahhabi* doctrine. The texts teach a dualistic vision, dividing the world into true believers of Islam (the "monotheists") and unbelievers (the "polytheists" and "infidels") [thus projecting threat and deterrence]. This kind of deterrence works, he claimed, because one is able to credibly threaten the center of gravity of the enemy: the threat of inflicting unacceptable losses upon him whether in a bar brawl or in nuclear escalation. The calculus of deterrence relies upon this: is it worth it? Is the price/earning ratio of the contemplated action so hugely negative that it would wipe out the capital? Deterrence works if the price to be paid by the party to be deterred hugely exceeds his expected earnings. But deterrence only works if the enemy is able and willing to enter the same calculus. If the enemy plays by other rules and calculates by other means, he will not be deterred. There was nothing the Philistines could have done to deter Samson. If the calculus is: I exchange my worthless earthly life against the triumph of Allah on earth, and an eternity of bliss for me, if the enemy wishes to be dead, if to him the Apocalypse is desirable, he will not be deterred. When Mahmoud Ahmadinejad was the Mayor of Tehran, suggested Murawiec, he insistently proposed that the main thoroughfares of Tehran should be widened so that, he explained, on the day of his reappearance, the Hidden Imam, Mohamed ibn Hassan, who went into the great occultation in AD 941, could tread spacious avenues. More recently, he told the Indian Foreign Minister that "in two years, everything will be settled," which the visiting dignitary at first mistook to mean that Iran expected to possess nuclear weapons in two years; he was later bemused to learn what Ahmadinejad had meant, to wit, that the *Mahdi* would appear in two years, at which point all worldly problems would disappear. This attitude, truly, is not new, nor should it surprise us: religious notions and their estranged cousins, ideological representations, determine not only their believers' beliefs but also their believers' actions. Reality, as it were, is invaded by belief, and belief in turn shapes the believer's reality. The difference between the religious and the ideologically religious, emphasized Murawiec, is this: "the religious believer accepts that reality is a given, whereas the fanatic gambles everything on a pseudo-reality of what ought to be. The religious believer accepts reality and works at improving it, the fanatic rejects reality, refuses to pass any compromise with it and tries to destroy it and replace it with his fantasy".[27]

Murawiec further contended that the accumulation of such deeds shows that they are not an epiphenomenon but are central to the purpose of the *jihadi*. They are aired 24/7 on TV channels such as *al-jazeera* and many others. They are avidly watched and celebrated, private and family screenings are arranged, images and video-films of assassinations, Daniel Pearl, Paul Johnson, "live" killing for the viewing public. Perhaps the worst symbol of all was the picture taken on October 12, 2000 in Ramallah: a young man shows his red hands dipped in the blood of two murdered Israeli soldiers to an exultant Palestinian crowd. There is a public demand to meet the supply: snuff movies are served as identity markers. They bespeak the triumph of a theology of death, a "manufacture of death" as the Ba'athist ideologues used to say (the purported division between supposedly "secular" Arab or pan-Arab nationalists and religious types is meaningless when the matter is life and death, as it is), and an "industry of death", as leading Saudi *ulama* proudly say. Murawiec counsels to "listen to the hypnotic threnody of the Muslim Brotherhood's", that is cited as gospel in the Hamas Charter chanted motto: "Allah is our goal, the Prophet our model, the Qur'an our constitution, the *jihad* our path, and death in the Path of Allah our most desired belief, Allah is the greatest". These are words to be taken seriously, even literally, as events have shown. Hassan al-Banna, the founder of the Brothers, repeatedly praised to heaven his Brotherhood's "art of death" *(fann al-mawt)*. "This is thanatolatry, martyropathology or nihilism", he suggests: when an entire society orients itself in this direction, that society is becoming suicidal. A society that gears especially its young toward killing and actively seeking death, is making choices that bring about its extinction. "We love death more than you love life." If one depreciates and deprecates life and conversely focuses all of one's desires upon death, the devoutly-wished passage into the glorious afterlife by means of *shahada* (martyrdom), "trading" (as the Qur'an states) one's own earthly life for one's afterlife is much easier, and taking the life of others is a mandate, it is an obligation, an offering. "Suicide-killing" according to Murawiec, (which this author has elected to dub *Islamikaze)* as practiced so much against Israel, India and more recently the United States, is caused by this collective pathology of the mind. There are secondary, contributing causes, but they are just that, auxiliaries to the ideology,[28] according to Murawiec.

Examples abound. In Canada at least three youths charged with terrorism expressed militant views and had misguided ideas about the Muslim faith, say some older men who pray at their *musalla* (a prayer place that is not a mosque). Hisham Syed, who considered himself a spiritual advisor to them, said he worried about one young man in particular, Amin Mohamed Durrani, aged 19, who had come under the influence of a fiery preacher at the *musalla*. The five youths arrested who are younger than 18 cannot be named for legal reasons. "I know he (Durrani) was reading a lot of twisted stuff on the Internet," he said. "There's a lot of nonsense on the Net that messes up people's heads." Syed added that he would get into political discussions with the young man that would become quite heated. Durrani, who has been charged with training and recruiting for a terrorist group, would often spend time with two younger friends who were also taken into custody. "They all hung out together," said Syed. Some of the youths charged have friends in common who played basketball together at the local mosque. Friends remember Fahim Ahmad, another of the 12 adults arrested, joining the youths at those games. Durrani and the two younger friends also prayed together at an informal place of worship called *Musalla-E-Namira,* close to the school, where security guards pointed out reporters and warned students not to speak to them. The modest prayer room is on the top floor of a two-storey *plaza,* alongside seedy storefronts and dumpsters. Worshippers use a back door that looks more like a warehouse entrance. Another of the high school friends who went there was a recent convert to Islam, whose parents were apparently upset when they caught him praying in the washroom at home and, according to some acquaintances, had an angry confrontation with people at the *musalla.* It was there that the friends gathered to listen to fiery sermons by an *amir,* or preacher, that were full of anti-American talk and literalist interpretations of the Qur'an. "He (the *amir)* was not a youth. He was definitely a senior," said a source not willing to be identified. They engaged in blazing political debates and often skipped classes to spend time at the *musalla.* But Syed worried that they weren't really learning about Islam. "They didn't do research or read their history books." Although in different grades at their high school, Durrani and the other two and possibly others from the school, had been "inseparable friends" for a long time.[29] That is the stuff and the personal relationship that makes the *Islamikaze* bombers devoted to each other as well as to their mission of bombing.

Inspired by rap music, Durrani dressed in urban gangster style. A second youth was a popular boy, the envy of his friends for dating the school's hottest girl. The third boy was bright with an interest in sciences, who volunteered with the school's Muslim association. But some school-mates said they noticed a drastic change in this group of friends toward the end of 2005. They started skipping school to attend the *musalla,'* lectures, and some started wearing traditional dress. "Not that there is anything wrong with that," said the source, "because dressing that way, for a good Muslim, makes you humble. But these were guys who were also acting strange." The popular boy often talked about politics, especially about the 9/11 attacks. "He talked a lot about the US and manifest destiny and that stuff," said Alex Tang, a student at Stephen Leacock School. "But he loves Canada. He'd rather live in Canada than in any place in the world," he added. The same youth was known for giving great speeches in class. "His teachers liked him. He talked like a college professor," said Tang. "He probably had all that knowledge from his friends, his parents and his outside schooling." "I used to go to Islamic school with him, but then he dropped out," said another friend who also attended the *musalla* with the youth. "We had to memorize the holy Qur'an. I guess he probably couldn't do it." The popular youth also started talking about his faith more openly. "Everything that happened to him, he'd explain through his religion," said Tang. "Even when he couldn't make it to prayer, he'd say it was God's will". When kids taunted him, Tang remembers, "He kept his cool, he'd just say something like, 'One day, God will punish you for what you've done.'" One source who had prayed at the *musalla* a few times with the *amir* and the youths said the inflammatory rhetoric made him too afraid to come back. And he noticed that the youths had stopped thinking for themselves. This group of friends became very involved with the Muslim association at school and would often forcibly introduce their viewpoints into discussions. "They started to bring their own views and interests," said the source. "Often they would bring lengthy printouts from the Internet to discuss issues from these printouts." Once they discussed at an association gathering whether "suicide bombing" was permissible in Islam. Their views were so violent that the other association members threatened to have them banned. Meanwhile, following their arrest, the future of the *musalla* is uncertain as the *amir* prepared to move the location of the prayer room and his classes. "He's moving, so he's very busy right now. I can't say why," said a worshipper at the *musalla?*[30]

The surprise that caught liberal Canada when the Muslim plotters of terrorism were arrested could have been mitigated if attention had been paid to the fiery preaching and incitement sermons which had been rife in Canada's mosques for years. Take a typical radical imam among Canada's Muslims: After daily prayer services, Qayyum Abdul Jamal would often retreat to a corner of the Ar-Rahman Islamic Centre in Toronto and deliver quiet lectures on religion or step outside into the parking lot to toss a football or bounce a basketball. But wherever he was, he was often surrounded by teenagers and young men, who seemed to relish the company of the 43-year-old radical thinker with anti-Western views. "He wasn't a fiery speaker," recalled Faheem Bukhari, who used to frequent the Mississauga center. "He was conversational. He'd go and sit and talk with these guys. He was a preacher." Six of the men arrested in an anti-terrorism sweep (see Chapter 4 on Canada) were among those who spent time with Jamal at the center and hung on his every word. Along with Jamal, they were targeted in a massive police operation aimed at dismantling an alleged homegrown terrorist cell. Police allege 17 people - 12 men and five youths

- were involved in a plot to launch terrorist attacks in southern Ontario and planned to make explosives using three tons of ammonium nitrate fertilizer - three times the amount used in the Oklahoma City bombing in 1995 that killed 168 people. Sources state that the suspects - Fahim Ahmad, 21, Zakaria Amara, 20, Asad Ansari, 21, Shareef Abdelhaleen, 30, Ahmad Mustafa Ghany, 21, and Saad Khalid, 19, worshipped at the center regularly. "These were very young youths going to the mosque with a fresh mind, a peace-loving mind from middle-class families," said Bukhari, who used to visit the center because his uncle was a founding member. Sources note that during the 2004 federal election campaign, Jamal told members that Islam "forbids" participation in politics and more recently accused Canadian soldiers of going to Afghanistan to rape Muslim women. However, others were quick to point out that simply having radical views does not mean he would have engaged in radical behaviour. And hosting barbecues for the young men and taking them out on bowling nights and camping trips does not mean there was anything nefarious involved. "These are completely wrong allegations," said Sam Lela, a member of the center, which is located next to a convenience store and take-out restaurant in a storefront strip mall on Montevideo Road. "We were completely shocked," he said after learning of the arrests of the seven members. "They're completely dedicated people, nice people. We could never believe these charges."[31]

When asked by reporters why he was so certain of the men's innocence, Lela said, "Because these people are so obvious, they are here all the time. Terrorists tend to be hidden .... Underground." Although many have described Jamal as soft-spoken, it was his outspoken *Wahhabist* views that had in recent years alarmed some of the directors at the center, which is non-sectarian. But because he was a volunteer who took on the role of "caretaker," his services were valued. The Ar-Rahman Center was set up in 1999 by immigrant families in search of a place to take their children for religious education and social activities. The center, which is in debt, was never able to hire a full-time imam or academic scholar to oversee teaching. Instead, a board of directors relied on a core group of volunteers to operate the activities. Although Jamal worked as a school bus driver and juggled a busy home life with four children, he had enough free time to go and open the doors for several daily prayer sessions. "He was a caretaker in a sense of day-to-day business," explained Mohammad Iqbal Alnadvi, imam at the Al-Falah Islamic Centre in Oakville and one of six directors at the learning center. Alnadvi joined the Ar-Rahman board because the centre was in need of someone to offer advice on an "Islamic perspective". He said Jamal often lined up speakers for the congregation, but "he was not in any policy-making or decision-making situations". Expressing "shock" over the charges, he was quick to distance Jamal's activities from anything the center sanctioned. "Maybe he established relationships with youth, but it was not his duty to arrange programs for kids," he said, adding that the center does not support Jamal's ideas.[32]

A sober evaluation of the state of the Muslim world today was provided by Martin Bright, who attended a gathering of Muslims in London, for a debate on the question of leadership, connected to the *Panorama* program that caused turmoil in the Muslim community when accusing Muslim leaders of being in denial about the scale of extremism in Britain. The meeting was organized by the City Circle, an impressive group of young, professional Muslims, which organizes regular debates and runs a series of youth projects in the poorest parts of the British capital. Discussion was intense and tempers flared. Most there felt that the BBC program had been biased and were affronted by the attack on prominent Muslim leaders such as Sir Iqbal Sacranie, secretary-general of the Muslim Council of Britain. As the sole defender of the program in the panel, Martin Bright was called a Muslim hater and a propagandist. But that the debate was held at all was evidence of the serious soul-searching that the program had provoked. The investigation that the *Observer* published in advance of the program came to similar worrying conclusions about the extremist links of the MCB (Muslim Council of Britain). As a result, the British media were swept up in a backlash against the program and accused of being part of an orchestrated Islamophobic campaign. At times, this accusation has been surreal. Bright attests to the fact that when he was interviewed a week earlier - on *Muslim Cable TV* - he was asked to declare his links to the Zionist media lobby. It is easy to understand such brittle reactions when many devout Muslims fear being targeted as extremists. But the central claims of *The Observer* and *Panorama* remain unchallenged: that the moderate credentials of the leaders of Britain's most powerful Muslim lobby group are open to question; and that the MCB grew out of sectarian Islamist politics of south Asia and that it fails to control its extremist affiliates. Bright felt that to say this was not to attack Islam or British Muslims; rather, it was an attempt to call to account the leaders of a powerful organization that has the ear of ministers and influence across Whitehall. Perversely, the program had the short-term effect of rallying many who have been critical of the Muslim Council of Britain in the past, to now, since it is under siege, espouse its cause. But Bright wrote that it would be catastrophic if this continued to be the case, since the organization is not capable of representing the broad diversity of the Muslim communities in Britain. For Bright, those were two fascinating weeks. He has lost count of the times he was "set straight" about Islam during this period.

A convert to Islam and former colleague told Bright that she now avoided shaking hands with men and that he was wrong to see such behavior as extreme. This was in sharp contrast to the young Pakistani TV journalist who told him that she objected to being told by the likes of the MCB to cover her head with a headscarf since, she said: "My modesty is in my heart." On the set of a Pakistani TV station, the host told Bright that he was a great admirer of Salman Rushdie, while a representative of the MCB bullied an imam who had dared suggest that he had been ashamed of Sir Iqbal Sacranie's boycott of Holocaust Memorial Day. Dozens of Muslims have called or e-mailed to tell him it is their duty to work towards the establishment of an Islamic state ruled by *shari'a* law, while as many have told him that Islam is a religion which celebrates the personal relationship of the believer with God. What Bright has learned is that there is no one monolithic version of Islam. All the more reason, then, for any representative body to reflect the fact that there are as many interpretations of what it is to be a good Muslim as there are Muslims. Bright became convinced that when the dust settles, Britain's 1.6 to 2 million Muslims will start to demand a real leadership robust enough to handle genuine criticism without crying foul. One would hope he is right, but meanwhile debates such as the one held on that Friday are a sign of hope in dark times.[33] At any rate, all these debates show once again that humiliated and frustrated Muslims are easy to inflame and hard to control.

2

Muslim Ambivalence Regarding World Terrorism

Abu-'Ubeid Qurashi, one of the aides of Osama Bin Laden, published after September 11 in the Arabic press and in the al-Qa'ida site on the Internet, a stunning article regarding his organization's strategy in its unseemly confrontation with the US and western civilization in general. This article demonstrates that not only do those champions of evil do their home work adequately, and that they are equipped with the requisite patience, sophistication and methodical thinking, the fruits of which were seen in the deadly precision of their operation against the Twin Towers, but that western democracies have something to learn in the war against terror. For it transpires that the Muslim terrorist organizations which have been waging war against the West directly are inspired by al-Qa'ida war doctrine, and it is not too early to try to comprehend their schemes. Qurashi, who has obviously studied the most recent western research in matters of the future battlefields and war doctrines, has come up with conclusions that are alarming: first, that the era of massive wars has ended, because the three war models of previous generations have been eroded; second, the fourth-generation wars of the twenty-first century will consist of asymmetrical confrontations between well-armed and well-equipped armies, who have a turf, a way of life and material interests to defend, and therefore are clumsy - against small groups armed with light weaponry only, who have no permanent bases and are on the move at all times. Thirdly, in these wars, the main target is not the armed forces, but civil society that has to be submitted to harassment and terror to the point of detaching it from the army that fights in its defense; and fourthly, that television is more important than armored divisions in the battlefield. The Twin Towers, the terrorist explosions in London and Bali, and the Israeli confrontation with Hamas and Hizbullah on its borders, show how these doctrines can be rendered operational.

This war doctrine lies in the gray zone between war and peace. Namely those who initiate this kind of war, e.g. by wanton terrorism, would not declare it openly, and would leave it to the defenders to announce war and thereby become the "aggressors". The terrorists themselves would create atrocities that are sure to attract the attention of television so as to "strike fear in the heart of the enemy" (a Qur'anic prescription), and make them retreat to their bases. But when the victim strikes back in self-defense, television can again be counted on to show the "abuses" of the "aggressor" and create sympathy for the cause of the terrorists. On television, the huge armies which crush everything in their path will always look more threatening than the "poor", "frustrated" "freedom fighters" who are "oppressed" and "persecuted" by far superior troops. Thus, the author could show that small groups of poorly equipped *Mujahideen* have been able throughout the past two decades to defeat superior and lesser powers: the Soviets in Afghanistan, the US in Somalia, Russia in Chechnia and Israel in Lebanon and then in Gaza. According to this analysis, the three major components of modern warfare are: early warning, the ability to strike preventively, and deterrence - exactly the elements that were paralyzed by al-Qa'ida on 11 September. As for the early warning, the writer claims that the terrorists have achieved a strategic surprise, in spite of American technology, on the scale of Pearl Harbor in December 1941, or of the Nazi attack against the Soviet Union in June 1940, the assault on the *Cole* in Aden in 2000, and the Suez crossing in the Yom Kippur War in 1973. On the basis of the above analysis, the terrorists were able to deliver a deadly blow on September 11, and levy on the Americans a very heavy economic and psychological price. The ability to deliver a preventive strike is linked, in the mind of Qurashi to the issue of early warning, because when the latter fails, then a preventive strike becomes irrelevant. But even if it had worked, there would have been no one to strike against in retaliation, as the terrorists are small groups, hidden and mobile. And finally - deterrence totally collapses in the face of the asymmetry between an institutionalized state which values life and a desire to live and prosper, and a group of *Mujahideen* who are indifferent to life, and indeed desirous to perish in the Path of Allah and attain the delights of Paradise. Thus, since nothing can deter them, they can always determine, against all odds, when, where, how, what, and whom to strike, without fearing that anyone will retaliate against them.[1]

It is harrowing to reflect on how effective this doctrine has been, and continues to be in our daily lives, starting with the Middle East, but going to the periphery of the Islamic world, in places like Australia and Canada. For example, the Hizbullah in Lebanon, which is linked to al-Qa'ida, not only ideologically, has had some successes, but has also exported this doctrine to the Muslim terrorist movements in the Palestinian Territories, such as the Hamas and the Islamic Jihad. Moreover, "secular" organizations such as the *Tanzim* and the *Aqsa Brigades* have been converted to these tactics, once Arafat's call for martyrdom, with himself at the helm, had become the favorite form of struggle against Israel. There is, however, a way to counter every deed or doctrine with a view to reducing its effect, thereby immunizing western society from deadly threat, and eliminating the terror it imposes on all civilized people. For example, if the terrorists intend to detach Western societies from their armed forces, an area where they have been partly successful by inculcating doubts into the public and by supporting protest movements from within, perhaps it is time for these societies to realize that they have been unwittingly used by their enemies to attain their ends: to dismantle national unity, to incite publics against their governments and to play into the hands of the terrorist subversive doctrine. If, as has been pragmatically demonstrated, television is a declared means to discredit western societies and their systems of defense, the media should not be allowed onto the battlefield until the end of hostilities. Perhaps it is better for governments to be accused of obstructing the media rather than to let them document the asymmetry between the established strong defenders of freedom and the weaker terrorists in the field.

If terrorism has adopted the recourse of fighting by using *Islamikaze* "martyrdom", because there is arguably nothing to be done against their "suicide-bombers", each of whom can terrorize and paralyze an entire public, then it is necessary to demonstrate, like President Bush, that we are facing not a war against individuals who are desirous of death, and whom we cannot bring to justice when they succeed in their task, but against those who train, dispatch, arm, indoctrinate, support, and finance them. Furthermore, as long as we keep them on the run, they will be less able to concoct and carry out their dark, cruel schemes against the West. That Islamists pursue their campaign of intimidation against the West is not new, but what does seem surprisingly new, compared with the legendary fighting spirit of the British, is the seeming capitulation of European capitals to their tormentors, and their baffling incomprehension of the Islamist phenomenon which has repeatedly declared itself so clearly inimical to them. Just consider the spirit of *dhimmitude* which has inundated the entire West due to its dependence on Muslim oil, and the humiliating consequences thereof. This state of mind, which dictates caution, surreptitious maneuvering as a survival mechanism, and a self-humiliating sycophancy toward the Muslim rulers in the hope of gaining their favor, has been inherited from many centuries of Islamic rule on vast swaths of Christendom, from Sicily to the Iberian Peninsula, from the Balkans to the gates of Vienna. This aggressive Islam which attempted, but failed, to Islamize Europe in the past, had also subjected large Christian communities to the *dhimmi* regime in the Near East after their conquest by the emerging new faith of Islam: like the Copts in Egypt, the Assyrians in Iraq, the Maronites in Lebanon, and countless other Christian communities which first became subjugated majorities and then systematically persecuted minorities in their own countries. This amounted, after many centuries of oppression and contempt by the rule of Islam, to a self-diminution of the *dhimmis* - a loss of their pride and confidence in themselves that they did not stand up to the standards set for them by their rulers, and a total distortion of their self-image and the image of their oppressors. So much so, that many Christians and Jews, years after being liberated from *dhimmitude,* continued to think and act as *dhimmis,* namely to hold themselves grateful to their Muslim masters, who beat, humiliated, and mistreated them. Any observer of the international arena today would have noticed how Western and Israeli policy-makers sycophantically submit to Muslim demands even when they are not compelled to.[2]

What is more, the spirit of *dhimmitude* has been adopted, or taken over, by many Western societies today which, for reasons hard to understand or explain, pretend not to hear or comprehend Muslim threats. Instead, western societies evince "understanding" in the face of those threats, and seem to be marching foolishly toward spiritual and cultural capitulation and enslavement. Take, for example, the regime of self-defense and of intrusion into the privacy of air-passengers, which has been imposed at airports worldwide in the past three decades due to Muslim terrorism. Instead of prosecuting and eliminating it at its roots, the West surrendered to it and adopted, at considerable financial, human and moral cost, measures to live with it in what has amounted to submission to a mammoth collective punishment of innocents.[3] Even more ominous has been the wholehearted and even enthusiastic support of Muslim fundamentalists, by Europeans on their own turf, when they rushed to sustain Bosnians, Kosovars and other Albanian Muslims in Macedonia, all of these being supported, financed and trained by revolutionary Iran; and when many Muslim volunteers from Chechnya to North Africa and the Middle East were recruited to fight a *jihad* for their cause. Again foolishly, the West permitted Muslim *jihad* to take root on the continent while emphasizing the problem of Serbian ethnic cleansing (abhorrent in itself). This caused a severance of Christian continuity between Russia and Central Europe to the Aegean Sea, by creating and sustaining a continuous string of revived Muslim presence from the former Yugoslavia to Turkey, hoping thereby to extend the Turkish model of "Islamic moderation" and thereby salvage European borders from a Muslim onslaught. As it turned out Kosovo was totally subtracted from Serbia under UN auspices, while in Turkey a Muslim fundamentalist party took over government in 2002.[4]

Following the London July 7 horrors, the British, who have for years given shelter to Muslim terrorists who clustered in London under the liberal policies of then Home Secretary Jack Straw, find themselves "surprised" and "shocked" that the wind of "liberalism" they had sown, now forces them to reap the whirlwind of terrorism. They have been talking about "criminals", instead of Muslim terrorists or simply *Islamikaze,* once again illustrating their *dhimmi* state of mind which refuses to recognize reality or wishes to avoid offending all Muslims. Criminals take their risks and try to survive and enjoy the fruits of their crime, but the *Islamikaze* have made evident that they do not expect any economic gains, for they pursue ideological goals for which they are ready to sacrifice their lives, if only they can force the West bend to their will. Instead of submitting to Muslim intimidation, as the West has shamefully done by yielding to "punishment" in airports for the past decades, and in Israel where, at the entrance to every public building, all have to submit to a thorough search, let us call a spade a spade, and blame the Muslim terrorists and the organizations behind them (by their own admission); instead the West only condemns their horrific *acts* of terror as if these were unforeseen events. Imputing this wave of evil to individual criminals or "suicide bombers" not only misses the point of identifying them and their organizations by name, but may even create some perverse sympathy for them by "understanding" their motives and deploring the poverty or the frustration that "caused" them to go to their death and bring down with them multitudes of innocent people.

The Muslim threat towards Europe and to the West in general, as delineated in the schemes of the terrorist organizations, is played out not only on the security field but also through the media. In 2002, journalist Martin Bright, cited above, in his professional capacity as Home Affairs Editor of *The Observer,* had for several years already taken a close interest in the Islamist community in Britain. He had also studied the rise of political Islam in North Africa as a graduate student at the School of Oriental Studies, London University (SOAS). By Islamist, he meant individuals who believed that political action should be guided by the Muslim faith and who were often in opposition to the regimes of their home countries. He also viewed Islamism as an extremely diverse movement in which he included militant extremists such as Osama Bin Laden's al-Qa'ida organization as well as groups and individuals who wished for peaceful, democratic reform and would condemn terrorism in all its forms. He observed that there were Islamist opposition groups in all parts of the Arab and Muslim world, many of which were persecuted by their ruling governments. Many Islamists therefore fled to Western countries as refugees. Precisely because of this diversity and a general ignorance about Islam in the West, it was all too easy for the police and security services to lump together genuine political dissidents and, in some cases, merely ordinary Muslims, with individuals most people would regard as terrorists. But since the events of September 11, this confusion has increased as Western security agencies have become more dependent on intelligence from countries within the Arab and wider Muslim world, who have used the occasion to target dissident members of their domestic Islamist movements who have found refuge in the West. Building on his knowledge of Islam, Bright also interviewed most of the high-profile Islamists based in Britain, for example Saudi dissident Khalid al-Fawwaz shortly before he was arrested in 1998, in connection with the bombings of the American embassies in east Africa. Bright was the first British journalist to interview Abu Qatada, the Palestinian/Jordanian scholar and master-terrorist, who was linked to several terrorist suspects across Europe since September 11, and he was also the first British journalist to interview Abu Hamza, the controversial imam of the Finsbury Park mosque in north London, (discussed at length in the Introduction). Bright has also written several articles opposing the new anti-terrorist legislation introduced by the Labour government, because he believed that terrorism was a crime that should be punished severely by the courts, but did not think that people should be persecuted for their beliefs especially when, as is the case with many Islamists, they are beliefs that are little understood. But after engaging with various security-related material he has seen, he revised his views. The material included a small number of government documents: one of them a Security Service document, court documents from the trials of various suspected terrorists, and press cuttings about

Islamist terrorism. By far the largest proportion of the material that caused him to change his view falls into the third category and Bright concentrates most of his following comments on these.[5]

From the press cuttings, taken as a whole, Bright concluded that they suggest the following:

1. That there is a serious threat to international security from Islamic extremists;
2. That Osama Bin Laden and his al-Qa'ida movement are at the centre of a loosely allied international Islamic terror network;
3. That the Egyptian Islamic Jihad has effectively merged with al-Qa'ida;
4. That there is a "British connection" to this network; and
5. That there is a threat to Britain that justifies the imposition of a state of emergency.

Unlike his many colleagues who together with the authorities and security agencies, elected to follow the cozy refuge of liberalism, multi-culturalism and political correctness, Bright took a hard look at the reality, and was alarmed enough to report what he saw to his readership. He was aware that information gathering usually came from three sources, each of which is compromised in its own way. The first source is the Islamist dissidents themselves, who would not describe themselves as terrorists even if they are committed to the violent overthrow of certain regimes. The second is the regimes these dissidents oppose and which believe them to be terrorists. Many of the individuals concerned in these press cuttings were refugees in Britain and have been allowed to stay precisely because the evidence provided by their home countries has not stood up to scrutiny. The third source is the British intelligence services and the police, whose off-the-record briefings form the basis of many of the cuttings that he studied. Much of the information contained in these press cuttings was almost absurdly circular. Information from intelligence briefings from foreign or the domestic services rapidly becomes common currency and is then repeated by journalists who are starved of any real information. Reputable journalists report the denials of the Islamists themselves, but the fact that someone denies being a terrorist is never considered to be much of a story. As increasing numbers of dissidents have been rounded up in Britain and elsewhere it has become increasingly difficult for journalists to check their stories properly by talking to people who really know about the world of extremist Islamic politics. So, journalists have been thrown back on an increasingly narrow set of sources: essentially the police and the intelligence services. Another difficulty that Bright encountered in assessing this material is that he had no way of knowing what status the Security Service gave to the information contained in the articles. Did the fact that they had been presented to the court mean that they believed every word contained in them is true? Or did they simply believe that any smear against an Islamist is a useful smear? Bright advisedly proceeded on the assumption that the information contained in the articles is taken seriously by the intelligence services and is thought to be largely accurate, and that any comments attributed to "security sources", "Whitehall sources", "intelligence sources" or "Home Office sources" have been accurately reproduced.[6]

Bright's pioneering work, which has broken the back of the terrorists' reliance on a confused and politically correct press to sow doubt and fear in the public, spotted two emerging themes: first, that Britain faced an Islamic terrorist threat justifying the introduction of a state of emergency, and secondly that members of the Egyptian Islamic Jihad and the Algerian Armed Islamic Group (GIA) involved in international atrocities, had been based in Britain at some point, although until July 7, 2005 there had never been a major Islamic terrorist attack on the British Isles or on British interests abroad. Until very recently the British intelligence services didn't officially talk to newspapers at all. Certain favoured journalists with connections to people working in the services, were passed information from time to time if it was thought useful to put it in the public domain. Sometimes the stories that resulted were true and sometimes not. In recent years, after intense pressure, MI5 and MI6 instituted a new system whereby each service has an unofficial press officer who talks to the media. Most media organizations then designate a journalist who will deal with each service. They are then given a telephone number and the name of the individual intelligence officer. In the case of the *Observer*, Bright was selected to deal with MI5. But unlike Bright who had previously specialized in Muslim affairs, his contact at the agency did not necessarily boast such expertise, but simply acted as a conduit for those who deal with the Islamic terrorist threat within the Security Service. Most journalists agree that there is less likeliood of confusion than with the old system, but it is far from ideal. Any conversations remain strictly off-the-record and, for the most part, any quotes are attributed to "sources". Since September 11, newspapers, including the *Observer*, have become increasingly reliant on these briefings for information. Most journalists feel that, on balance, it is better to report what the intelligence services are saying, but whenever the readers see the words "Whitehall sources" they should have no illusions about where the information comes from. In the period immediately following the events of September 11 and up to the new internment legislation (2005-6), these journalistic briefings were used to prepare journalists for what was to come. Immediately before suspected terrorists were taken into custody journalists were told that the choices had been very carefully made and that these men constituted a "hardcore".[7] By making journalists privy to upcoming arrests, the anti-terror authorities blunted their anticipated usual criticism of the "abuse of human rights" or "police brutality", thus also scuttling the terrorists' capitalizing on turning the press and the public against their government.

An example provided by Bright illustrates the complexity of this relationship between the agencies and the press. It concerns an article entitled "MI5 searches for terror cells based in Britain",[8] printed less than one week after the attacks on the World Trade Centre and the Pentagon. The reporters in question are respected investigative journalists and were, at the time, in charge of investigations for the *Independent*. The article shows that even journalists as experienced as they are were forced to fall back on intelligence sources when assessing the Islamist threat in Britain. They reported that at least three terrorist cells linked to Bin Laden were at large in Britain and that the UK had been a major base for his operations. They added that there are believed to be dozens of terrorists in Britain associated with Bin Laden. One "intelligence source" was then quoted as saying "There is no reason why what happened in America couldn't happen in Britain or any European country. The terrorists are in place, and there is very little to stop them." A source, this time from "Whitehall", added: "The problem is, that these groups are amorphous and hard to identify until they commit a terrorist act." This is a terrifying potential scenario and the two journalists concerned were right to report what was said to them - indeed, it is hard to imagine anything that was more in the public interest, yet more pleasing to the terrorists who yearn to terrify the unsuspecting public. But it seems a little disingenuous of the intelligence services to present this as independent evidence of the threat, when the journalists are simply reporting what they had been told. Bright too was told by "Whitehall sources" that Britain came third in al-Qa'ida's list of targets after the United States and Israel. Bright had no way of knowing if this was true and there appeared to be no evidence of specific threats. What he did know was that al-Qa'ida's rhetoric as seen in the various *fatwas,* interviews and statements from its leadership, suggested that the United States and Israel are the main focus of its attention.

Apart from general threats against "allies of the United States", Bright himself found only one serious threat to British people in the thousands of words from al-Qa'ida documents among the bundles he received. The first came in a statement issued on October 10, 2001 on *al-Jazeera* TV by al-Qa'ida spokesman Abu Ghaith, that followed allied air strikes on Afghanistan. Al-Qa'ida ordered British and American troops to leave the Arabian Peninsula and added: "We also say, and advise the Muslims in the United States and Britain, the children and those who reject the unjust US policy, not to travel by plane. We also advise them not to live in high-rise buildings and towers". This threat had been taken very seriously by the security services, but how far al-Qa'ida had the capability to carry it out it was not then known.[9]

The evidence provided in the bundles of documents received by Bright was contradictory. A government statement dated October 4, 2001 proclaimed that the UK and UK nationals were potential targets. "Al Qa'ida retains the capability and the will to make further attacks on the US and its allies, including the UK", it said. But this appeared to go against briefings given to the British press at Scotland Yard at the end of September 2001. As reported in the *Independent* on September 29, 2001 "threat assessments carried out by the security services have concluded that there is no evidence of a plot to commit a major attack on a British target. They have also told ministers that most of the key British-based supporters of Mr Bin Laden have been either extradited or arrested". There is a world of difference between a generalized threat and an imminent risk of attack and, in their selective briefings, the intelligence services could not seem to make up their mind which it was that the British were facing. However, within Islamist and wider Arab circles it has always been understood that the British authorities have traditionally taken a tolerant line towards Islamist dissidents. Much to the irritation of the French government and many Middle Eastern regimes, until recently it has been accepted that opposition figures were welcome as long as they committed no crimes on British soil. It was believed that such figures were a useful source of intelligence and the more cynical commentators believed they also acted as protection against attack - a kind of Islamist human shield. Bright does not know if this had genuinely been the strategy of the intelligence services in the past, though it strikes one as an eminently shrewd one. It also demonstrated a respect for freedom of expression and freedom of worship that are at the heart of British ideas of democracy.[10] But these are precisely the soft spots in Western democracies that the *jihadists* are looking for and against which reporters like Bright alert the public to be on guard, since British openness and hospitality will at some point be used against them by the Islamists.

Martin Bright pursued his unflinching reporting, his courageous commentary and his acute sensitivity to upcoming events, to make the public aware of the double-talk, cynicism, hypocrisy and impotence of the leadership of organized British Islam, upon which governments had showered praise as "moderate" and bestowed honors that they did not deserve. While the Muslim Council of Britain's condemnation of the London bombings was qualified by the government as a model response for mainstream Muslims, Bright tells a different and disturbing account. Like his colleague John Ware of the BBC, but preceding him in many of these revelations, Bright tore the masks from the faces of the MCB and its Chief, Iqbal Sacranie, by revealing that the organization which won the favor of Whitehall, in fact has its roots in extremist Pakistani Islam, and that far from unifying mainstream Islam, has been crowding out other genuinely moderate Muslims. He documented the links between MCB and the Pakistani *Jamaat-i-Islami* on the one hand and the Birmingham-based *Jamiat Ahl-e-Hadith* on the other, which is an extremist group whose website states: "The disbelievers are misguided and their ways based on sick or deviant views concerning their societies, their universe and their very existence." It urges its adherents not to wear Western hats, walk dogs, watch sport or soap operas and forbids "mingling and shaking hands between men and women". He disclosed that *Jamaat-i-Islami* activists in Pakistan have been involved in protests against images of women on advertisements in public places. The organization's founder, Maulana Mawdudi, was a fierce opponent of feminism who believed that women should be kept in *purdah* - seclusion from male company. Although the MCB's leadership distances itself from some of these teachings, it has been criticized for having no women prominently involved in the organization. Bright also referred to Salman Rushdie's article in The *Times* in which he warned that Sacranie had been a prominent critic during the *Satanic Verses* affair and advised that the MCB leader should not be viewed as a moderate. Rushdie also criticized Sacranie for boycotting the Holocaust Memorial Day ceremony. The origins of the Muslim Council of Britain can be traced to the storm around the publication of the *Satanic Verses* in 1988. India was the first country to ban the book and many Muslim countries followed suit. Opposition to the book in Britain united people committed to a traditionalist view of Islam, of which the founders of the Muslim Council of Britain was a part.

The MCB was founded in November 1997, shortly after Tony Blair came to power, and it has had a close relationship with the Labour government ever since. Its detractors claim it was the creature of Jack Straw, but his predecessor as Home Secretary, Michael Howard, also played a role in its establishment as a semi-official channel of communication with British Muslims. The MCB remains particularly influential within the Foreign and Commonwealth Office, which has a little-known outreach department working with Britain's Muslims. The FCO pamphlet on Muslims in Britain is essentially an MCB publication and the official ministerial celebration of the Muslim festival of *Eid ('Id-al-Ad'ha*, the Feast of Sacrifice marking the end of the Pilgrimage to Mecca) is organized jointly with the MCB.[11]

The Observer has also learnt that the MCB used its influence in Whitehall to gain a place on the board of trustees of the Festival of Muslim Cultures, planned for 2006 at Alton Towers. This extravaganza was designed to demonstrate the diversity and vibrancy of Muslim culture. The festival was funded by the British Council with Prince Charles as its patron, but it was told that it will need to be compliant with Islamic *shari'a* law in order to gain the MCB's full support. The organizers were concerned that the festival would lose political backing if they invite performers who were seen to be "un-Islamic". According to *The Observer,* the Foreign Office insisted that the festival organizers involve the MCB before they would give them their full backing. As a result, an MCB nominee was taken on to the festival's board of trustees. The chairman of the festival's trustees, Raficq Abdulla, said: "We will welcome the MCB's trustee and hope his contribution will prove valuable. But we insist that the festival is not dominated by any ideology. The aim is to capture the values of Muslim cultures and bring them into the British mainstream. We are not here to be the mouthpiece of any Muslim organization".

The event was finally cancelled, ostensibly due to "insufficient sale of tickets", but it was an occasion both to reveal the intrusion of the MCB into the event, which may have caused its annulment, and for some journalists to poke fun into the whole affair. Indicative of this mood was the write up in the *Spectator*[12] which mocked:

> I am beginning to think that Islam's lord of misrule, the Dajjal, He who will bring about the final conflagration and darkness and cause a great stench to emanate from the earth, has taken up an administrative post at the Alton Towers leisure facility. On 17 September this year Alton Towers is to be handed over to the Muslims for a day. There will, therefore, be no music, no gambling and of course no alcohol. The rides will be segregated between men and women.... There will be prayer mats scattered around, so that you can give thanks to Allah for not having been thrown head first out of the

big dipper. Who knows, perhaps they will adapt some of the rides for the day: maybe the chamber of horrors will be full of Hasidic Jews wreathed in sinister smiles.... Tickets, though, are available only through a company called "Islamic Leisure", and the whole business is advertised on the website belonging to the Muslim Public Affairs Committee (MPAC). And quite apart from the antagonism the proposed event has engendered within the godless Kufr press by which I mean the Daily Mail and the Sun and so on, it has also caused one or two problems for devout Muslims, some of whom think it inappropriate to disport themselves in such a temple of decadence, even if the best of the decadence will have been expunged for 24 hours.

The article revealed that a fervent debate was taking place at that time on the message board of the MPAC. One blogger pointed out that the Prophet never went to leisure parks; and that money is going to a *Kufr* enterprise. The majority of remarks complained that women were to be allowed to the park at all, never mind being segregated from the men and "forced to don the usual sackcloth and ashes". The former leader of the Muslim Council of Britain, Sir Iqbal Sacranie, was taken up on his remark that homosexuality was damaging to society, and the author also castigated the Muslim community claiming that to ring-fence an entire day at a public leisure complex because "you cannot face being anywhere near the rest of us, that is as eloquent a statement of separateness, of apartheid, as you could wish to get". It says, simply: 'We find you repulsive to the degree that we cannot share our space with you. We abhor you and the way you live your lives'. In which case the rest of us may find it all too easy to respond: "Well, clear off, then". And Rod Liddle to conclude: "the hand of *Dajjal* has been at work. In the Qur'an, incidentally, Dajjal represents the rest of us: the Jews and the cockroach infidels. Hell of a nice chap. You should meet him".[13]

This opposition to the MCB is connected to the strain of Islamic ideology favoured by its leadership and many of its affiliate organizations, which is recognized as inspired by Maulana Mawdudi, who though little known in the West is hugely significant as a thinker across the Muslim world. His writings, which call for a global Islamic revival, influenced the Egyptian Muslim Brother Sayyid Qutb, usually credited as the founding father of modern Islamic radicalism and one of the inspirations for al-Qa'ida.[14]

In Mawdudi's worldview all humanity was split into believers (practicing Muslims) and non-believers, whom he describes as "barbarians". He was deeply critical of notions such as nationalism and feminism and called on Muslims to purge themselves of Western influence. In 1941 he *formed Jamaat-i-Islami* and remained its leader until 1972. His writings do not advocate terrorism, but the language of his *Jihad in Islam,* written in 1930, may seem violent to a Western reader: "The objective of Islamic jihad is to eliminate the rule of an un-Islamic system and establish in its stead an Islamic system of state rule. Islam does not intend to confine this revolution to a single state or a few countries; the aim of Islam is to bring about a universal revolution." Abdul-Rehman Malik, contributing editor of Muslim magazine *Q-News,* wrote: "Mawdudi saw the world in the same way that Sayyid Qutb saw the world: they both divided humanity into true believers and those in a state of ignorance *(jahiliyya).* Many of the affiliates of the Muslim Council of Britain are inspired by Mawdudi's ideology". Malik said that its leaders needed to be clearer about its position on "suicide bombers". "You cannot be equivocal about innocent people. An innocent person in Tel Aviv is the same as an innocent person in Baghdad or London. The MCB has never clarified any of the critical issues and now the chickens are coming home to roost."[15]

One has to also mention that the significance of "innocent" has never been clarified by any Muslim authority, except for Sheikh Qaradawi. He determined, for example, that Muslims are always innocent, for even those who fight among them do it for the cause of Allah, while in Israel there are no innocent civilians, because all Israelis are subject to military service, therefore they are all permissible targets. The same problem exists in general when one talks about "innocent civilians" in times of war. Are all non-combatant persons necessarily "innocent"? How about those who, arms in hand, and red or black bands on their foreheads, demonstrate in the streets of Beirut or Gaza in favor of Hamas or Hizbullah? How about civilians who aid those terrorists transporting weapons, supplying food, transmitting messages and propagandizing for them? Are they also innocent? When one probes people in the street who say that they support al-Qa'ida and Bin Laden, are they innocent people if injured in war? One cannot pretend to innocence when one goes out and lends vocal and practical support to a terrorist, but when one is hurt, either while extending help to the terrorists or allowing them to operate from one's home, to shout "foul!" because one is an "innocent civilian". Innocence is a state of mind, not a statement of propaganda.

The MCB's Inayat Bunglawala said he had a deep respect for Mawdudi and defended the MCB's affiliation to Khurshid Ahmad's Islamic Foundation: "Mawdudi is a very important Muslim thinker. The book that brought me to practice Islam was *Now Let Us Be Muslims* by Mawdudi. As for *Jamaat-i-Islami,* it is a perfectly legal body in Pakistan. There is no suggestion that the Islamic Foundation has done anything wrong. They have done fantastic work in publishing literature on Islam, including works for children." A spokesman for the Islamic Foundation confirmed that Khurshid Ahmad was chairman of its board of trustees. "The Islamic Foundation does not have links with the *Jamaat-i-Islami*. We promote assimilation, integration and encourage community cohesion. We do publish books by Mawdudi, but we feel these are books of merit to British Muslims." Sacranie has explained that he believed that recent attacks on the Muslim Council of Britain were inspired by a pro-Israel lobby in the British media: "The MCB carries out its activities through its affiliates. There are more than 400 organizations involved, representing 56 nationalities. Yes there is a following for Mawdudi in the UK. I am not a scholar, but in many areas I am inspired by what he has to say and in others I am not." But he cautiously avoided pinpointing where he agrees with Mawdudi and where he does not, thus letting his interlocutors guess. He sounded like a politician who would admit that he "made mistakes, like any human being" but would resist tooth and nail acknowledging any concrete error that is imputed to him. Bright thinks that there is no suggestion that Sacranie and other prominent figures in the Muslim Council of Britain are anything but genuine in their condemnation of the terrorist bombings of 7 July. But their claims to represent a moderate or progressive tendency in Islam are becoming increasingly difficult to sustain. The MCB's reaction to the Festival of Muslim cultures, which was to mark the first anniversary of the London bombings, was significant. Sacranie was clear: "If any activities are seen to contradict the teachings of Islam, then we will oppose them. If you organize a festival in the name of Islam then it must be Islamic. We will advise them accordingly". Small wonder then, that under the double pressure of the British media and MCB, the organizers sought the way out of actually cancelling the Festival.[16] Many other lessons can be learned from the rhetoric around that festival that never was.

Another ambitious planned event for 2006 was the The "IslamExpo" held July 6-9, 2006, the first anniversary of 7/7, at the Alexandra Palace, London, to promote the very creed which was seen as responsible for the deaths of 52 Londoners a year earlier. The organizers probably thought this would deflect any unfavorable media coverage and adverse public opinion from the commemoration ceremonies of the first anniversary, while enabling them to set the agenda in any discussion on the anniversary of the bombings. The list of speakers included Frank Gardner from the BBC, an Arabist, who was shot and left semi-paralyzed by some *jihadis* in Saudi Arabia some years ago when his cameraman was killed. At the time, he pleaded for his life by showing them a copy of the Qur'an which he carried, but to no avail. Even though severely wounded, he was not helped by a single onlooker from the fast-gathering crowd. (I fail to understand why such a man remained in awe of these people and their religion/ideology.) Under the title "Eighty thinkers & experts from 22 countries to debate at IslamExpo", the organizers publicized the upcoming debate at what was slated to be "the scene of one of the largest Islamic cultural events in the world". The intensive program of lectures, seminars, workshops, panels and debates covered a broad spectrum of subjects which included religion, art, culture, history, economics and politics.[17] The colorful (though clearly ironic) array of titles ranged from "the roots of terrorism: religious or political?", "Muslim Youth between national identity and the *ummah*", and *"Jihad:* holy war?", to "Muslim contributions to physics & medicine", "the art of the Islamic garden", and "Al-Andalus: when East & West lived side by side". The "impressive" list of speakers featured such world-renowned names as Professor John Esposito (Georgetown University), the famous apologist for Islam, Mr Wadah Khanfar, the General Manager of *Al-jazeera* Satellite network, who acts as Bin Laden's PR man as well as Frank Gardner (BBC), Seumas Milne *(The Guardian),* Professor Tariq Ramadan (Oxford University), Professor Jacques Waardenburg (Lausanne University), Norman Kember (Christian Peacemaker Teams), Rageh Omaar (former BBC correspondent), Professor Merve Kavakci (George Washington University), Dr. Azzam Tamimi (Institute of Islamic Political Thought), who we have met above, and Alastair Crooke (Conflicts Forum). The IslamExpo was opened by Culture Secretary Tessa Jowell, and Mayor of London and friend of the ultra-jihadist Qaradawi, Ken Livingstone.

The event was presented as promoting a "better understanding" of Islamic faith, history and society with the aim of "strengthening the values of dialogue, openness and tolerance". In the words of the organizers, "in this climate of tension full of talk of clashes of civilizations, the need to build bridges between cultures has never been greater. That, we hope, will be IslamExpo's legacy". Further announcements were made by the organizers, to wit that as part of IslamExpo there would be an economic conference at Cabot Hall, Canary Wharf on the same day July 6, 2006) "to promote London as the center of investment for the Islamic world"; and that as a "ground-breaking event for London and the UK, this is the first expo in Europe devoted to exploring Islamic culture, history, innovation and civilization through theatre, exhibitions, shopping, film, music, and family activities". The event was expected to attract in excess of 40,000 attendees from across UK society.

A multitude of businesses from around the world exhibited at Islam-Expo, and more than 150 exhibitors from Britain and across the globe, from the Middle East, Europe, Asia, Australia and America were present to represent their products and services. Products on show included books, DVDs and other digital products, rugs, music, clothing, toys and educational materials for children, health products, properties, holiday packages, scarves, foodstuffs, and lots more. Many overseas businesses launched their new products at IslamExpo. For example Ahiida Zanettie, a business woman based in western Sydney (Australia), created a fashion range of active lifestyle gear for Muslim women that combines modesty with modernity. This innovative product, called *Hijood* in reference to its hooded *hijab* shape, was first presented in Britain at IslamExpo. Ms Zanettie's project and participation at the exhibition were facilitated by an Australian government organization. Labour MP Sadiq Khan, who spoke at the event, said: "It's important to debunk some of the myths that exist about Islam and to explain the true teachings of Islam. It's also a great opportunity to debate the role and challenges that British Muslims face in the political arena." Other speakers included Mayor Ken Livingstone, Sebastian Coe, chairman of the London Organizing Committee of the Olympic Games, Culture Minister Tessa Jowell and Professor Tariq Ramadan, from Oxford University.

Most "creative" and inventive were the themes chosen for the symposia. Some were innocent in appearance, but pregnant with hidden messages that promoted multi-culturalism or simply constituted good PR exercises by the mere presence of celebrities like Sebastian Coe and Ken Livingstone. One title, for example, was "The London Olympics: A Triumph For Multiculturalism"; others included "Islam and the West: Toward Better Relations", "Muslims in Britain: Facts & Challenges", and "The Islamic civilization: Scientific Traditions in Islam", or "Muslim Contributions to Medicine & Physics". To make more palatable the explicit Qur'anic xenophobia and cult of hatred, recourse was made to the "Hidden Qur'anic Treasures Unveiled". The subservient status of women was subsumed under the presumptuous "Extraordinary Women of Islam", and *"Hijab:* Obstacle to Success?", and the ambition to see Arabic become the *lingua franca* of the world, translated into "We All Speak Arabic". The aggressive and expansive meaning *of jihad* was camouflaged under the innocent *"Jihad:* Holy War?", and the social backwardness of Islamic countries where most population lives in abject poverty, oppression, sickness and ignorance, was discussed under the lofty title of "Social Justice in Islam". One wonders why so many Muslims stream to the West to benefit from its social welfare, if the social situation is so good in their lands? Politics too were not absent, subsumed under "bridges to the West". The Palestinian issue was not examined scientifically through a multi-party panel that would argue various aspects of the issue, for debate on this and other topics was curtailed. There was just a one-sided verdict: "Palestine 58 Years After the *Nakbah*" ("disaster"). And for those who still doubted the delights that would descend on them when the *Pax Islamica* is implemented on earth, "Earthly Paradise: The Art of the Islamic Garden" awaited them. Lest someone dare again deprecate the Prophet of Islam, his preponderant role in world history was assured in the title "Muhammad: Seal of the Prophets". The sad fact is while no democratic regime has emerged in the entire Muslim world, yet another imaginative title came to the rescue: "Democratic Change in the Muslim World: Prospects & Obstacles".

The organizers also used the occasion to address some of their most burning issues in the West, with a view to lending legitimacy to any misconduct they might be accused of in the future. For example, "Islamic Schools: A Vessel of Integration or Isolation?" attempted to legitimize the activities of *Wahhabis,* Mawdudi and all the affiliates of MCB. "Islamophobia: The New Face of Hatred of the Other" was used to deflect the anger in the West resulting from the hatred that Islamists spread against Jews and Christians in the world. It is exactly in that spirit of teaching the West to "think positive" about Islam that Islamists draw attention away from terrorism and bigotry. Unlike the reality of conservatism and fundamentalism enshrined in the affiliates of MCB, who follow Sayyid Qut'b and Mawdudi, Islamists want people to believe that with lectures such as "Reform and Revivalism in the Islamic Tradition", they can escape public scrutiny. Their condemnation of the government which they befriend on the surface, and of the society to which they wish to erect bridges, is encapsulated, not so subtly, in "Iraq: The Record of Three Years of Occupation". Perhaps the apex of cynicism given the squalor in many parts of Cairo, Lagos, Karachi or Khartoum is the attempt to teach to the much cleaner and hygiene-conscious West the "Ethical Foundations of Islamic Environmentalism". There is also political cynicism involved in such titles as "Muslims & the Left: Partners for a Better World". What Left?: the Labour Party that they criticize for the war in Iraq, or the extreme Left with which they find common grounds in their hatred of Jews, Israel and Zionism? Even the popular topic of nutrition in Western nations that suffer from over-eating and obesity was picked up by the Muslims in whose countries there is under-nourishment and starvation, to proclaim "Nutrition Science from the Qur'an". Either that branch of science was not very successful in Islamic lands, or people stopped heeding the teachings of the Holy Book.

International issues were also tackled. To cover up the status of *dhimmi,* the Christians and Jews, as subservient and second-rate citizens under Islam, even when the Christians were a majority ruled by a Muslim minority of occupiers, the spurious precedent of Muslim Spain was resurrected: "Al-Andalus: When East and West lived side by side", forgetting to add "under Islamic rule" to that title. Africa, in which Islam made rapid conquests and also excelled at the slave trade, suddenly became a gentle cultural issue: "Timbuktu: A Centre of Islamic Scholarship". Panel Discussions too were held to sing the praises of Islam: "To be a Muslim Artist: An audience with a host of world-renowned Muslim artists"; "Reporting Islam: World-Renowned Journalists Share Their Experiences of Covering the Muslim World". It is quite a feat how Abdel Bari Atwan editor-in-chief of *Al-Quds Al-Arabi*, a notorious anti-Israel and enthusiastic supporter of Bin Laden and other terrorists[17], could star in this latter panel and share his biased journalism with Western journalists who are used to different standards of reporting and commentary. Panels were also set up to glorify the role of Muslim women, "Role models: An Audience with a Host of Successful Muslim Women", one of them a relative of Sheikh Qaradawi, the icon-Sheikh of Muslim radicals; and "A Woman's Journey to Islam", by Western women who converted to Islam. And finally, to halt the leakage of Muslim youth to Western ways, a reinforcement of Muslim identity was suggested in "Muslim youth between British identity and the *Umma"*, with the fiery Tariq Ramadan leading the way.

There is no prospect of resisting and surviving this wave of Muslim manipulation of facts and events unless one defines these facts and events unequivocally. No other group of people, no adherents of any other faith have so relentlessly vowed to destroy Western culture as the modern Islamists have. There are plenty of poor and frustrated people in the *favelas* of South America, the shack cities of Asia and the jungles of Africa. But in none of them is this unstoppable desire to kill Westerners and Jews as evident and manifest as in the case of *Islamikaze.* Western societies have punished themselves enough in their squeamishness that avoids acting firmly against them; the West has tried in vain to skirt the issue of Islamic terrorism in the hope that it might disappear. Only shedding the remnants of the *dhimmi* spirit in all Western minds may help achieve that aim. To that end, a clear Western definition of what is terrorism has to be announced, not negotiated, because Muslims will never submit to it. In their eyes, terrorism is what others do to them, for example President Bush and PM Blair are terrorists and aggressors in Iraq and Afghanistan, and Israel in the Palestinian territories and Lebanon. What Muslims do is only self-defense and therefore they can never be accused of terrorism. They have long ago embraced the goal-oriented definition of terrorism, meaning that any violent act committed by Muslims against the West is justified by definition, because they are oppressed, humiliated and frustrated by the West, and in their eyes being a Westerner means that one cannot be an "innocent civilian", because in one way or another all citizens serve the Western machine of oppression. The West pursues the means-oriented criterion, namely that regardless of the goals or motives of terrorists, noble as they are to terrorists, innocent civilians cannot be harmed intentionally and indiscriminately, and if they are this is terrorism. Due to their refusal to accept the Western definition, Muslims can never be made to take steps against world terrorism unless they are its direct victims themselves. For example, Saudi Arabia, Jordan and Egypt have for years supported the Hamas and other terrorist organizations, or turned a blind eye to their horrors, in spite of their indiscriminate attacks against civilians who travel on buses or eat in restaurants, as their targets were in Israel and the West. Saudi Arabia, Jordan and Egypt joined the battle against terrorism only when home-grown terrorists turned against their own regimes at home. Only in recent years do they admit that what threatens them is terrorism which has to be battled ruthlessly everywhere. But even under this new circumstance, what happens in Israel remains justified in their eyes.

For Muslim fundamentalists there is even a Qur'anic justification of terrorism *(irhab),* since the Holy text prescribes to Muslims to sow *irhab* in the hearts of the enemy. And if the enemy is invariably identified as Israel or the West in general, that in itself allows a theological justification of terrorism. Of course, when President Bush declared after September 11 that all those who do not battle terrorists or who give them shelter are themselves terrorists, all Muslim states who feared the wrath of the US declared they would join the fight, but in fact duplicity set in. Iran, Syria, the Palestinian Authority, Lebanon, Pakistani Kashmir and others continue to give shelter to terrorism (according to Western definitions) or to finance and encourage it, while at the same time declaring that they fight terrorism (Islamic definitions). We should not be fooled by this double-talk which reflects the Muslim state of mind. Even when they dispatch, *or post-factum* approve of, acts of obvious terrorism by "self-sacrifice", which they call "martyrdom", i.e. a religiously sanctioned act (*"Islamikaze"*), they insist that martyrdom for the sake of Allah and in His Path cannot by definition be termed terrorism. That is the reason why whenever a major terrorist attack by Muslims is perpetrated against the West or Israel, there is rejoicing in the Muslim streets, regardless of the numbers of innocent civilian victims, be they Muslim (as in Iraq) or otherwise (as in New York, London or Tel Aviv). That is also the reason why all UN attempts to come to one unified definition of terror in order to optimize the world battle against it have fallen on deaf ears, as long as all Muslim countries insist that "resistance" against "occupiers" is not terrorism, and they reserve to themselves the right to define who is an occupier, be it Israel in Palestine, India in Kashmir, Russia in Chechnya, or the US and Britain in Iraq. Rather, the notion of Muslim terrorism is altogether denied (for Muslims are not considered terrorists unless they threaten Muslim regimes), and their acts of violence are praised as a necessary act of self-defense by Muslims at large.

Muslim terrorism is "legitimately" directed against nations of Unbelievers, Muslim nations presently headed by "renegade" Muslims who have "sold out" to the West; individual Unbelievers who are considered legitimate targets if they are members of anti-Islamic or un-Islamic entities that are identified as "enemies of Islam"; and Muslim individuals who are regarded as "heretic" *(kafir)* or "apostate" *(murtadd)*. Moreover, when Sheikh Yussuf al-Qaradawi, the arch-Muslim fundamentalist who supports this discourse and terrorism, is accepted and embraced by the Mayor of London, Ken Livingstone, unable to see "anything wrong" with this radical Muslim who does not shun violence, Muslim terrorists regard Livingstone's act as an ideological capitulation of the West before the new waves of Islam. During the first week of July 2003, the European Council for Fatwa held its 11th conference in Stockholm to discuss questions concerning the Muslim community in Europe. The issue of the definition of terrorism was brought up for discussion again after the previous Dublin conference, a year earlier, had come to a deadlock. The main speaker, al-Qaradawi, who is much heeded in Sunni radical circles worldwide, differentiated between colonialist and international terror, contrasted with political terror and terrorism such as *Islamikaze* (martyrdom) operations, these latter not only permitted by Islamic law, but condoned and recommended by him. His main arguments were summed up by a major Arabic medium published in London:

1. The martyrdom operations against Zionists are not included in the category of prohibited terrorism, even if its victims are civilians, thus once

again testing the validity of terrorism not by its disgraceful means of mass murder of innocent civilians, but by its goals, thereby justifying the act, regardless of whether the victims are in Tel Aviv or London, when the goal is identified as worthwhile.

2. Israeli society is a "colonialist, racist and occupying power" and its society is completely militarized, therefore everyone is a legitimate target. It is an "invading" society whose members had come from the outside to occupy and settle Palestinian lands. This means that any Muslim place that can be identified as "invaded" or "militarized", like Afghanistan or Iraq under the US, those Muslim lands must act in self-defense and attack relentlessly and indiscriminately the enemies, be they military or civilians. This is called a *jihad* of personal necessity *(fard 'ayn),* not one of communal choice *(fard kifaya),* and the Believers must subscribe to it.

3. Wherever the battle for the domination of Islam is waged, any act against Muslims, even in self-defense, is tantamount to "aggression" in Muslim eyes, for Islam, the Path of Allah, cannot be resisted and those who resist it are legitimate targets for annihilation. In other words, suffice it for Muslim clerics to declare *jihad* against any European territory resisting its takeover, to justify any act of terror against it. They have achieved that in Bosnia, Kosovo and partly in Macedonia, courtesy of the same Europeans and Americans who are themselves targeted; therefore persistence in the pursuit of that goal is bound to bear fruit.

4. Even when the enemies hide behind innocent Muslims (Muslims are by definition always innocent) as human shields, it is permissible to kill the innocent Muslims for the sake of the overall Muslim good when that serves Muslim goals and protects the universal *ummah* of Islam; how much more so if it is non-Believers who serve as human shields. The significance is harrowingly simple: if civilians, like office workers or government officials, are perceived as shielding enemies of any sort, they are legitimate targets, like in the New York, Madrid and London massacres. In fact, al-Qaradawi specified, since every modern war is a total one, and the domestic front, including laborers, industrialists and farmers stand behind their armed forces, then all civilians are liable to massacre.

5. *Islamikaze* martyrdom is the most valuable weapon of the Muslims, that even America's billions cannot buy, that Allah has placed in the hands of the Believers as the weapon of the weak and wretched in the face of world powers. Therefore those who oppose this mode of fighting are mistaken. The martyr does not value his life when it is sacrificed for the sake of the Muslim community and is assured of Paradise in return. Unlike the usual suicidal type who commits his act as a retreat from life, the martyr

dies in attack and his act emanates out of his desire to attain his goal and please Allah.[18]

The Hamas organization, which follows masters like Qaradawi, and implements the Islamists' strategy to the letter, gave vent to their thinking in proclamations by its leadership in exile in Syria. In an interview with *Spiegel Online,* Musa Marzook laid out his plans and intentions without hesitation or compunction. He said that his organization remains committed to violence against Israel, regardless of the PLO obligations towards it, and that the agreement with Fatah on the foundation of a Palestinian state does not mean that his organization will recognize Israel. Hamas, he explained, would remain committed to violence against its occupier, making it clear that he meant the entire expanse of Palestine, including Israel. Typically, only the suffering of the Palestinians was his concern, and accusations were hurled at Israel for killing Palestinian civilians, but his mentality of denial never saw any wrong with what Palestinians terrorists were doing, for everything is justifiable for the sake of liberation or of walking the Path of Allah. Conversely, the violence of his organization will always be considered a defensive reaction to others, for their own defensive steps are by definition acts of aggression against the Muslim *ummah*. " If Palestinians are killed, Israelis will be killed. That should be clear to all Israelis", he said, but he did not say or imply, that if Israelis do not kill then the Hamas would stop too, for Muslims are allowed, indeed obliged, to kill others in "self defense" if they are perceived as oppressors, occupiers, or offenders of Islam. He in fact confirmed that "No matter what, the violence will not stop. We are on the weaker side and we do whatever we can. The Palestinians have no other choice".[19]

This matter of Palestinian terrorism under the pretext of retaliating for "occupation", while it sounds logical to naive minds in the Middle Eastern context, one cannot mistake its fallacy once one considers what British Islamists say in Britain about that issue which is not so obviously theirs; in so doing they out-Hamas Hamas. Indeed, radical Muslims in Britain have blasted Hamas for failing to carry out a "real" Islamic holy war, and have called for a *jihad* against Israel following the escalation of Israeli-Palestinian clashes in July, 2006 in the Gaza Strip. A number of British-based Muslim organizations have called on followers to wage war on Israel. "What the Jews are doing in Palestine today will no doubt disturb any true Muslim," a statement authored by 'Abdul Aziz al-Dimashqi' declared on the website of the Saved Sect group. He continued:

"However, what hurts us equally as much is to see the Muslims in Palestine calling for an independent Palestinian state, Palestinian constitutions, man-made law, democracy, freedom and so on. Hamas have no intention of establishing the *shari'a* (Islamic code), and are only concerned with having their own nationalistic state," the statement said. In a direct warning to Hamas, the *jihadists* organization wrote: "The Messenger of Allah also promised humiliation and disgrace for those who abandon *jihad* and become busy with the worldly life and seeking wealth." The group also said that there are few "real *mujahideen* (holy fighters) in Palestine at the moment". In other words, the problem for this group of British Muslims is not Israeli "occupation", and the establishment of a Palestinian state, but the need to pursue *jihad* for its own sake. Calling on Muslims around the world to answer the call to *jihad,* the statement concluded: "If a terrorist is a person who resists occupation, calls for the implementation of Islam and fights for his rights, then we are terrorists." In an earlier statement, the same group made known that "Israel is a cancer, Islam is the answer". During protests against the Danish cartoons of Islam's Prophet, Muhammad, members of the organization held similar signs declaring that "Europe is a cancer". British police, who finally woke up to the universal danger of these mad fanatics, have since made a number of arrests of those suspected of organizing the demonstration. "Fight, don't boycott", they shouted from the top of their lungs. "The only solution and divine method to liberate Muslim land is *jihad. Jihad,* in *shari'a,* means fighting, not boycotting Coca-Cola or Fanta, and definitely not voting for man-made laws as suggested by many hypocrites," the Saved Sect declared. The organization also said that *jihad* was a means to bring about its long-term vision of a vast Islamic state occupying the whole of the Middle East: "The *Khilaafah* (Caliphate, or Islamic empire) is undoubtedly the permanent solution for the Muslim *Ummah.*" In pro-*jihad* forums used by British Muslims, anti-Israel hatred peppered discussions. "I'm so fed up with these dirty, filthy Israeli dogs. May Allah curse them and destroy them all, and may they face the same fate as Banu Qurayzah!" wrote one user on the *Muntada* forum/club, the short form for *Muntada Ansar al-Islam* Islamist forum. Banu Qurayzah was the name of a seventh-century Jewish tribe living in the Arabian Peninsula whose members were murdered by Islam's prophet, probably due to Muhammad's intolerance.[20]

As the verdict was read out for those arrested during the disturbances, a man in the public gallery shouted: "I curse the judge, I curse the court, I curse the jury, all of you." One of them said he regretted the chants but described them as "just slogans, soundbites". Choudary, a former spokesman for *al-Muhajirun,* said he was not surprised by the verdict because Muslims were treated as second class citizens in the UK and denied fair trials. "When we have peaceful demonstrations, then slogans that have been used normally, are taken out of context", he said. "This is a failure of capitalism, of democracy and the freedom of speech."[21] Abdul Saleem, 31, was found guilty of stirring up racial hatred during the protests. The court was told that the British Telecom engineer was the "cheerleader" of hundreds of protesters at the demonstration. The father-of-five was filmed chanting "7/7 on its way" and "Europe you will pay with your blood". Saleem told the trial that while his words could be seen as "threatening'", that was not what he intended and he was repeating slogans "because everyone else was saying it".[22] Abdul Muhid, 24, was found guilty of soliciting murder. He led a crowd chanting "Bomb, bomb the UK", and produced placards with slogans such as "Fantastic four are on their way" and "3/11 is on its way", referring to the terrorist attacks on London and Madrid. Muhid, a father of two, had a previous conviction for smashing a bus shelter in Walthamstow market which displayed an advertisement which he said "offended his religious beliefs". Muhid said that the protest had been intended to show the "hurt and distress" felt by Muslims after the cartoons were published. David Perry said: "Of course the UK had already been bombed. There was another significance to 'Bomb, bomb the UK.' The drawings had not appeared in any UK newspapers. This was supposed to be a demonstration against the publication of drawings in newspapers abroad. This behavior shows what the demonstration was about - it was an exhortation and encouragement to terrorism."[23] Rahman, Javed and Muhid were each sentenced to six years in prison in July 2007 for soliciting murder, and Saleem was sentenced to four years. In the face of these words of horrific incitement to kill the innocent, that are pronounced on European soil and supported by multitudes of European Muslims, small wonder that home-grown terrorists all over the continent are preparing themselves to die for their cause, or just to kill without dying if they can achieve it. Other Muslims see the conflict between the West and Islam as the "pre-ordained eternal destiny of Muslims", and therefore they counsel preparation to face it. On the occasion of the 1 March, 2006 launch of *al-Risalah* (the Message), the new 24-hour Arabic language news channel, Saudi Prince Waleed bin Talal told a press conference that his channel would "counteract the misconceptions about Islam in other societies", as well as project Islam as a religion of moderation and tolerance and provide a platform for dialogue on religious, social and economic issues. This channel was to be the forerunner of a similar English language channel aimed at Western audiences. A measure of the intention of the founders to implement all these lofty goals was given in an interview with a Saudi Muslim cleric, Sheikh Ahmed al-Qubeisi, who said, *inter alia:*

> I cannot talk about jihad when the world considers a plundering occupier to be a man of peace, and the owner of the occupied land to be a terrorist. The world demands today from anyone whose land has been occupied - but only from among the Muslims - that they shut up. If any of them complains, or picks up a gun to kill those who killed his family, and destroyed his land with missiles - he is considered a terrorist. On the other hand, those who plundered, occupied, colonized, killed, executed and dropped nuclear bombs and depleted uranium shells, are considered men of peace who spread democracy . . . How can one talk about jihad in such conditions?... The West's conflict with Islam and the Muslims is eternal - a pre-ordained destiny that cannot be avoided until the Day of Judgment.... In Islam, jihad is conducted in order to spread its principles, justice and views. This is exactly what America is doing today when it spreads democracy. When Islam spread monotheism, it was at a time when idols and people were worshipped. It is one and the same. What was said there is being said here. If this is correct, then that was correct too. If that was a mistake, then this is a mistake too. Hence, we have reached the following conclusion: the term violence or jihad, or you could call it aggression or colonialism, means that you take control of the resources of others, out of economic or political greed. On the other hand, Islam does this to bring people to worship Allah and to install justice among all people.[24]

A *Times* lead article[25] asserts that there are limits to what government can do to change Muslim attitudes. Tony Blair berated moderate Muslims for not doing enough to challenge extremists in their communities, and insisted that this was not a task for the Government. "You cannot defeat extremism through what a government does. You can only defeat it within a community", he was reported as saying. His remarks came after the accusation by Sadiq Khan, a Muslim Labour MP, that the Government had failed to carry out most of its promises to help Muslims fight extremism, and had left them disillusioned and bitter at the lack of any action plan to integrate Muslims more fully into British society. But this is another delusion that Muslim leaders almost everywhere cultivate especially when it concerns Muslim minorities, namely to throw accusations at the government, society and the world, only exempting themselves; thus they avoid taking responsibility. The Jews, the Hindus and the Sikhs did not need government assistance and they were absorbed without making trouble or wrecking the public order. The *Times* saw the problem from different angles:

> There is a confusion here. The Prime Minister and Mr Khan are talking about different issues. One factor contributing to the alienation of many young Muslims and their

frustration with mainstream society is low achievement: across Britain, Muslims, on average, are less well qualified, earn less, have higher dropout rates, suffer greater unemployment and live in poorer neighborhoods than other Britons. This is an area where Mr Khan and others believe that the Government should focus its intervention. The problem, however, is that such dirigiste policies rarely bring results: and it is far from clear that simple government decrees can lift Muslim attainment in schools, encourage the spirit of entrepreneurship or promote integration across the tense racial and religious divisions that mark the geography of some northern towns. But economic hardship alone is not the issue. The profiles of the London bombers and their extremist associates show that many came from solid, respectable homes which would normally be seen as middle class with middle-class values and attitudes. Improving social conditions does not drain the pool in which terrorists swim. A more important factor, to which Mr Blair was referring, is the cultural, social and religious framework of Muslims growing up in Britain. Thus, are low ambitions or meager successes in commerce related to prevailing attitudes regarding the education of women, social isolation or cultural incongruity, all highlighted by an inability to speak English? In some areas, government intervention can make a difference: it can refuse visas for foreign imams, make it harder to import brides from abroad, insist on access to English classes. But the mind-set and beliefs of a community are not under the aegis of government; adapting such mind-sets to life in Britain must be the responsibility of scholars examining Islam's confrontation with modernity as well as those who have moved away from their religious roots. Government intervention in the vigorous theological debate in many Muslim communities in Britain is perilous and can be counter-productive. Even the attempt to embrace Muslim leaders has its drawbacks: the more they are photographed at Downing Street, sit on official committees or accept honors and medals, the less credibility they have on the streets. There is a generation gap among Muslims, far wider than that found in other communities, which young Muslims, torn by the conflict between Western and Islamic values, find difficult to bridge. It is encouraging that Muslim leaders have just launched a national forum to counter extremism, specifically recognizing its dangers in their midst. It must be here, and not in Whitehall, that strategies are elaborated to overcome this problem. The question many will ask, however, is: why has this initiative taken so long?[26]

The Times lead article was referring to the announcement by Muslim leaders in Britain of a national task force to fight extremism, and called for efforts to end false justifications for acts of violence. The move was announced after the publication of a *Times/ITV* News poll, which suggested that a significant minority of British Muslims believe they are at war with the rest of society, with 13 per cent saying that they regarded the July 7 bombers as martyrs. Tony Blair said that the poll showed the overwhelming majority of Muslims to be decent, law-abiding people who wanted to put an end to extremism, and that people within the Muslim community needed every help in mobilizing themselves to combat the extremists' ideology and methods. But with Muslim "moderates" like MCB, ul-Haq and Sacranie, how in the world can the extremists be defeated? Blair appeared to indicate that the language of *jihad* used by terrorists could be blunted by some moderate discourse, as if *jihadi* talk were the language of the "extremists", but not of common Muslims. The problem is that the language and expressions of both extremists and "common Muslims" ultimately derive from the same historical and religious roots, and may be used with different connotations by different groups which, therefore, could result in a confusion of concepts; this would be the most benign explanation, giving everybody the benefit of the doubt. However this ambiguity equally lends itself to deliberate manipulation. What Blair could fight for, with little prospect of success, is a reformed Islam that would offer an alternative to *jihad by* creating new meanings for it or shedding its militancy altogether. But who would dare to tamper with the Holy *Shari'a* Law which has divine sanction and was bequeathed to Muslims for all generations to come? Blair wanted to show the extremists that their attitudes towards the West and towards the western way of life are wrong and misguided, but this is precisely the problem in Beeston, as in the satellites *cites* of Paris, and the dark alleys of Karachi and Cairo. As the Prime Minister made his comments, 17 organizations representing Sunni and Shi'a Muslims in Britain signed a declaration stating that violence had no place in Islamic beliefs, teachings and practice and proposed a national Muslim forum on combating extremism. If it were so, then why are most acts of violence today performed by Muslims? How was Islam born and how did it expand unless through sanctification of conquest, violence, subjugation of other cultures and massacres among them, which have resulted, most recently, in the wiping out of most Eastern Christianity and many Jewish communities in the Middle East and North Africa? Some British Muslims, the declaration admitted, were uneasy, arguing that Islam was not to blame for extremism. However, it added: "We acknowledge this may be true, but we emphasize that Muslims must accept that there are extremists and terrorists who justify themselves by reference to Islam". Mr Blair, appearing before Commons Select Committee Chairmen, said there was an impression that Muslim leaders sympathized with extremists' grievances but disagreed with their actions. But those who "disagreed" did nothing to eradicate violence. Mr Blair begged to differ with critics who said that the Government was to blame for not doing more to combat extremism in Muslim communities. He said, "I am not the person to go into the Muslim community and explain to them that this extreme view is not the true face of Islam." But he would be prepared to meet again with those who had served on the working groups set up after the July 7 bombings. Mr Blair defended the police raid on a home in Forest Gate, East London, in which one man was shot. He suspected that most Muslims would recognize that Forest Gate, in a sense, had to happen, because when police receive information, they can do nothing but go and investigate. But for Muslims in Britain and the world, that was another manifestation of their conspiracy theory, that the West is out to get them.[27]

A survey for *The Times* indicated that the population at large is in a state of misunderstanding of Islam, the result of the fiery language of *jihad* and of the different ways of the Muslims which the public understands less and less and fears more and more. A quarter of the public regards Islam as a threat to the British way of life. The survey suggests that the gulf of understanding and empathy between Britain's Muslim and non-Muslim communities is mutual, and that more than a third of British Muslims (36 per cent) believe that British values threaten the Islamic way of life. The greatest social difference between British Muslims and the rest of British society is over the wearing of Islamic dress in schools. Three-quarters of Muslims (76 per cent) think that pupils should be free to wear religious dress whatever a school's uniform policy, but only two-fifths (42 per cent) of the general population agree. Commentators expressed concern at this picture of a Muslim community at loggerheads with the greater population over their differing cultures. David Dabydeen, Professor of Cultural Studies at Warwick University, explained that the findings on the wearing of religious dress in schools were particularly revealing. "I think that aspects of Islam are so backward they are practically medieval, particularly when it comes to attitudes towards sexuality and gender", he said. Professor Dabydeen also asked why the Muslim community, according to the results, felt threatened by mainstream society. "For Muslims to feel threatened is ridiculous.... It is not in any sense an anti-Muslim issue. This is a plural society that has tolerated many different cultures, and I see very little evidence of mosques being burnt down or attacked." Sir Iqbal Sacranie, the former secretary-general of the Muslim Council of Britain (MCB), retorted that the issue of religious dress in school was one of fundamental freedom. It was highlighted when Shabina Begum, 17, a schoolgirl from Luton, was refused permission to wear a full-length Islamic gown in class. Many Muslims, according to the survey, do feel strongly about the issue of the *hijab,* but that is because they see it as an issue of freedom of choice, which is of course false, because none of them came to Britain from a Muslim country that had a freedom of choice. But when in the West, freedom of choice suddenly became sacrosanct for public propaganda; yet in the homes of many of those same Muslims, marriages are not by choice, nor are other discriminations against women in the Muslim community which is strongly authoritarian by tradition.

Therefore it is easy for Sacranie to say that if a pupil (that is, actually, his/ her parents) wishes to wear a particular item, such as the *hijab,* it can easily become part of a school's uniform, and accommodate the wishes of pupils of any faith. While it is an elegant way to Islamize the western educational system, such an attitude is frowned upon by the British public.[28]

Despite these divides, the poll also suggests a remarkable level of agreement between Britain's Muslim and non-Muslim communities. Two-thirds of Muslims admit that their community needs to do more to integrate with British society, almost as many as the three quarters (74 per cent) of all Britons who say the same. More than nine in ten Muslims (92 per cent) say that their community makes a valuable contribution to British society, a view shared by most of the general population (59 per cent). Nearly as much of the population at large (54 per cent) as do Muslims (57 per cent), find public displays of drunkenness unacceptable. Slightly more Muslims (29 per cent) than the general public (21 per cent) say the same about women wearing low-cut tops and short skirts. Half the general population (51 per cent) believe that Islam treats women as if they are inferior to men but a third of British Muslims (36 per cent) think that the values of British society degrade women. Simon Mundy, director of the Centre for the Cultural Environment at King's College London, said: "Citizens, the general public, have proved over the last year to be infinitely more tolerant and less hysterical than the Government has. The way people talk to others around them who are different is considerably more understanding and liberal than the Government has proved to be." Shahid Malik, Labour MP for Dewsbury, agreed: "This is really Neanderthal, instinctive stuff, based on prejudice not on a knowledge of each other's cultures," he said.[29] Others make the point that the single biggest mistake made by western governments was to engage Muslims through their "umbrella" groups or clerics. They say that since Muslims chose to immigrate to Britain, which has a parliamentary-party system, they should only seek to influence government policies by being active within the system and joining one or other of the parties. If they are addressed as Muslims, they are concomitantly absolved of the need to integrate. Their concerns should not be treated as "particularist" or "special" in any way. In fact, they ought to, though they, not usually, do have the same general concerns as the rest of society, and should therefore operate through the political parties. But Sacranie and his likes could not care less about British society; their agenda is centered on Muslims in Britain and elsewhere. Holders of these views also emphasize that it is a conceit to believe that there is such a thing as a "moderate" Muslim. They also believe that Government ministers are the least likely to be able to distinguish between Muslims of the "extreme" or "moderate" tendencies, if such a distinction could be made in the first place.

Similar phenomena have been taking place also in Canada and Australia, the seemingly farthest periphery of the Muslim diaspora, but little notice has been given to them, even though the same stories, persons and events described here for London would remind Canadians and Australians of what they have encountered to date. In the summer of 2006, when the transatlantic plot to down American and British passenger planes was revealed, Canada was taken by surprise because it was not prepared for that sort of potential terror (see Chapter 4). Similarly: when in Australia gang rapes by Muslims took places on the Sydney beaches in early 2007; when Muslims used violence against Jewish and Israeli targets during the *Intifada* in 2000-1; when the Chief Mufti Hilali made outrageous statements in early 2007 regarding the rights of the incoming Muslim immigrants to the land; or that the public square should be sanitized to accommodate the Muslims by "covering the uncovered meat" of Australian women - the naive and good-hearted Aussies ought to have realized that what was long ignored is finally coming to their shores. In fact, in early 2007, the annual conference of *Hizb-ul-Tahrir* (the Liberation Army) which convened in Sydney, should have stood as a resounding alarm clock had the public paid any attention to it.

3

Down Under: The Land of the Fair Go

Like the US and Canada, Australia has been a country of immigrants since its inception, and in order to maintain its "WASP-ish"-European-Christian culture it carefully balanced and monitored the origins of the new immigrants. Naturally, being located where it is, its access for Muslim minorities was much harder until the past few decades, when the facility of air transportation brought in many "refugees" (real and fictional), who sought shelter and were accepted by that land of abundance, liberalism and hospitality, taking in many Muslim immigrants. Their numbers amount to less than half a million of a total of over 20 million, but their vocal presence came to the fore during the outbreak of the *Intifada* in the Middle East (October 2000), when Muslim immigrants demonstrated against the US and Israel (in itself legitimate, but for the use of violence), hurled rocks against the Israeli Consulates and burned institutions of their Jewish compatriots. The situation worsened after the Bali Incident in 2002 when the Australians suddenly realized that their blissful isolation far from the trouble spots in Europe would no longer protect them from Islamic-oriented violence. Australia was dealing with a combination of a growing restive Muslim population, together with the adjacent geographical presence of the largest Muslim country in the world - Indonesia - previously considered by them as a strong ally and partner. This new realization, backed by attempts of Muslim "boat people" to break the strict immigration policies and venture into Australia illegally, brought the relationship between Canberra and its Muslim population to boiling point.

Australian fears, triggered by the cruel mass killing by Muslim terrorists of over 200 vacationing Western civilians in Bali, half of them Australian, created an escalating anti-Muslim mood which was reflected in Australian domestic policies and politics. Indeed, a day after a group of mainstream Muslim leaders pledged loyalty to Australia as a way of reversing this escalation, in their meeting with Prime Minister John Howard, he and his ministers made it clear that extremists would face a crackdown. His Treasurer and heir apparent, Peter Costello, hinted that some radical clerics could be asked to leave the country if they did not accept that Australia was a secular state and its laws were made by Parliament. He addressed Australian Muslims on national television:

> If those are not your values, if you want a country which has Shari'a Law or a theocratic state, then Australia is not for you. I would be saying to clerics who are teaching that there are two laws governing people in Australia, one the Australian Law and one the Islamic Law, that this is false. If you cannot agree with parliamentary law, independent courts, democracy, and would prefer Shari'a Law, and have the opportunity to go to another country which practices it, perhaps then that is a better option.[1]

Asked whether he meant that radical clerics would be forced to leave, he said that those with dual citizenship could possibly be asked to move to other countries. His stance was echoed by Education Minister Brendan Nelson who also told reporters that Muslims who did not want to accept local values should "clear off". He made it clear that people who do not want to be Australian, and do not want to live by Australian values and understand them, had no place in the country. Prime Minister Howard himself also angered Australian Muslims when he declared that he supported spies monitoring the nation's mosques.[2] The Prime Minister met in February 2006, for the first time, with his Muslim Advisory Group, following his and his ministers' declaration about Islam. That meeting was attended by the Grand Mufti of Australia, Sheikh al-Hilaly who, incidentally, objected to the presence in the group of Muslim Youth Representative Mustapha Kara-Ali, who was accused of promoting extremist aspects of Islam linked to the Muslim Brotherhood, within the Aussie Muslim community, under the innocent acronym of FAMSY (Federation of Australian Muslim Students and Youth). FAMSY has operated in Australia since 1968 and defines itself on its website as a "national student and youth Islamic organization with branches throughout most states of Australia". But in fact, it is the umbrella movement that unites all Muslim university and youth groups. One of their members is Zachariah Matthews, who has been involved with the movement since 1992 and has spoken at its annual conferences. In 2003, the *Sydney Morning Herald* investigated Abdul Rahim Ghouse, one of the key-members of the organization, who supposedly had business dealings with an al-Qa'ida financier. He also headed the "International Free Anwar Campaign", referring to the Malaysian Islamist and former Deputy Prime Minister who was jailed between 1998 and 2004 by his bitter opponent Prime Minister Mahatir on apparently trumped-up charges. Some of this network's members were linked to the University of Florida Professor Sami al-Arian who has been arrested and convicted for raising funds for the Hamas and conspiracy to commit murder via *Islamikaze* attacks in Israel.[3]

At the 1997 annual conference of the group at the University of Sydney, the founder of the Muslim Brotherhood in the US, Ahmed Alkadi, attended. He had served previously as the Secretary of the Brothers in the US from 1984 to 1994. He revealed his way of recruiting members from small prayer groups: "first you change the person, then the family, then the community, then the nation". In 1998, FAMSY invited Sarraj Wahhaj, an American convert to Islam, and again in 2001, as he was so popular. Wahhaj had gained attention during the Sheikh Abdul-Rahman trial in the US, following the first Twin Towers attempt, where he was the Sheikh's character witness. Both men had met at Sarraj's Mosque in New York where the blind Sheikh had reportedly suggested to his devout audience that they should even rob banks to benefit Islam. Sarraj was continually under the watch of the FBI since he was suspected of co-conspiring with the Sheikh to destroy New York landmarks in 1993, after he expressed the opinion that the constitutional government of the US would eventually be replaced by Islamic law: "In time, this so-called democracy will crumble and there will be nothing. And the only thing that will remain will be Islam". He was not the only Muslim fundamentalist who was invited by FAMSY, knowing that he despised the West and wished to transform it into a Muslim realm. Another was Kamak Helbawi, a former senior member of the Brotherhood in Egypt who fled to the UK in 1997 and helped to found the World Assembly of Muslim Youth (WAMY), a Saudi-backed organization. In the 2003 Conference of FAMSY, another American convert to Islam, Mahdi Bray, who specialized in recruiting Muslim inmates in American jails, was invited to speak before the audience. Previously, he had mounted large-scale demonstrations in America against the Jews, warning them that the Armies of Muhammad were coming to slaughter them as in the days of Khybar, the oasis in Arabia whose Jews were exterminated or enslaved by the army of the Prophet.[4]

In 2004, the guest of honor at the FAMSY Conference was Shaker al-Sayed, who had previously encouraged *jihad* by every individual Muslim and lashed out viciously at Jews. In 2005 the guest hero was Anas al-Tikriti, whose father was Saddam's schoolmate in Tikrit; thereafter he headed the Muslim Brotherhood in Iraq. Anas himself is a founding member of the Muslim Association of Britain (MAB), which admits openly its links to the Brotherhood. In May 2006, FAMSY planned a "Peace Conference" in Melbourne, where Tikriti was again to be the main speaker. The website of the conference promoted it by announcing its support for the "Stop the War Coalition", arguing that while the US and its allies (including Australia) were trapped in their illegal war in Iraq, the Australian government, in the name of fighting terrorism, "has been attacking civil liberties and demonizing Muslims in the community". In other words, while Muslims in Australia and elsewhere claim their civil rights, they also proclaim the coming end of the countries whose liberties they enjoy. Zachariah Matthew, mentioned above, is cited as telling his young Muslim audiences that "the West is so unfair to the Muslim world that it is understandable how an extreme margin would strike out in frustration and revenge",[5] beyond the concrete problems of Iraq, Afghanistan and Palestine. This close collaboration between FAMSY and the Brotherhood, and through it with al-Qa'ida, is precisely what causes concern in Australian government and media circles, in the face of the radicalization of Muslim students and their sometimes naive local supporters, who are sowing havoc and unrest on Australia's campuses. To top it all, following the race riots in Sydney in 2005, a woman arrested for plotting to plant a bomb in the city was found to be a recent convert to Islam. Jill Courtney, 26, was charged with conspiracy to murder and causing explosives to be placed in a public location. A court granted a request by her lawyer that she be assessed by a psychiatrist. Police and journalists believed that she was acting out of love for a jailed Muslim murderer, Hassan Kalache, who killed a rival drug dealer in 2002 and told Jill that he would marry her if she retaliated for the race riots with a bomb.[6]

A whole string of court cases throughout the country illustrated to the stunned and easy-going Australians, who are used to answering: "How are you?" with "No worry", that terrorism had reached their remote confines too. Terror suspect Faheem Khalid Lodhi allegedly bought two maps of the Australian national electricity grid using a false name and business name. Rose Bakla, who worked at the Electricity Supply Association of Australia in 2003, told the New South Wales (NSW) Supreme Court she remembered the man who paid $170 cash for two diagrammatic maps of the national supply grid. "The gentleman said that he was starting up a business and he wanted to display these in his office," she told the Court. She described him as in his "mid-30s, early 40s" with a medium build, dark features and dark hair. The jury heard that he filled out the sales form as M. Rasul [significantly meaning "messenger", either for his "sacred" mission, or borrowing the epithet of the Messenger of Allah -Muhammad], a partner in Rasul Electrical. Prosecutors claimed the man was Faheem Khalid Lodhi, 36 (in 2006), a Pakistani-born architect who was put on trial on four terror-related charges and later convicted. Lodhi was accused of planning to blow up three military bases around Sydney and the national electricity grid. The jury heard that during a search of his office, security agents recovered a receipt for the maps made out in the name M. Rasul of Rasul Electrical. It is alleged that the name and business name are false. Ms Bakla said the diagrammatic wall map, which carried a disclaimer about its accuracy, outlined grids of the electricity and energy sectors. "People could use it for a guideline as to what the electricity lines were within a country," she said. However, Mr Lodhi's lawyers argue the map was purely schematic and would have been useless as a tool for anyone contemplating a terrorist attack. They also contend Mr Lodhi had entirely legitimate business purposes for buying the maps. The court heard from Sydney baker Rashid Altaf, who admitted he had shared a unit with a man named "Jamal" in 2003. Prosecutors alleged that Jamal was French citizen Willy Brigitte, who allegedly trained with the outlawed terror group *Lashkar-e-Taiba* in 2001 (see below). Mr Altaf said Jamal had two visitors soon after he arrived in the unit; one was a "Bengali" butcher who worked at the local *halal* butchery and the other said he was from Sialkot in Pakistan and was an architect. In his opening address, Crown prosecutor Richard Maidment alleged Mr Lodhi and Brigitte shared two mutual contacts: one was in Pakistan and the other was Sydney butcher Abdul Rakib Hasan.[7]

The authorities were alerted in October 2003 by Hasan's boss when a suspicious fax containing prices of chemicals which can be used in explosives arrived at his office. A 15-page book of notes handwritten in Urdu, containing instructions to make petrol bombs, cyanide gas and hand grenades, was found in a raid the following day. A computer disk containing more than 600 files relating to Islamic extremism and military training manuals was found in a simultaneous search of his home. Lodhi is the third Australian convicted under federal anti-terrorism laws passed in direct response to the September 11 atrocity in the United States. He was convicted by an NSW Supreme Court jury of six men and six women after five days of deliberation which at one stage had reached deadlock. He was cleared of a fourth charge of using aerial photographs of military bases for a purpose connected with terrorism. Lodhi, an Australian citizen, was remanded in custody until June 29, 2006 when he was convicted and sentenced. This Sunni Muslim had denied all of the charges, saying that he had migrated to Australia in 1998 to "do something better for my life," and saying that killing innocent people was against Islam. He argued that, struggling to find work as an architect, he had considered setting up his own export business and chemical manufacture company. "This country is my country. These people are my people," he told the court. In court papers, Lodhi was accused of "the intent of advancing a political, religious or ideological cause, namely violent *jihad*". Lodhi has been also linked to Frenchman Willie Brigitte (see below), who was deported from Australia in late 2003, accused in a leaked French intelligence dossier of planning a terrorist attack "of great size". As pointed out above, both Lodhi and Brigitte were alleged to have trained with *Lashkar-e-Taiba*, a militant Pakistani group that Australia has banned as a terrorist organization.[8]

Another British-born Muslim convert, Jack Roche, became the first person convicted under Australia's anti-terror laws in May 2004, when he pleaded guilty of conspiring with al-Qa'ida to blow up the Israeli Embassy in Canberra. He was sentenced to nine years in prison. In February 2005, yet another Muslim activist, 32-year-old Joseph Thomas - dubbed "Jihad Jack" by local media - received a five-year prison sentence for intentionally receiving money from al-Qa'ida and having a false passport. In November 2005, police arrested 18 Muslims in coordinated pre-dawn raids in Melbourne and Sydney in an operation officials said headed off a catastrophic terror attack, possibly targeting Australia's only nuclear reactor. As of summer 2007, they were awaiting trial on charges ranging from being members of a terrorist organization to conspiring to carry out a terrorist attack. Each charge carries a maximum sentence of life imprisonment.[9]

In another case that made headlines in the country, Australia's most wanted terror suspect, Saleh Jamal, pledged loyalty to Osama Bin Laden and threatened to "chop up" Prime Minister John Howard, as Lebanese authorities prepared to deport him in May 2006. Jamal's firebrand comments came before his imminent re-arrest by Australian police, who will use one of six arrest warrants prepared during his two years in a Beirut prison for firearms trafficking and entering Lebanon on a false passport. The part-time butcher fled Sydney in March 2004 while on trial for five counts of attempted murder during the 1998 shoot-up of the Lakemba police station in the city's southwest. He has since been the subject of intense interest by counter-terrorism police. Jamal was captured in Lebanon after the Australian Security apparatus (ASIO) intercepted a phone call he made to his wife. The spy agency believed the call suggested he planned to become a suicide bomber. Since there is no extradition treaty between Australia and Lebanon, the question remained open of whether and when he would be extradited after he served his term in Beirut. From his Beirut prison, Jamal told *The Australian* he would fight every step to deport him, insisting he never again wanted to set foot in Australia and describing the Prime Minister as an "evil man". "I feel sorry for the Australian people," Jamal said. "I love Osama Bin Laden, I love [al-Qa'ida's leader in Iraq] Abu Mus'ab al-Zarqawi, I love al-Qa'ida. I will never go against their word. If the Australian people want me, Saleh Jamal, then they're going to cop the consequences. I don't want to go back to Australia. I don't want to see Australia." Jamal threatened to kill Mr Howard:

> If I was given the opportunity I'd chop him up too, without any doubt, or remorse, because he's a very evil man. If he was just to listen to people, he'd be a better person. He was the one who wrecked Australia. His people don't want war against terrorism, against Muslims. He's the Prime Minister of Australia, not the puppet of George Bush. There are 50 people in Australia who want to die [for an Islamic cause]. The Australian Government should think really, really hard. Death means nothing to these people. I wouldn't want to be in a country where sheikh Osama bin Laden, may God protect him, wages war against them. Do you know how easy it is to get 100 blokes, to talk to them for 10 minutes to do that, to get them to meet their lord? They'll destroy anything. Look at each person killing 10 people, that's 1000 people.[10]

NSW police mounted a terrorism case against Jamal, who is closely linked to six of the men charged in November 2005 in Sydney with terrorism offences as a result of the nation's largest ever counter-terror probe, Operation Pendennis. Jamal is accused of being central to the fledgling days of the investigation, when NSW police and Australian Federal Police monitored him using a small boat on Sydney Harbor to allegedly examine the Shell oil refinery, Harbor Bridge and Walsh Bay before New Year's Eve celebrations in 2003. He is also facing arrest warrants for his alleged role in the Lakemba shooting, using a bogus passport to leave Australia, and two other attempted murder cases. But Jamal insists he has no case to answer in Australia, after his two co-accused in the Lakemba shooting were found not guilty during a Supreme Court trial in 2005. It was feared that the fact that some Australian media put the epithet "terrorist" between quotation marks when referring to these terrorist activities, would not help juries to convict the suspects either.[11] These frequent reports in the Australian press regarding Muslims prosecuted by the local court system, have sometimes produced cultural clashes between the parties. A case in point unfolded in May, 2007 in connection with the nine Sydney men who were accused of plotting a terrorist bombing campaign in Australia; they caused an uproar as they refused to stand up before the judge in court.

Islamic scholars were summoned and rejected the notion that there are restrictions on Muslims standing in court, after nine Muslim terror suspects remained seated before a NSW Supreme Court judge, saying that their religious beliefs prevented them from getting to their feet. The nine Sydney men, accused of plotting a terrorist bombing campaign in Australia, refused to stand before Judge Anthony Whealy as they entered their pleas of not guilty, to the charges against them. Solicitor Adam Houda, who acted for three of the men, said that their objection to standing was part of a religious observance. But an Islamic law academic and two Islamic organizations said they knew of no religious observance that prevented Muslims from standing in a courtroom. Mr Houda told the court: "The accused have a problem with standing up…. not to be disrespectful but it's a religious observance." Justice Whealy said that he was not concerned by the refusal but suggested it might not be a wise course of action when the trial started. "A jury might take a different view and regard it as a discourtesy - judges are made of more robust material," he said. After the hearing, Mr Houda said the men's refusal to stand was based on an Islamic teaching that all men were equal and no person should be elevated above another. But Sydney University of Technology Islamic law lecturer Jamila Hussain said she knew of nothing which prevented a Muslim from standing in court: "I think it might be a figment of their imagination. It sounds like a weak excuse to me. I have never heard of it before." The men, five of whom wore traditional Islamic robes, smiled and whispered to each other during the court hearing. They waved to supporters and some of them, as they were led out of court, exchanged shouts of "Allahu akbar" (Allah is the Greatest—the war cry of Muslim fundamentalists) with friends in the public gallery. Lebanese Muslim Association director and spokesman Abdul El-Ayoubi said Muslims should not bow to anyone but Allah but he knew of no restriction on standing in court. The Islamic High Council of Australia, *Dar-ul-fatwa,* also said it knew of no religious objection to standing before a judge. Convicted terror plotter Faheem Khalid Lodhi, discussed above, had stood for the judge and jury during his trial before Justice Whealy, and, similarly, the Bali bombers stood before the judges in their criminal trials in the Muslim nation of Indonesia.[12]

Mr Houda told *The Australian* that there was no law which required his clients to stand and they had meant no disrespect to the court by their actions. He contended that the religious basis for not standing came from a *hadith* in which the Prophet Muhammad told his followers not to stand in his presence, he said. He explained that the men followed the teaching because of their level of religious observance. The accused men—Omar Umar Shariff Baladjam, 30; Khaled Cheikho, 34; Moustafa Cheikho, 30; Mohamed AH Elomar, 42; Abdul Rakib Hasan, 37; Mohamed Omar Jamal, 22; Mirsad Mulahalilovic, 30; Khaled Sharrouf, 26; and Mazen Touma, 27—pleaded not guilty to conspiring to carry out acts of preparation for a terrorist act. It was alleged they were involved in stockpiling hundreds of litres of the volatile chemical acetone and had proposed to use it in a holy war against Australia. Their trial was expected to begin in February 2008 and run for up to a year. Commonwealth prosecutor Wendy Abraham said the Crown case would last for six to eight months. No time estimate was made about the length of the defense case and there are expected to be at least three months of pretrial legal argument. Defense barrister Peter Lange told the court that recorded evidence (on CDs) would take 80 days to listen to. Criminal law specialist Bernard Brassil said prospective jurors would be advised about the trial's expected duration. The accused men reserved the right to challenge the legality of the charges against them. Justice Whealy said he wanted the trial to begin in early 2008, as he was aware that the accused, who were arrested in anti-terror sweeps in late 2005, had been in custody for a long time, in "fairly difficult conditions". Media reports have suggested the trial will cost taxpayers about $4.5 million in legal bills alone. Islamic Friendship Association spokesman Keysar Trad supported the idea that some Muslims chose not to stand out of a sense of equality. "The Prophet used to say, 'Don't stand up for me when I walk in. Don't over-honour me'", Mr Trad said. University of NSW legal academic David Brown said people were not legally bound to stand before a judge. "There's no law as such" Professor Brown said. "The judge is in control of his own courtroom . . . there is an understanding the judge should be shown respect."[13]

Mounting terrorism on the one hand, and the wish of peaceful Muslims to lead a tranquil life on the other, have generated divisions within the Muslim organizations in the country. Some Muslim leaders have dubbed the nation's umbrella Muslim body a "dictatorship" and threatened to break up its newly elected executive committee. Four member organizations of the Australian Federation of Islamic Councils (AFIC) have turned against their umbrella group, rejecting its election results in early May 2006 and labeling it undemocratic, an "immoral farce" and a "conspiracy" to cement the old guard's control of the country's 400,000

Muslims. In a letter in Arabic obtained by *The Australian* the Muslim Council of NSW president, Neil Kadomi, called on the previous AFIC executive committee not to relinquish power to the new board until a "legal and *shari'a*-compliant solution to the problem" was reached. "What took place during the congress is a farce that is devoid of morals and a nefarious scheme to take over the biggest Islamic body that represents the Australian Muslim Community," the letter states. Mr Kadomi, who, according to the letter, is backed by the Islamic councils of ACT, Tasmania and Christmas Island, asks why New South Wales and Victoria - the two states that contain the largest Muslim populations - were not given "important office-bearer positions". Kadomi replied that "AFIC has taken the path of isolation and exclusion that is based on dictatorship and fascism. This is contrary to the democratic process".[14]

AFIC's new vice-president Waqar Ahmad hit back at Mr Kadomi and AFIC's chief executive, Amjad Mehboob, for trying to destabilize the new executive. "After many years, the true hold of a selected group is finally broken," he told *The Australian*. Dr Ahmad said people such as Mr Mehboob and some former members of AFIC's executive, including Ameer AH, had for many years "resisted transparency and accountability, (and) failed to streamline administrative procedures". He labelled the Muslim Council of NSW a "joke" and said Mr Kadomi was controlled by Mr Mehboob. Mr Kadomi's letter is the latest in a series of blows to AFIC, which represents nine state and territorial Islamic councils and advises the Howard Government on Islamic issues. In April 2006, a survey of the Muslim community, carried out by AFIC's state of Victoria member organization, had found the national council to be "secretive, sexist, unrepresentative and irrelevant". The Northern Territory's Dr Ahmad said Mr Kadomi's letter was a "case of sour grapes . . . and an attempt to destabilise the democratically elected team". While the three Islamic organizations that have supported Mr Kadomi in his letter would not be suspended or expelled, Dr Ahmad had said that Mr Mehboob's position as AFIC chief executive would be reviewed "very carefully" in the future. Mr Kadomi refused to comment to *The Australian* about the letter.[15]

But internal divisions had to be put aside in the face of the perceived attacks on the Qur'an that were launched by none other than the Archbishop of Sydney, George Pell. Indeed, Australia's most influential Catholic has stated that the Qur'an is riddled with "invocations to violence", and that the central challenge of Islam lies in the struggle between moderate and extremist forces as the faith spreads into a "childless Europe". Archbishop Pell explained that reading the Qur'an, the sacred text of

Islam, was vital "because the challenge of Islam will be with us for the remainder of our lives - at least". But in a speech to US Catholic business leaders, Dr Pell noted that Western democracy was also suffering a crisis of confidence as evidenced by the decline in fertility rates. "Pagan emptiness" and western fears of the uncontrollable forces of nature had contributed to "hysteric and extreme claims" about global warming. "In the past, pagans sacrificed animals and even humans in vain attempts to placate capricious and cruel gods. Today they demand a reduction in carbon dioxide emissions."[16]

Dr Pell said that the September 11 terrorist attacks had been his personal wake-up call to understand Islam better. He had tried to reconcile claims that Islam was a faith of peace with those that suggested the Qur'an legitimized the killings of non-Muslims. "While there was room for optimism in fruitful dialogue between faiths and the common human desire for peace, a pessimistic response began with the Qur'an itself. Errors of facts, inconsistencies, anachronisms and other defects were not unknown to scholars but difficult for Muslims to debate openly", he said. "In my own reading of the Qur'an, I began to note down invocations to violence. There are so many of them, however, that I abandoned this exercise after 50 or 60 or 70 pages." Recently Dr Pell courted controversy when he drew a link between Islam and communism. His speech on Islam and western democracies was delivered in Florida on February 4, 2006 but only appeared on the archdiocese's website in May. Dr Pell wrote that every nation and every religion, including Catholicism, had "crimes in their histories". In the same way, Islam could not airbrush its "shadows". Claims of Muslim tolerance of Christian and Jewish minorities were largely mythical and he wondered about the possibility of theological development in Islam when the Qur'an was said to come directly from God. "Considered strictly on its own terms, Islam is not a tolerant religion and its capacity for far-reaching renovation is severely limited," he said. However, he added, like Christianity, Islam was a living religion and the existence of moderate Islam in Indonesia was proof of the softening impact of human intervention. Democracy and moderation did not always go hand in hand and an "anorexic vision of democracy and the human person was no match for Islam".[17] Consternation was deep in Muslim circles in Australia, with the moderates probably acknowledging in their hearts what the Cardinal said, and the infuriated militants hardly daring to contradict him while new cases of Islamic terrorism were filling the pages of the Australian press as a matter of routine. This turmoil did not prevent Muslim students, clerics and other ideologically committed spokespersons to speak their minds, despite the damage they might cause to their community. A former president of the Muslim Student Association of the University of Sydney, Usman Badar, was cited as decrying: "The conflict is so clear, so stark that there is no middle ground. How do you come to a middle ground on whether sovereignty belongs to the people or to Allah? You can't."[18]

Schools in Australia have begun welcoming Badar and other speakers who, as the *Sydney Morning Herald* reporter Miranda Devine wrote, "appear to be fully assimilated, second-generation Australians" who wear conventional Western clothing and speak fluently in "broad Australian accents" as well as Arabic. "But they belong to a political group called *Hizb ut-Tahrir* (Party of Liberation) that calls for the creation of a global Islamic state, or caliphate, under strict *shari'a* law," wrote Devine. "The message from these young men is one of division, non-assimilation and rejection of the values of the *'kafir'* - non-Muslims." This radical Islamist movement, which is now being invited onto campuses of one of America's most dependable allies in the war against terrorism, has been banned in Germany, Holland, Russia and many Muslim countries. There is a new wave of sophisticated, articulate Islamic fundamentalists attempting to spread the word among moderate Muslims in Sydney. Young men, wearing regular clothes, with neatly trimmed beards indeed appear to be fully assimilated, second-generation Australians.[19]

At a public lecture at Bankstown Town Hall in April 2006, *Hizb ut-Tahrir* organizer Soadad Doureihi, his brother Wassim, and Usman Badar, president of Sydney University's Muslim Student Association in 2005, outlined their utopian goal of the ultimate overthrow of western democracies. "Islam can never coexist one under the other or one within the other," Soadad told the crowd. "When the state is established, when people see the mercy of Islam, they embrace Islam in droves." The April 8, 2006 lecture, to about 200 men and 50 women, was entitled "Should Muslims Subscribe to Australian Values?" *Hizb ut-Tahrir (HT)* has been invited to speak at Sydney Boys High at least twice, and often addresses students at Sydney University. Borrowing its methodology and ideology from Marxist-Leninist groups, *HT* calls itself a political party which works to "change the situation of the corrupt society so that it is transformed into an Islamic society", according to its website. It opposes integration and assimilation of Muslims into Australian society. Wassim told the Bankstown crowd: "The pushing to integration and assimilation is to get us to think and believe and feel in a certain way that Islam will not condone…. On the collective level everyone accepts that you have to have one set of laws and no Muslim in this country is demanding today the implementation of *shari'a* law…. In this country, yes, we believe this is the best way forward but … our current struggle is the implementation of Islamic law in the Muslim world and that will serve as a model for the rest of humanity. [But] if governments want to interfere in the individual, personal affairs of any citizen, they are going to create the conditions of civil unrest and chaos like in France."[20]

Soadad had a message for youth: "They must be aware of the plot of the *kafir* (Unbeliever), the plot of the Western society to enforce on them a palatable Islam…. Secularism is a clear assault on the fundamental belief of a Muslim. Democracy is a clear assault on the fundamental belief of a Muslim also." *HT* says it advocates non-violence, and yet, terrorism expert Rohan Gunaratna, from Nanyang Technological University in Singapore, told a conference in 2004, that "key members of the al-Qa'ida organization [such as Abu Mus'ab al-Zarqawi] formerly belonged to the *HT* organization…. The upper echelons of organizations that are of key interest to us, and operating at a violent, extremist, radical level, consist of former members of *HT*. In Australia, *HTs* threat is its anti-integration message". An audience member in the Bankstown gathering asked: "The reality is that many of us live in Australia as citizens. We, or our parents and families, have accepted this citizenship with the full knowledge of Australia's social construction and her values. Can we not as Muslims hold these Australian values [while] keeping our Islam intact?" Badar, a graduate of Malek Fahd Islamic High School in Chullora, who was such a good student that he appeared on the 2002 HSC all-rounders list, answered: "It comes back to the theory that Western values [and Muslim values] - [and] their opposition, are in such stark conflict that there is no middle ground….Yes, our parents came here. I wouldn't say they were fully aware of the Australian values and systems, way of life and so on…. But what's more important is why did they come here? What were they running away from? Was the country in which they lived not providing for them? What was the cause of the conditions in that country? They were running away from the very same values…. If you are saying they came here so we should accept or follow those values, there's a clear contradiction. The simple matter of fact is that there is no middle ground." The bottom line is that there is no middle ground. *Hizb ut-Tahrir* is a fringe group, rejected by most Australian Muslim leaders, all right, but its message is alluring to the young and the disenfranchised. Is the answer to ban it? Wassim says the more the group is attacked, the more it grows. In his words: "The more we come under pressure the more we return closer to Islam."[21]

Once tolerated in Britain, *HT* has, according to Devine, also been banned there. Those familiar with this movement's message, methods and terrorist connections know how dangerous it is. Muslims living in western nations "must be aware of the plot of the *kafir*, the plot of the Western society to enforce on them a palatable Islam," said another *Hizb ut-Tahrir* spokesman Soadad Doureihi in an April 8, 2006 public speech in Bankston, Australia. "Secularism is a clear assault on the fundamental belief of a Muslim," Doureihi told his Sydney audience of 200 men and 50 women, many of them Muslims. "Democracy is a clear assault on the fundamental belief of a Muslim also." In the society advocated by Doureihi and *Hizb ut-Tahrir* there would be no equal rights for those of other faiths or for women. No speech or writing would be permitted that questioned Islam, and no democratic votes would be taken to choose national leaders or determine government policy. All would be controlled by a small group of Muslim theologians, as (despite the figurehead president) it is today in theocratic Iran. *Hizb ut-Tahrir* in Australia claims to advocate nonviolence. But to judge this tree by its worldwide fruits, this movement radicalized many future terrorists. These *Hizb ut-Tahrir* "graduates" include one of the founders of *Fatah* who, prior to that, was a founder of *Hizb ut-Tahrir*. Another former *Hizb ut-Tahrir* member became the "spiritual leader" of *Islamic Jihad*. This organization has been the "finishing school" for several top members of Al-Qa'ida, the group behind the September 11, 2001 attacks in the United States that killed nearly 3,000 Americans. According to terrorism expert Rohan Gunaratna of Singapore's Nanyang Technological University, one former *Hizb ut-Tahrir* member who became a leader of Al-Qa'ida is Abu Musab al-Zarqawi.[22]

After *Hizb ut-Tahrir* separates young Muslims from their larger society, the most fanatical followers often are led to contact its ideological fellow travelers. These radical kinsmen in parallel Caliphate movements, such as Al-Qa'ida, then try to recruit and hook the most susceptible youngsters on the "harder stuff of zealous religious fanaticism, terrorism, assassination, the promise of 72 virgins in Paradise and *Islamikaze* bombing. Such are the Islamist "drug pushers" of *Hizb ut-Tahrir lo* which Australian schools are now exposing their Muslim and religiously adrift other students. At least some of those purpose-craving students will become addicted to the dogma, certitude and comradeship these passionate anti-democratic propagandists offer, and a few will likely use their Australian passports as future agents of global terrorism. These agents of *Hizb ut-Tahrir* aim to banish free speech and democracy for the rest of society, but they are eagerly exploiting Australia's freedom and toleration to advance their totalitarian agenda.

What are the tangled roots of *Hizb ut-Tahrir* and its polarizing ideas? The movement *Hizb ut-Tahrir,* as *DiscoverTheNetwork.org* explains, aims to replace existing governments with theocratic Muslim rule and to bring about a worldwide Islamic government under a single ruler called the Caliph. *Hizb ut-Tahrir* aims to restore and expand the Caliphate, the last vestige of which collapsed when war hero Mustafa Kemal ("Ataturk") and his "Young Turks" overthrew the last Sultan of the Ottoman Empire and his underlings in 1923-24. The eventual worldwide rule of the new Caliph, *Hizb ut-Tahrir* teaches, will be that of a human being, fallible and prone to sin and error. "The post of the *Khaleefah* is decided by people and not by Allah." The Caliph is selected, and can in theory be removed and replaced, but not by a democratic vote of the whole body of believers. This power of election and removal will be held by the *Ummah,* "the nation of Muslims," a vague notion by which *Hizb ut-Tahrir* means an elite committee of the wise and powerful, comprised entirely of men. *(Hizb ut-Tahrir* does not specify how this ruling committee of Islamic scholars or Ayatollahs will be chosen.) *Hizb ut-Tahrir* explicitly rejects Western notions of both democracy and capitalism as defective, and as instruments with which the West has colonized and subjugated Islamic nations. They argue that the Muslim world became weak and fell under the hegemony of Western unbelievers. Restoring the Caliphate and expanding its rule to the entire planet, the Liberation Party teaches, will usher in a new global Muslim Golden Age of peace and divine harmony. The movement - *Hayat al-Tahrir al-Islami* ("the Islamic Life of Liberation") - was founded in Jordanian-controlled East Jerusalem in 1951 by Sheikh Taqi-ud-deen Al-Nabahani, who is discussed below. He was "an associate and contemporary" of the anti-Semitic, pro-Nazi Grand Mufti of Jerusalem Sheikh Haji Amin Al-Husseini, who spent much of World War II in Berlin.[23]

Hizb ut-Tahrir al-Islami ("the Islamic Party of Liberation") emerged as a "political party" from this society in 1952-53 and was led by Al-Nabahani until his death in 1977. His place was taken by Palestinian cleric Sheikh Abd-el Qadim Zaloom, a former professor at Al-Azhar in

Cairo, who led it until his death on April 29, 2003, publicly naming no successor as head of the *Hizb.* The Liberation Party today reportedly has tens of thousands of secret members across the Muslim world and in at least 40 countries, attracted by its zealous vision of a triumphant Islamic future and their own frustration with today's ascendant Western world. The "genius" of Al-Nabahani, wrote Heritage Foundation researcher Ariel Cohen, "was in marrying Orthodox Islamist ideology to Leninist strategy and tactics". *"Hizb ut-Tahrir",* Cohen writes, is a "totalitarian organization, akin to a disciplined Marxist-Leninist party, in which internal dissent is neither encouraged nor tolerated." A would-be member undergoes two years of indoctrination, becoming a full member only after he "melts with the Party." Members belong to compartmentalized cells and know the identities of only the others in that cell. "When a critical mass of cells is achieved," writes Cohen, "according to its doctrine, *Hizb* may move to take over a country in preparation for the establishment of the Caliphate."

The branch of *Hizb ut-Tahrir was* established in the United Kingdom by Sheikh Omar Bakri Mohammed, who was discussed above, and who joined the party as a teenager in Lebanon during the early 1970s. He also created another organization that aims to create a global Islamic Caliphate, *Al Muhajirun* ("The Emigrants", a name that referred to the early followers of the Prophet Muhammad, who emigrated with him from Mecca to Medina), which he has led from an office in London. *Al Muhajirun,* the Sheikh has said, was established in Mecca but launched publicly in Jeddah, Saudi Arabia, with 40 founding members on March 3, 1983, a date chosen because it was "the 59th anniversary of the destruction of the Ottoman Caliphate". Expelled from Saudi Arabia for radical political activity, the Sheikh arrived in Great Britain, the asylum of many Islamic fugitives from their countries' authorities, on January 14, 1986. He immediately proceeded to establish both *Al Muhajirun* and *Hizb ut-Tahrir* on fertile British soil, and from there to other Western countries, including Australia. In October 2000 the Sheikh co-signed and issued a "Warning to All Jews ... in the UK" that "if you support Israel financially, verbally or physically you will become part of the [Middle East] conflict." In other words, he explicitly warned Jews in democratic Great Britain, the mother of parliaments, that if they opened their mouths in support of Israel, they risked being attacked in England by Islamist terrorists. In 1999 the Sheikh became chief sponsor in Great Britain of the *International Islamic Front* (IIP), a group persuading and assisting young British Muslims to undergo "guns and live ammunition" combat training and then go overseas to fight *Jihad* ("Holy War") in Chechnya and the Balkans.[24]

Sheikh Bakri Mohammad, whom we have met in London above, described himself as the head of the "political wing" of the IIP with no "structural link" to Bin Laden; bearing in mind that the latter issued in 1998 a *fatwa* declaring it a Muslim's "individual duty" (*fard 'ayn*) to kill Americans, and that he created a new organization called the International (or World) Islamic Front for Jihad Against Jews and Crusaders in whose name Osama Bin Laden and his associates have operated since, the connection between the two becomes inescapable. The Sheikh himself acknowledged that "the military wing of the International Islamic Front is run by Osama Bin Laden".[25]

The very word "Islam" means "surrender" or "submission" (to Allah). Muslims refer to the combined nations where Islam is the dominant religion as *Dar al-Islam,* which literally means "the Zone of Submission." Like *Hizb ut-Tahrir,* *Al Muhajirun* aims to restore the Caliphate, a monolithic form of religious-political rule of all the world's Muslims that existed during the succession of the four "rightly guided" Caliphs who ruled after the death of the Prophet Muhammad. Every Muslim on Earth would look to this single ruler, and with Islam's global conquest all human beings will become citizens of a single Nation of Islam. The new Caliph, *Al-Khalifah* in Arabic parlance, or "leader" as on *Al Muhajirun's* website, "whose foreign policy is to conquer the whole world by *jihad,*" will thereby bring the dawn of a world of peace, love, economic fairness and divine harmony. By striving "to establish *Al-Khilafah* in order that Islam dominates the world and becomes the World Order," reads the website, *Al Muhajirun* teaches that its followers are following the will of Allah. Under this coming worldwide "Domination of Islam *(Izhaar ul Deen)"* people will not necessarily be forced to become Muslims, but they will be taught "to accept it as a political way of life and a solution for their [and society's] problems." "When the state [of the global Islamic Caliphate] is established, when people see the mercy of Islam," Soadad Doureihi told his Australian audience on April 8, 2006, "they [will] embrace Islam in droves." Australians and others in the West will at best, in other words, either bend their knee to Islam and convert or live the rest of their lives on their knees in *dhimmitude* as second-class citizens with fewer rights and higher taxes than Muslims. Until that day arrives, the website frankly proclaims that one of *Al Muhajirun's* tactics will be "To formulate a fifth column as a community pressure group which is well equipped with Islamic culture to bring about ruling social, economic, judicial, penal and ritual systems in order to become capable of implementing Islam fully and comprehensively in society." The weapons to be used to establish global Islamic political power range from debate, media appearances and the law, to the funding of *jihadists* and recruiting of *Islamikaze* bombers.

How dangerous is what *Al Muhajirun* and its connected Caliphate groups teach young Muslims? In early 2004 a group of Islamist protestors from its offshoot organization the "Islamic Thinkers Society" staged a protest in front of the Israeli Consulate in New York City carrying signs depicting an Islamic flag atop the White House stating: "Islam will Dominate". The protestors chanted in Arabic: "The mushroom cloud is on its way! The real Holocaust is on its way!", as Steve Emerson of the Investigative Project on Terrorism reported on CNN. Other chants included: "Israel won't last long.... Indeed, Allah will repeat the Holocaust right on the soil of Israel". "Islam is the fastest growing religion in the UK, with up to two million followers and more than 1,000 mosques across Britain," wrote Ori Golan. "In many cities across Britain, Muslims live in segregated communities, with separate education, social and cultural networks. It is within these closed communities that the extremists find recruits for al Qa'ida and other terror groups."[26]

Most British Muslims, of course, are not Anglo-Saxon converts but Islamic immigrants from lands like India, Pakistan, the Middle East and other parts of the world once ruled by the British Empire. Their children, born in the West, are brought up as Muslims and often carry the passports of Western nations. Osama Bin Laden has said that the goal of Al Qa'ida is to "unite all Muslims and to establish a government which follows the rule of the Caliphs." Sheikh Omar claimed to have resigned from *Hizb ut-Tahrir* on January 16, 1996 over a theological issue. But on the first anniversary of the September 11, 2001 Al-Qa'ida terrorist attack on America, Islamist cleric Abu Hamza Al Masri marked the day by scheduling a conference to launch a new organization (reportedly funded by *Al Muhajirun* with a six-figure cash donation) to be called the *Islamic Council of Britain* (ICB). ICB's stated goal is to "implement *shari'a* law in Britain." The poster advertising this conference at Sheikh al-Masri's Finsbury Park mosque in North London featured a large photograph of the World Trade Center towers, one already ablaze, the other about to be hit by another skyjacked airliner. In large letters the poster read: "September the 11th 2001: A TOWERING DAY IN HISTORY",[27] just like a poster of the Hamas which showed Manhattan burning against a background of a war of annihilation against Israel.[28] Among the most prominent guests invited by Sheikh al-Masri to attend his conference was the British founder of both this political party and *Al Muhajirun,* Sheikh Umar Bakri Mohammad, who reportedly said: "The people at this conference look at September 11 like a battle, as a great achievement by the *mujahideen* against the evil superpower. I never praised September 11 after it happened but now I can see why they did it." (Conference flyers described the 19 skyjackers of 9/11 as the "Magnificent 19"). Of Osama Bin Laden and his Al-Qa'ida terrorists, Sheikh Umar reported: "We don't perceive them as the US perceives them; we see them as a sincere devoted people who stood firm against the invasion of a Muslim country." That September 11 preceded the "invasion of Afghanistan and Iraq", and was not the result of it, was a small detail not worth bothering about. Also invited was the British spokesman for *Al Muhajirun,* Anjem Choundary. The third such distinguished guest invited to this conference was the British representative of the *Hizb ut-Tahrir,* Dr Imran Waheed. On July 7, 2005, four Islamist terrorist bombs exploded in a coordinated attack in London. Fifty-six people were killed and more than 700 were injured. Some of the bombers had been born and raised in Great Britain but radicalized by Islamist preachers and organizations. And now, carefully-groomed propagandists for *Hizb ut-Tahrir* are engaging with students in the schools and universities of Australia. Can a crop of Islamist terrorists be far behind? Soadad's brother Wassim, another *Hizb ut-Tahrir* advocate of the imposed global Islamic government, told his Australian audience on April 8, 2006, "The pushing to integration and assimilation is to get us to think and believe and feel in a certain way that Islam will not condone." And "If governments want to interfere in the individual, personal affairs of any citizen, they are going to create the conditions of civil unrest and chaos like in France."[29]

In addition to violent anti-Israel riots of Australian Muslims, who use the same anti-Semitic themes as their European coreligionists, they also engage in active peddling of hatred against the Jews, incite to violence and glorify terrorism. When the government reformed sedition laws in 2005 in order to stop direct incitement to terrorist violence, some of the media and academia raised hysterical claims that the laws went too far and would stifle legitimate political reporting and debate. But it soon became clear that in some respects these laws do not go far enough. The government committed itself to reviewing the laws with a view to addressing the existing loopholes, which under existing legislation allow free circulation of literature inciting to hatred, violence and terror. These activities are led by *jihadists* who oppose democracy and are committed to overthrow it and undermine it; therefore the law ought to protect democracy from the *jihadists* rather than *jihadists* from democracy. Unlike Europe, where the immigrants fail to dilute themselves within existing societies in a process of integration thereby creating a state of friction with their host cultures, Australia remains committed to multi-culturalism with integration, like Canada and to some extent the US; it must be remembered that each of these nations, in contrast to Europe, feature a constitution of what was since its inception, an immigrant society, and which remains constantly in the making. But multi-culturalism does not mean freedom to propagate hatred. At a Muslim bookstore in Sydney, which prides itself as being the largest in the country, one of the children's books offered for sale is *The Emergence of Dajjal, The Jewish King* by Mohamad Yasin Owadally. This Malaysian publication argues that every Jew is party to a plot to "control the whole world, from east to west, under the leadership of *Dajjal*", the Muslim equivalent of the evil apocalyptic anti-Christ. Any peace-process, the text argues, is the result of superpowers preparing the path for the Jews. This signifies in Muslim parlance that every Jew is the existential opponent of Islam, and Muslims should oppose all Jews at every turn. The idea that every world problem is the result of a Jewish conspiracy goes back to that infamous and spurious text, *the Protocols of the Elders of Zion*, which remains popular among Arabs, Muslims and anti-Semites across the globe. The introduction to that book, which is available at a give-away price, states *inter alia*: "The Christian world . . . has already been snared and lies prostrate at the mercy of the ruthless inhuman cabal. And now Jews have to march towards the Islamic world.... It is a great honor, a privilege to contribute what one can in the *jihad* against this menace." Another Muslim store sold a new stock of Henry Ford's *The International Jew,* which includes the text of the *Protocols,* preceded by anti-Semitic invective, printed in Johannesburg, South Africa. When one adds to that the injunction of Sheikh Abdullah bin Muhammed Humaid: "When you meet those who disbelieve, smite at their necks till when you have killed and wounded many of them and taken the rest captives", and you have a harrowing framework for the operation of this industry of hatred in the heart of a free democratic nation.[30]

The Advertiser, an Australian newspaper, has come out with some startling revelations about an Al-Qa'ida man, a French national, captured in Australia and then taken for interrogation by the French. According to a report published by the newspaper on 18 October, 2005, Willie Brigitte, the captured man, has told French investigators of his extraordinary journey from failed butcher to linchpin in an Al -Qa'ida plan to launch

a terror attack on Australia. He has detailed the high-altitude paramilitary training he undertook in a vast camp overlooking the Himalayas in
which he and thousands of *jihad* warriors were schooled in terrorism. He
has told of how Osama Bin Laden's allies have penetrated the Pakistani
Army to thwart US efforts to crack down on terrorist training operations in the remote Pakistani mountain regions that border Afghanistan,
known as Waziristan. A year after the French national was captured in a
western Sydney apartment with documents indicating he was planning
to launch an attack on Australian targets, his interrogation transcripts
are said to have come into the possession of the Australian newspaper.
The transcripts are said to give a rare insight into the functioning of the
networks of people prepared to join the Islamist *jihad* against the West.
Brigitte told investigators about the camp where he was trained in the use
of explosives, small arms and terrorism tactics, explaining that it was a
sophisticated three-tiered mountain complex close to the Indo-Pakistani
border. He was grouped with foreign recruits, including American and
British citizens of Pakistani origin. "There were between 2,000 and 3,000
mujahideen," Brigitte told French anti-terror judge Jean-Louis Bruguiere.
"I remember it was very impressive because we gathered every morning
and shouted *Allah Akbar* !! (Allah is the greatest! - the war cry of Jihad
fighters). What was more, the site was imposing since one could see the
outline of the Himalayas." The camp was run by *Lashkar e Taiba* (LET),
a *jihadi* organization already mentioned above. Brigitte explained that
LET included soldiers from the Pakistan Army who worked to sabotage
efforts by the West to fight Bin Laden and his allies.[31]

"There was complete complicity between *Lashkar e Taiba* and the
Pakistani Army," Brigitte said in a secret interrogation in the Paris judicial
chambers of Judge Bruguiere on 3 December 2003. "Furthermore, the
weapons were provided by the army. The munitions were brought in by
night between the first and second levels (of the camp). There was everything - munitions, arms and food. We had the feeling that these weapons
came from the Pakistani Army. There were American Ml6s, French
FAMS, Kalashnikovs and Makarovs. All the identification numbers
had been removed." Brigitte said on several occasions he was ordered
to remove any evidence of military activity. The camp leaders had been
warned that a raid by a coalition of CIA agents and Pakistani soldiers was
imminent. "I can remember four raids by the Pakistani Army," Brigitte
said. "They always asked the foreign volunteers, of whom I was one,
to clean up the camp and particularly to collect the cartridge cases and
cartridges. There were no more than 15 Pakistani soldiers who came to

carry out these checks with the same number of Americans. We were told that they were CIA agents who had come to check for the presence of foreign *mujahideen*." Brigitte stayed at the camp for six weeks before returning to Paris early in 2002. His flatmate in Paris, Ibrahim Keita, said Brigitte had returned under orders to organize a sleeper cell there. "Brigitte did explain to me he had been sent back to France in order to make contact with a certain number of people," Keita told Judge Bruguiere. "They were individuals who had either already fought or who had taken training in camps like him, as I understood it." Brigitte was acting under orders from his mentor at the LET camp, known as Sajid Abu Braa, a 30-year-old Pakistan Army soldier in charge of foreign recruits. Abu Braa, who traveled with two personal bodyguards, was a close associate of the camp's leader, known only as Zakerahmane. In Afghanistan, Zakerahmane was Bin Laden's right-hand man. Brigitte was arrested at his Sydney flat on 9 October 2003 and officials found maps of Australian nuclear sites, and the Perth headquarters of Australia's elite SAS unit. He was repatriated to France on October 17, where, as of 2004, he was still imprisoned in Paris's Fleury Merogis Jail.[32]

A new battle has been launched on the Australian domestic front between the conservative federal government, which is fighting terrorism outwardly and strengthening national consciousness and Western culture inwardly, and the labor provincial governments which if left to them would probably forget Australia's heritage in favor of rootless cosmopolitanism, minority rights at the expense of the dominant culture, and immigrant narratives of history at the expense of the national ethos that was won by more than two centuries of history. Two centuries after he dropped anchor in Botany Bay, Captain James Cook has sailed into a political storm in Australia, the country he put on the map. Once honored as an Australian hero, the eighteenth-century English navigator has been sidelined - even vilified - in recent decades in a nation embarrassed by its bloody colonial past and the cruel treatment of its indigenous population. But the Australian government vowed to reverse the tide of political correctness that had swept Cook, who claimed Australia for the British Crown in 1770 together with other European "colonizers", from the national school curriculum. Julie Bishop, the federal education minister, announced that there would be a radical overhaul in the way history is taught in Australian schools, in order to see a return to the narrative form of history, free of political interpretation. "Every school child should know when and why Capt. James Cook sailed along the east coast of Australia, who was our first prime minister, why we were involved in two world wars and how federation came about," she said. Miss Bishop accused politically correct educators of hijacking history, presenting Australia's past through a filter of Marxist, feminist and Green interpretations, and one might add minority, especially Muslim history. "There is too much indoctrination and not enough pivotal facts and dates," she complained. Her comments echoed the views of John Howard, the prime minister, who recently called for a "root and branch" overhaul of the way history is taught in Australian schools. He also wants to see pupils saluting the Australian flag at morning assembly, a practice last seen in the 1960s. In some parts of Australia, history is no longer taught as a separate subject, but has been absorbed into a broader social studies program. In Western Australia, history is part of a program called "time, continuity and change". In South Australia, it is part of the society and environment studies unit. Mr Howard believes that history should once again be a compulsory part of the syllabus, for at least some of the time a child is at school. Well known for his love of British institutions - especially cricket, the monarchy and the Westminster system of government - Mr. Howard told one of his audiences that school children should have "some understanding" of British and European history, the Enlightenment and the influence of Christianity on Western civilization. Only then might they comprehend the dangers that loom to their civilization from the invasion by minority immigrants with proclaimed intentions of over-throwing government and local law. Although the education minister has commissioned two historians to map out how history can return to the national curriculum, the Canberra government faces stiff opposition from the Labor-controlled state governments who run the schools. The federal government, however, is likely to have the last word since it funds the state school system, and its success in this endeavor might become a model for other Western governments who are meekly surrendering their national histories to please the politically correct, and the Muslims who cannot identify with the respective national ethoses and narratives.[33]

New Zealand was also dragged into the Muslim problem, though by itself it does not have any Islamic group to be concerned about. It turns out that the roommate and flying-school classmate of a September 11 hijacker was banished from New Zealand, where he had been using a suspended US private pilot certificate to obtain a commercial license. Rayed Mohammed Abdullah is one of a dozen pilots whose licenses were suspended after the attacks on New York and the Pentagon. The Federal Aviation Administration having revoked Mr. Abdullah's license after a lengthy appeal process, Mr. Abdullah then used an alias to enter New

Zealand in February 2006 to obtain an English-language based commercial pilot's license. Federal officials declined to comment on their role in his deportation, but press reports state that the FBI alerted New Zealand officials to his presence. "I can tell you there are no US federal charges that I am aware of on Rayed Abdullah," said Richard Kolko, FBI special agent. "It is our standard procedure. We do not confirm or deny the existence of an investigation, nor do we confirm status on the terrorist watch list." "However, the prevention of terrorism is the FBI's number one priority. It is clear that in the post-9/11 world, we cannot succeed in this task without efficiently sharing information with our domestic and international law-enforcement and intelligence community partners. The FBI has excellent relations with New Zealand through our Legal Attache office in Australia, and it is routine for us to work together in matters of current interest," Mr Kolko reported.[34]

Dave Mackett, president of the Airline Pilots Security Alliance, has said that it's "almost impossible" to get a commercial pilot job because of a "severe" vetting process. "Any time you have a roommate of a terrorist training to be a commercial airline pilot, it's a great concern," Mr. Mackett said. "But I don't think we worry so much that they will become pilots with hostile intent. A person with minimal skills, on a good day, can fly an airplane into a building." Another pilot said he can imagine numerous scenarios "that would scare the public and disrupt the infrastructure" if a terrorist were to obtain such a license. "He is probably trying to get enough [flying] time to get a corporate job and then fly a larger 'C' jet into something of substance for another terrorist event," the pilot explained. That "can be done without drawing attention or raising security concerns." Ravindra Singh, a Manawatu Aero Club flight instructor who flew with Abdullah on five training flights, told the *Manawatu Standard* newspaper that the Saudi man left the US five months after the terrorist attack because "no one was allowed to fly after 9/11". The paper also reported that Mr. Abdullah's family has not heard from him since his deportation from New Zealand in early 2006. Mr. Abdullah had shared an apartment with Hani Hanjour and took flight lessons with him at an Arizona flight school. Hanjour, who also had a commercial license, is thought to have been the pilot who crashed American Airlines Flight 77 into the Pentagon. Laura Brown, spokeswoman for the Federal Aviation Administration, reported that Mr. Abdullah's license was suspended and eventually revoked at the request of Homeland Security officials out of "security concerns." Miss Brown says the number of foreign-born pilots seeking private pilot licenses dropped after the terrorist attacks, when the application process stiffened. There are 600,000 licensed pilots in the United States. Jennifer Marty, spokeswoman for the Transportation Security Administration, has explained that more than 41,000 applications have been processed since October 2004, and about 100 applications have been denied. Kathleen Vasconcelos, spokeswoman for the Aircraft Owners and Pilots Association, has confirmed that instructors and employees of the nation's 2,000 flight schools are trained in security awareness. "There is more scrutiny of foreign students since September 11…. We are hearing from flight schools that the number of foreign flight students has decreased since 9/11, most likely because of the cost and time involved in complying with new rules."[35]

The US Government's 9-11 Commission Report on the attacks regarding Rayed Abdullah states that Abdullah lived and trained in Phoenix, Arizona, with Hani Hanjour, and was a leader at the Islamic Cultural Centre in Phoenix where, the FBI says, he "reportedly gave extremist speeches at the mosque". A website sourced to the 9-11 report states that Abdullah attended the same Phoenix flight school as Hanjour and the pair used a flight simulator together on June 23, 2001. A 2004 report in the *Arizona Daily Star* names him as Rayed Mohammed Abdullah. But the Rayed Mohammed Abdullah Ali who wandered into the Manawatu Aero Club in March gave no suggestion of a fundamentalist outlook. The clean-cut Muslim told the club's chief flying officer, Captain Ravindra Singh, he had obtained his private pilot's licence in the US and spent several years there before returning to Saudi Arabia to work in his father's textile business.[36] He wanted to pass the International English Language Testing System (IELTS) exam so he could return home to train for his commercial pilot's license. He wore a baseball cap, smart shirts and baggy trousers and favoured burgers over *halal* food. Captain Singh, a former Indian Air Force officer trained in intelligence, says Ali had a Yemeni passport and he was naturally suspicious at first. "At the time of September 11 he would have been in the US. I asked him some very direct questions about his US flying experience and found he was quite intelligent and a moderate person. He was not at all fundamentalist - he was against those people." Singh and other instructors accompanied Ali on several flights in a Cessna 152 aircraft. "I found his standard to be very good," Captain Singh said. "He wanted to fly in Saudi Arabia or the [Arab] Emirates and was doing instrument training in the US before September 11 but said that since then everyone had treated him with suspicion. I'm 99 per cent sure he was genuine." Ali told Captain Singh he was born and raised in Saudi Arabia but traveled on a Yemeni passport because his father was from Yemen, and Saudi Arabia had refused to give him citizenship. When he returned to Palmerston North, he told Captain Singh he had missed an application deadline and been unable to sit the IELTS exam in Auckland. He planned to re-enroll in Palmerston North, where it was cheaper to fly than in Auckland. Others could not comment on what happened after Ali returned to Saudi Arabia. Nor could they comment on what specific information the Government had on him or where it came from. "We're satisfied he is the right man",[37] he said. Cases like this are numerous, where innocent men can arouse suspicions and be unjustly arrested and deported, but on the other hand too many culprits slip through the net because of a clamoring for civil rights and the ultra-caution of law-enforcement authorities.

The Melbourne-based leader of the *Ahl Sunnah Waljammah* association, Mohammed Omran, and his Sydney counterpart, Abdul Salam Mohammed Zoud, called for a conference in July 2006 at RMIT University (previously The Royal Melbourne Institute of Technology, Melbourne, Australia) under modified names - a ploy their critics claim is designed to escape media attention. The promotional flyer for the Annual Australian *Da'wah* Conference identified Sheikh Omran as Sheikh Abu Ayman and Sheikh Zoud as Sheikh Abdul Salaam. The pair are widely known in the broader community - and listed in their now defunct newspaper *Mecca News* - as Omran and Zoud. Sheikh Omran told *The Australian* that he was known as Sheikh Abu Ayman - meaning the father of Ayman in Arabic - by the Muslim community, and was not attempting to escape the media radar by appearing under another name at the Melbourne conference. But a member of John Howard's Muslim Community Reference Group, Mustapha Kara-Ali, said that Sheikh Omran and his group were renowned for using "phony" names to avoid "spurring certain media reactions". "Because when you say Omran, the surname Omran is going to be very controversial," Mr Kara-Ali said. "When you say Abu Ayman, there could be 100,000 Abu Aymans." He said both sheikhs Zoud and Omran teach *Wahhabism*, a fundamentalist version of Islam spread and financed by Saudi Arabia, which inspired the former *Taliban* regime in Afghanistan and is preached by the world's most notorious terrorist, Osama Bin Laden, leader of al-Qa'ida. "The (conference) organizing group headed by Omran is an Australian Trojan horse," Mr Kara-Ali said. "Year after year this fringe group continues to adapt its cover while it unashamedly maintains the same core support to Bin Laden and his ideology. Omran's conspiratorial pussyfooting over the issue of terrorism is producing more Bin Ladens in the suburbs, and it's turning more of Australia's youths towards the path of destruction and terror." Mr Kara-Ali said Sheikh Omran's organization has a "hidden agenda" to "further recruit" more Australian Muslims and "disenfranchised youth" into his radical sect. But a spokesman for Sheikh Omran stated that Mr Kara-Ali's claims were "ridiculous" and divisive. He said the organization was open about its annual *Da'wah* (proselytism in Arabic) conferences, which are partly held for "recruiting Muslims and non-Muslims combined". "It's a calling for the true teachings of Islam," Sheikh Omran's spokesman said, its purpose was not to attract "terrorists into the fold".

RMIT University distanced itself from the conference, which was held at its Brunswick campus, in Melbourne's inner north. An RMIT spokesperson stated that the university was not involved in organizing the conference, which was expected to attract hundreds of people. He explained that Sheikh Omran's organization had rented the RMIT conference halls for the same events in 2002 and 2003 and that they were being used for "peaceful" purposes.[38]

The outrageous interviews in early 2007 by Sheikh Hilali, the Chief Mufti of Australian Muslims headquartered in Sydney, which prompted members of the local Muslim leadership to remove him from his post for fear of an Australian backlash, apparently did little to quiet the concerns of the general population. Large swaths of the Australian major cities, especially Lakemba at the heart of Sydney, have become "Muslim" neighborhoods which show little signs of acculturation to the environment. Though the total number of Muslims approaches the half million mark, out of a total of just over 20 million (ca 2.5%, which is very low compared to France - 10%), their concentration in the major cities and their visibility, vociferousness and sometimes use of violence, make them more salient than their proportion in the population. In early 2007 a case of gang rape of Australian women by Lebanese Muslim immigrant youth, became a *cause celebre.* When the event was coupled with Hilali's observations to the effect that Australian women should dress less "provocatively" so as not to expose themselves as "uncovered meat", general indignation among Australians kept mounting. Hilali also hurled at the Australians that they were less deserving of the land than the immigrant Muslims, because the newcomers paid their way while the early Australians came as sentenced convicts; this brought public outrage to the boiling point. Public anger and the Muslim backlash produced a mood that was publicized in the local media:

> Muslims are outraged that prospective citizens will have to acknowledge the Judeo-Christian tradition as the basis of Australia's values system. Australia's peak Muslim

body said the proposed citizenship question - revealed in the *Herald Sun*-was disturbing and potentially divisive. The Australian Federation of Islamic Councils president Dr Ameer Ali said the "Abrahamic tradition" or "universal values" would be less divisive ways of describing the nation's moral base.

Dr Ali said the use of the term Judeo-Christian was the result of "WW II guilt", and before 1945 Australia would have been called only Christian. "That question must be rephrased," he said. Dr Ali was backed by Democrat senator Lyn Allison, who said the answer to the question was highly debatable. But Immigration Minister Kevin Andrews stood firm on the merit of the question. Mr Andrews said Australia's Judeo-Christian heritage was indisputable historical fact. "We are not asking people to subscribe to the Judeo-Christian ethic," he said. "We are simply stating a fact that this is part of the heritage of Australia in terms of its foundation. This is not an exercise in political correctness. It is trying to state what has been the case and still is the case."

But Health Minister Tony Abbott confused the issue, by saying that the modern Australian values system was secular, or of no particular religion. The *Herald Sun* revealed[39] twenty key questions, developed in consultation with Mr Andrews, that are likely to be asked of would-be citizens. Mr Andrews said the test, to begin by September 2007, would help immigrants integrate into society better. "We celebrate diversity and people are free to continue their own traditions, but we are also very insistent that we have to build and maintain social cohesion," he emphasized.

Dr Ali said he would request a meeting with Mr Andrews to discuss the question. "It is the wrong message we are sending," he said. Senator Allison said the test was pointless: "I don't see what it's going to achieve ... It doesn't say anything about people's character, whether they are going to be good citizens." Opposition immigration spokesman Tony Burke responded that Labour agreed in principle with the test, but wanted details.[40]

This is neither a simple matter nor a formal exchange of opinion, because while there is a Judeo-Christian tradition of openness, tolerance and democracy, the Muslims are not bound by it, since they claim that Islam is a new beginning, original and without any connection to Judaism and Christianity that preceded it. For them, the entire world was Muslim in the era of Abraham, until Jews and Christians distorted the old faith and forged their new false religions which are at variance with "true" Islam. Therefore, an "Abrahamic tradition" as they would have it, far from bridging over the three monotheistic faiths and drawing them closer, would on the contrary dramatize the yawning gap between the previous faiths of the Judeo-Christian tradition which "went astray", and the newly installed Muslim faith which has no link to the other two. Unlike the Jewish and Christian faiths which are ready to include Muslims in the Abrahamic faith, for the Muslims, the Abrahamic faith means only Muslim, nothing else, nothing more, to the exclusion of all others. The debate over this issue will determine to a large extent the degree of Muslim acculturation into Australia and other Western countries in the final analysis.

All these tensions culminated in early 2007, when Attorney General Phillip Ruddock said there was not enough evidence to ban the *Hizb ut-Tahrir* group despite the outrageous stands it took and its continuing call for Australia to become part of a Caliphate or *"Khilafah"*. The controversy rose in anticipation of its conference in Sydney, as an advertisement posted on internet site *youtube.com* showed crowds of Muslims marching, praying and protesting to dramatic and warlike music and explosions. In what appears to be a call to arms, the video features slogans attacking the United States and capitalism, and features militant anti-Western Iranian leader Mahmoud Ahmadinejad shaking his fist, before the slogan "embrace the revival". "The Muslim world has awakened from its slumber and is ready to resume its political destiny"; and "From the darkness will emerge a new light," the video says. Articles published on the group's website claim that Israel is an illegal state, that "Iraq is an occupied land" and its residents have a duty to resist the Coalition. In one article dubbed "The Clash of Civilisations", an anonymous author claims a clash of Western and Islamic civilizations is inevitable, and that Muslim scriptures show Islam "has come to dominate this Earth" and that Muslims "must sacrifice everything to achieve this". "This means we must establish the *Khilafah* in order that we can challenge the capitalist nations intellectually, economically, politically and militarily until we defeat them, thus liberating their peoples from the darkness and subjugation and fulfilling our own covenant with Allah," the article says. The site also called on Australian Muslims to come to the aid of Islamist fighters in Somalia against Ethiopian forces. But Phillip Ruddock said the organisation could not be banned as a terror group under current laws.

"We looked very closely at the organization some time ago to see whether or not it met the criteria to be banned as a terrorist organization in Australia," he told *Southern Cross Radio*: "It doesn't mean that we agree with what it's saying, but there are strict criteria for banning organizations and when those enquiries were undertaken we didn't have sufficient evidence. Mr Ruddock said the organization's aim of creating an Islamic state were clear in the latest video advertisement, but it had also reportedly said it wanted to do so by peaceful means. This is quite strange, since the messages and symbols of the organization are so violent, that simply stating that that "it wanted peaceful means", had no significance beyond avoiding a friction with law enforcement agencies. Government agencies would examine the latest propaganda to see whether it changed the situation, but agreed many people would see the material as provocative, said the Attorney General, reflecting the popular mood. "There's no doubt in the context of a great deal of violence that's been pursued in other parts of the world, that people might assume when they're advocating that Australia have *Shari'a* law and a Caliphate that should be a role model for the rest of the world, that people might be alarmed," Mr Ruddock said. "If they look at some of the approaches by organizations such as al-Qa'ida and so on, there may well be a concern they might be heading in the same directions. "But by their own activities, there is no evidence for banning them as a terrorist organisation."[41]

Judging from fiery Muslim declarations of late, partly emanating from within the Muslim community, tempers seem far from calming down. Melbourne Islamic cleric Mohammed Omran has been accused by his own estranged son-in-law of preaching extremism and hatred, in a bitter war of words following his separation from Sheikh Omran's daughter. The accusations have been levelled by 26-year-old Ali Kassae, a former member of Sheikh Omran's fundamentalist *Ahl -al Sunnah Wal-Jama'ah* association, who was married to Sheikh Omran's daughter, Zaynab, until they separated in August 2006. Mr Kassae claims he has been prevented from seeing his children since the split, and has been threatened and abused by other members of Sheikh Omran's group. He also accuses Sheikh Omran's organisation of inciting violent attacks on people who disagree with them. Mr Kassae, who moved to Australia from his native Syria as a nine-year-old, blames the break-up of his seven-year marriage on the extremism of Sheikh Omran and his group. "I couldn't stand their attitude and beliefs," Mr Kassae said. "I had left that culture behind. I just wanted to live an Australian life. Then I was forced into the culture again." Mr Kassae said he and other group members were "taught to hate" by being shown violent propaganda videos about conflicts involving Muslims in places such as Palestine. One DVD, shown to *The Australian,* which Mr Kassae said was distributed among members of *Ahl al-Sunnah Wal-Jama'ah,* declares: "You should hate them as they hate you, invade them as they invade you, fight them as they fight you. Whoever dies will be granted the mercy of God and paradise. Jews have no place in Palestine. Jews shouldn't be there. Jews should die. We should proclaim jihad until they all die, until every single one of them is dead." A spokesman for Sheikh Omran said the cleric completely rejected Mr Kassae's statements, claiming his estranged son-in-law had a "mental illness". Sheikh Omran's organisation has been under close scrutiny by the Aussie security apparatus for years and several of its members are known to have undergone training with the militant group *Lashkar-e-Taiba* in Pakistan. In 2000, members of the group were raided by NSW and Australian Federal Police. Mr Kassae said he was visiting a fellow *Ahl al Sunnah Wal-Jama'ah* member in Sydney's Wiley Park, when armed police burst in. "There was an AK-47 loaded next to me with an 80-round magazine," Mr Kassae said. "The house was full of weapons. It was like they were preparing for war." The police seized an AK-47 assault rifle, handguns, shotguns and grenades, according to Mr Kassae. [42]

In an affidavit filed in the Federal Magistrates Court in Melbourne in November 2006, Zaynab Omran cited her husband's paranoia about the Aussie security agency (ASIO) among the reasons for their marriage break-up. "He thought that I was in contact with ASIO or the CIA about him, and thought people were out to get him," the affidavit reads. "He would leave pornography magazines everywhere, and told me that this was to confuse ASIO or the CIA if they ever raided the house." Mr Kassae was a troubled street punk who had dabbled in drugs and had run-ins with the police when he was recruited into Sheikh Omran's group by his brother-in-law, an *Ahl al-Sunnah Wal-Jama'ah* member. Sheikh Omran, who knew Mr Kassae's mother, proposed that the 17-year-old marry his daughter, Zaynab, then aged just 15. "I was ripped out of my life and put in this life," Mr Kassae said. "I was just a kid trying to grow up. I wasn't into it for the religion. I was a child. I looked at them as role models." The newlyweds went to live with Sheikh Omran's family in Melbourne, where Mr Kassae worked on construction sites before setting up his own mobile phone business. A reference from one employer described him as "always reliable, punctual and respectful". Mr Kassae said that Sheikh Omran put him in charge of "security" for his organisation, which involved looking after visiting sheikhs from overseas, and helping to organise the weekend bush camps where *Ahl al Sunnah Wal-Jama'ah* members would engage in paint-ball skirmishes, described by one participant as "jihad training". By Mr Kassae's account, his life was totally controlled by Sheikh Omran and his group. "I wasn't meant to have any friends but them, I couldn't talk to anybody but them, I couldn't do anything without their permission. It was like, 'You want to be part of this family - this is how it's got to be. This is who you've got to be now, and this is what you've got to do.' Basically, they wanted me to be a sheep - he's the shepherd and I'm the sheep." Mr Kassae claimed he became increasingly disturbed by Sheikh Omran's puritanical interpretation of Islam.[43]

"I couldn't hack their understanding of Islamic teaching," said Kassae. "Their teaching was inappropriate. It was like they were God's angels given a key to Paradise. So who are we? Slaves from hell?" Mr Kassae explained that the group was paranoid about anyone they suspected of talking to ASIO, including Sydney man Mamdouh Habib, who was believed by some members to be an ASIO informant. Mr Kassae has told Mr Habib's lawyer that a meeting was held in Lakemba in Sydney's southwest in 2000 where it was agreed to "do something about this guy (or) he will destroy us". A group of *Ahl al Sunnah Wal-Jama'ah* members later physically attacked Mr Habib outside the association's Haldon Street prayer room. Mr Habib was treated at Bankstown hospital for cuts and bruises to his head. Mr Habib was arrested as a suspected terrorist in Pakistan in late 2001 and held by the US at Guantanamo Bay in Cuba until his release without charge in February 2005. In November 2005, Mr Kassae was accused by fellow *Ahl al Sunnah Wal-Jama'ah* members of being an informant, after several of the group's followers were arrested in ASIO raids in Sydney and charged with terrorism-related offences. Ostracised within the group and with his marriage failing, Mr Kassae said he became depressed and took to drugs again. In May 2006, after an amphetamines binge, he was admitted to the mental health unit of the St George hospital, in Sydney's south, where he spent a month being treated for drug-induced psychosis. His wife cites his mental illness as the key reason for their break-up, stating in her affidavit: "There were many incidents leading up to our separation, including him disappearing for several days without explanation, and being extremely paranoid about things that were going on." She also claims he was abusive towards her and their two children, now aged five years and 15 months. In November 2006, a federal magistrate granted Zaynab Omran sole parental responsibility. A spokesman for Sheikh Omran said that Mr Kassae's drug abuse and mental problems were the reason for his marriage failing. "We appeal to Ali to seek medical help for his mental illness. We totally refute and reject the statements he has made," the spokesman said. Mr Kassae claimed that since leaving the organisation, he had been threatened numerous times after members spread rumours that he was working for ASIO or the CIA. In February, Mr Kassae was attacked by two men in the southwest Sydney suburb of Belmore and stabbed in the back. He was treated in the acute care facility of the Royal Prince Alfred Hospital. A NSW police report on the incident said Mr Kassae had been accused by his assailants of spying for ASIO. No one has been charged over the incident. "Since leaving (the organisation), I've committed an even bigger crime. I've been judged - I'm a disbeliever and I should be taken apart," Mr Kassae said. "All I wanted was a future, a wife and a family and a home. And they took that away from me." [44]

These highly publicized and revealing domestic skirmishes within the Muslim community, avidly read and heeded by a concerned and challenged Aussie public, when coupled by news about the participation of Australian Muslims in global *jihad,* become stringent signals of alarm. This time the news was connected to conflict ridden Somalia. Somalian spiritual leader Hersi Hilole warned that originally Somalian young men returning to Australia from their *jihad* mission against the Ethiopian-backed Somalian Government, were more likely to consider becoming involved in a terrorist attack on Australia. "Now when they come back, how are they going to join the rest of society?" Sheikh Hilole said. "There is a great danger that they could carry out any kind of terrorist activity here." Sheikh Hilole, chairman of the Somali Community Council of Australia, said hard-line clerics in Melbourne continued to "prey" on young Somalian men, whose welcoming attitudes to *Wahhabism* - a puritanical interpretation of Islam espoused by Osama bin Laden - were a result of the ideology's prevalence in their home country. He said the Somalian spiritual leaders preaching *Wahhabism* had gone further "underground", following an Australian Federal Police investigation into claims that some Somalian community members were sending money home to assist the Islamic Courts movement that has been accused by the US of harboring al-Qa'ida operatives. The AFP investigation, revealed in *The Australian* in April 2007, is continuing. "Some of these religious leaders who are teaching these radical ideas to the young people now have gone underground," Sheik Hilole said. *The Australian* revealed that a Somalian man from Melbourne, Ahmed Ali, who traveled to Somalia in December 2006 to fight alongside the Islamic Courts movement after telling his mother he was going to Dubai, was believed to be working as an interpreter with al-Qa'ida. Mr Ali's mother also accused Melbourne's ultra-radical Islamic spiritual leader Mohammed Omran of radicalising her son. A spokesman for Sheik Omran rejected her claims. [45]

4

Under the US Shadow: The Canadian Case

The mass-arrest in Toronto, in Summer 2006, of 17 Muslim co-plotters who were scheming a major act of terror, awakened the Canadians the way September 11 shook up the Americans, and 7/7 snatched the British out of their torpor. A Muslim religious leader in Toronto who knows some of those charged in the suspected bomb plot commented that the young men underwent rapid transformations from normal Canadian teenagers to radicalized introverts. Sayyid Ahmed Amiruddin became acquainted with Saad Khalid, 19, and some of the other alleged conspirators at a local mosque. Khalid was arrested at a warehouse, where he and another suspect took delivery of what they thought was ammonium nitrate, a fertilizer, the same substance used in the deadly Oklahoma City bombing in 1995. At the time of writing (September 2007) fifteen others are also facing charges connected to the alleged plot. Amiruddin says Khalid used to come to his mosque to pray, sometimes in the company of Zakaria Amara and Fahim Ahmad, two of the alleged ringleaders. "They would enter into the mosque to pray, and prayed in a very aggressive manner, they would come in military fatigues and military touques and stuff. It looked to me that they were watching a lot of those Chechnyan *jihad* videos online and stuff." Amiruddin is a teacher of Sufism, that is mystical Islam that shuns the ideology of violent *jihad*. Amiruddin believes that the group was seduced by hardline propaganda financed by the Saudi government which promotes a strict *Wahhabi* brand of Islam inimical to Sufism. He explains that the Saudis have flooded Canada with free Qur'ans, laced with *jihadist* commentary. "In the back of these Qur'ans that are being published in Saudi Arabia, you have basically essays on the need for offensive *jihad* and the legitimacy of offensive *jihad* and things like that. Very alarming stuff," he said. Amiruddin reported that many mainstream Muslim organizations in Canada are really part of the problem, simply standing by as extremist propaganda spreads in

147

the mosques. He cites the *Al-Rahman* center in Mississauga, Ontario, which he links to the *Al-Maghrib* (the West) Institute, the source of a popular educational website. He complains that nominally the website is run out of Ottawa, but Amiruddin says it is really a Saudi operation. Recruiting young teens, Amiruddin notes that Khalid underwent a rapid transition from a clean-cut Canadian teenager to a longhaired, radicalized introvert. He says the young men would pray by themselves, and try to recruit younger teens to the fundamentalist *Wahhabi* view. Amiruddin says Khalid stopped coming to the mosque after he befriended 43-year-old Qayyum Abdul Jamal, another key suspect, who once preached that Canadian forces were in Afghanistan to rape Muslim women. Amiruddin also has a theory as to why Khalid may have been open to such influences. "His mother passed away and let's say within the first month of his mom passing away, his girlfriend, who was not Muslim, dumped him. And then from that, within a year, you have this radical turnaround.... Fahim Ahmad also was in love with a girl who constantly rejected him. Maybe he was just looking for love? I can't say for certain, but this was something I found common with these young guys."[1]

Canada, like Britain and other Western countries, has its liberal laws and cautious law enforcement agencies so subservient to human rights issues, in general accordance with western policies, that the existential issue of grave danger to their populations becomes a secondary consideration. As a result, suspect Muslim elements are unwittingly encouraged to pursue their subversion under the existing legal safety net. For example, the son of a suspected al-Qa'ida financier became free to re-apply for a Canadian passport after a court ruling that Ottawa was wrong to deny Abdurahman Khadr's application on the basis of national security. But the win could be short-lived for Khadr, since the ruling by Federal Court Justice Michael Phelan also made it clear that the federal government could thereafter revoke the newly granted passport on those same grounds. Thus, first the government is obliged to provide a passport to a suspected terrorist, and then it has to fight through the courts for its revocation. That decision didn't stop Khadr, and his lawyer Clayton Ruby, from denouncing the March 2004 resolution by former foreign affairs minister Bill Graham to deny the application on the basis of a law that had not as yet been passed. "Not bad for a dictatorship, not good enough for Canada", Ruby opined, "The grounds on which [Graham] made [his decision] were expressed in no Canadian law that then existed, namely [based on] national security grounds". Ruby said he's confident Khadr's new application will be approved - and he vowed to head back to court if Ottawa tries to take it away again. Abdurahman Khadr is the second eldest son of Ahmed Said Khadr, an associate of Osama bin Laden who was killed in a firefight with Pakistani forces in 2003. Khadr returned to Canada two years after being arrested as a presumed member of al-Qa'ida in November 2001. "For me, to have my passport is just to feel like a full citizen," said Khadr, who calls himself the "black sheep" of his family. "To travel is a choice, it's another right that I'm given in this country. Where I'm going to travel to, I don't know". Khadr's brothers Abdullah and Omar have both been charged with terrorist activities and they were awaiting trial as these lines were written (2007).[2] This is how the rule of law becomes self-defeating in the liberal West.

One of the most popular ways to recruit prospective terrorists among the young Muslim population is via the plethora of websites that have been set up. On a cold night in October 2005, police stormed a West London (Ontario) apartment and found Younis Tsouli at his computer, allegedly building a web page with the title "You Bomb It". Initially, the raid seemed relatively routine, one of about 1,000 arrests made under Canada's terrorism act during the last five years. But on this occasion substantial evidence was allegedly found in the West London homes of two accused co-conspirators: a DVD manual on making suicide bomb vests, a note with the heading "Welcome to *Jihad"*, material on beheadings, a recipe for rocket fuel, and a note with the formula "hospital = attack". As investigators sifted through computer disk information the picture that emerged was dramatic. Police had apparently stumbled on the man suspected of being the most hunted cyber-extremist in the world. Tsouli, a 22-year-old Moroccan, is widely named as a central figure in a cyber-terrorist network that has inspired suspected homegrown extremists in Europe and North America, including the 17 people recently arrested in the Toronto area. On the massive, 750 gigabytes of confiscated computer and disk information found on Tsouli's computer files is an Internet trail believed to link some of the 39 terror suspects arrested in Canada, Britain, the United States, Sweden, Denmark and Bosnia. A source with close knowledge of the Tsouli case has told the *Toronto Star* of evidence that he used the Web address *Irhabi 007* (meaning, the Qur'anic terrorist - and 007 the added halo of James Bond), as his cyber-persona, to become the most notorious extremist hacker on the World Wide Web. "*Irhabi 007* was like the Godfather of cyber-terrorism for Al Qa'ida," says Evan Kohlmann, an Internet terrorism consultant and determined *Irhabi 007* tracker. Since coming upon the cyber-extremist scene in late 2003, *Irhabi 007s* Internet exploits have become the stuff of legend for the scores of militants reading and chatting on Al Qa'ida-inspired sites. He almost single-handedly brought the hardcore network into the modern computer age, solving its most pressing propaganda challenge: how to distribute heavy multi-media files, such as videos of beheadings, to the growing ranks of *jihadis*. A self-starter, believed to have worked mainly from his home, he hacked and linked his way to become the administrator of the password-protected forum, *Muntada al-Ansar al-Islami* (The Islamic Club of the Supporters [of Islam]); the main Internet mouthpiece of Abu Mus'ab al-Zarqawi, al-Qa'ida's leader in Iraq until he was killed in Summer 2006 by a US aerial attack. But his downfall has been as dramatic as his rise. Says Aaron Weisburd, another *Irhabi* tracker: "While he was at large, he was a leader, an opinion-shaper, a solver of problems, and an inspiration to his friends and associates. Now that the authorities have him and his hard disk drive, he has become a major liability". The West London raid resulted in terrorism related charges against Tsouli, Waseem Mughal, 22, and Tariq Al-Daour, 19.[3] They were all awaiting trial when these lines were written (summer 2007).

Among the items allegedly found in Tsouli's computer is a video slide film on how to make a bomb and another showing sites in Washington, D.C. The images of the American capital were reportedly filmed by two Georgia men who were arrested by the FBI in March 2006 and accused in US court documents of having traveled to Toronto to meet "like-minded Islamists". Tsouli immigrated to London (Ontario) in 2002. At the time of his arrest, his father said Tsouli often spoke of the West waging a war against Islam. Bachir Tsouli, then deputy head of Morocco's tourism office in London, said his son had few friends and spent most of his time at his computer. "What can you do on the computer?", he asked, probably naively, in an interview with the *Daily Mail* newspaper. "He hasn't been to Iraq or to training camps in Afghanistan. Tomorrow they will be saying he is a friend of Osama bin Laden." No one has accused him of that, but experts who tracked *Irhabi 007* believe he had links to al-Zarqawi, and credited him with having turned the web into a powerful tool for global *jihad*. During the past years, al-Zarqawi's followers produced scores of videos on "suicide bombings", attacks against US forces in Iraq, beheadings of hostages, propaganda tracts and terrorist "how to" manuals. The problem was distribution: how to post and move heavy files on the Internet without sites crashing or being shut down. *Irhabi 007* met the challenge. In May 2004, he helped distribute the video of al-Zarqawi's beheading of American contractor Nicholas Berg. It was quickly copied on Internet sites and downloaded half a million times within 24 hours.

"He got his name on the map with the Nicholas Berg beheading video", says Ned Moran, intelligence analyst with the Virginia-based Terrorism Research Center. *Irhabi 007's* distribution technique became clear two months later, when he hacked into an FTP computer site used to transfer large files by the Arkansas Highway and Transportation Department. He posted 70 *jihadi* propaganda files on the site, including videos featuring Osama bin Laden. He then posted links to the files on the *Muntada* site and urged *jihadis* to download quickly. Arkansas authorities didn't catch on until 24 hours later. By then, the material had replicated exponentially, with those who downloaded it passing it on to others in an almost endless chain. *Irhabi* used skills largely unknown in the cyber-*jihadi* world. He spread them around, posting his own hacking manuals for a new generation of more computer-savvy *jihadis* to increasingly use the Internet as a tool to recruit and plot attacks. *Irhabi* wannabes suddenly began appearing on chat forums, tagging 007 at the end of their web personas. In October 2004, his status in their eyes reached heroic proportions when he provided almost immediate links to a "suicide bombing" video posted by Abu Maysara al-Iraqi, widely considered one of al-Zarqawi's closest aides. The initiative led Maysara to break silence for the first time and post praise for *Irhabi 007's* work, Kohlmann says. "Bless the terrorist, *Irhabi 007*" said the message, translated by Kohlmann, founder of *globalterroralert. com.* "In the name of Allah, I am pleased with your presence my beloved brother. May Allah protect you". Says Kohlmann: "It's kind of like Bruce Springsteen picking someone out in a concert and saying, 'I love this guy.' That's what the effect was - people went crazy."[4]

In September 2005, a Terrorist Research Center report described *Irhabi 007* as "heavily involved" in maintaining Al Qa'ida's on-line presence. It found evidence on al-Zarqawi's *Al-Ansar* site listing *Irhabi* as its "administrator." The speed with which *Irhabi* posted links to videos from al-Zarqawi's Iraqi cell led observers to speculate he was getting a heads up from al-Zarqawi's people. Tsouli was suspected of stealing identities to register his websites. His *http://www.irhabi007.org* domain name was registered to the name, telephone number and Pennsylvania home address of a first lieutenant deployed in Iraq, according to the center's report. He also registered a Canada-based domain name, *http://www.irhabi007. ca.* By the end of 2005, *Irhabi 007* had a whole army of cyber-terrorism trackers on his trail. Few were as persistent as Aaron Weisburd, director of Internet *Haganah* (Defense), dedicated to making on-line life miserable for cyber-*jihadis*. In 2004, Weisburd turned in *Irhabi* to his service provider and had him cut off. An incensed *Irhabi* posted Weisburd's home address in Illinois on the Internet and took part in chat-room discussions on slicing Weisburd like a salami. "I get to keep a finger or an ear," *Irhabi* wrote, "a little souvenir." Weisburd reported the threat to the FBI and stepped up his efforts. "I take all threats seriously", he said in an e-mail exchange with the *Toronto Star.* "And like any American 'good old boy' I have more than one loaded gun nearby." In July 2005, *Irhabi* made his first mistake, leaving his IP (Internet Protocol) address, which can be used to track a user's location, on a site which was being set up to issue a threat against Italy. Weisburd examined another *Irhabi* Web page and found a second IP address. He then posted a message on the *Haganah* site warning that *Irhabi's* files were infected. *Irhabi* responded by posting a graphic to prove they were not. His IP number was blotted out, but not well enough. Weisburd's associate deciphered it. The three IP addresses all pointed to London's Baling area, the place where Tsouli would be arrested 15 months later. Weisburd passed the information on to US and British police but heard nothing back. In September 2005, a month before Tsouli's arrest, a frustrated Weisburd posted this message on his site: *"Irhabi 007* is in Baling. Or at least that's where the bastard was when we located him (18 months ago)." Since Tsouli's arrest, Weisburd says police have asked him to resubmit the information he passed on months before. The events that led to the arrest of the presumed *Irhabi* began with police forcing their way into an apartment in Sarajevo on October 19, 2005, arresting 18-year-old Swedish citizen Mirsad Bektasevic and Abdul Kadir Cesur, a 20-year-old Danish-born Turk. Almost 20 kilograms of explosives were in the apartment, according to the indictment filed in a Sarajevo court. A Sony VHS tape was also found giving instructions on how to make a bomb. Says a voice on the tape, believed to be that of Bektasevic: "These brothers are ready to attack and, God willing, they will attack the infidels who are killing our brothers and Muslims in Iraq, Afghanistan. This weapon will be used against Europe, against those whose forces are in Iraq and Afghanistan". Their arrests sparked back-to-back raids in London and Denmark, where a total of nine men were arrested, including Tsouli. The last number dialed on his cellular phone was Bektasevic's Bosnian number three days earlier. Since then, arrests have also been made in the US, Canada, Britain and Sweden. Postings on the Internet by *IrhabiOO7* stopped with Tsouli's arrest.[5]

Up until the arrest of the 17 in Summer 2006, complacency among the Canadian media, authorities and intellectuals, who feared indictment for "racism", or wished to "maintain public order", had prevented serious investigative reporting about the impending threat of Muslim terrorism.

Whether escapism or denial, it was pathetic watching the media indulge in a cover-up instead of uncovering the dramas that were reported from the Continent. *The Toronto Star* was derided in the blogosphere for repeating that it is "difficult to find a common denominator" which binds the 17 terrorists. While the authorities were expected to cling to these absurd storylines, one would have expected that the media would expose the fallacy of such notions. And yet, the *Star* has seen fit to congratulate itself on its coverage. Perhaps they would have their reading public believe that the *jihadis* were linked by their love of football, or for their kindness to animals, or even their concern for global warming. Instead of mentioning the common Muslim heritage of the arrested terrorists, the three reporters of the *Star,* all of Muslim descent according to their names, went to the investigators' offices, where an intricate graph plotting the links between the 17 men and teens charged with being members of a homegrown terrorist cell, covered at least one wall. And yet, the reports insisted that "it is difficult to find a common denominator, except that they represent the broad strata of our community". When coming from the Muslim organization of Canada, this cynical remark represented an attempt at decriminalization of the terrorists (presented as just representatives of the broad strata of supposedly decent citizens), an exoneration of the Muslim community who gave rise to those home-grown terrorists in the first place (they had no other common denominator to bind them), and the usual escape from responsibility.[6]

Other media were more conscientious in their reporting. A top Canadian intelligence official said that many potential terrorists already reside in the country and have trained in al-Qa'ida training camps, reinforcing publicly what many security analysts have warned of for years. In testimony before a Senate committee studying Canada's role in Afghanistan, Jack Hooper, the Canadian Security Intelligence Service deputy director, explained that there are people living in Canada who fought alongside Afghani *mujahideen,* or holy fighters, during the Soviet occupation of that country in the 1980s. "I can tell you that all of the circumstances that led to the London transit bombings . . . are here and now in Canada," said Hooper, CSIS's operations director. The Senate Standing Committee on National Security and Defense held a full day of hearings on Canada's military mission in Afghanistan, and how it relates to security at home. The hearings came at a time when Canadians and some lawmakers voiced growing concern over the deaths of Canadian soldiers serving in Afghanistan as part of a NATO force charged with weeding out *Taliban* fighters. Parliament voted earlier in June 2006 to extend Canada's mission in Afghanistan until 2009. One of the recent 16 Canadian troops killed in the country since the 2001 US-led invasion was Captain Nichola Goddard, who died on May 18, 2006 following fighting between insurgents and Canadian and Afghan forces in Qandahar. Canada had then about 2,000 soldiers based in Afghanistan, most of them in Qandahar. In outlining the domestic threat, Hooper said that a Vancouver man trained the bombers involved in the 1998 bombings of the US embassies in Nairobi, Kenya, and Dar e-Salaam, Tanzania. Hooper did not provide further details about the man but pointed out several other examples of people who had lived in Canada, and later taken part in terrorist attacks. A common thread (the common ground the *Star* could not find) was time spent at training camps in Afghanistan. "When we talk about the homegrown terrorist phenomenon, these are people ... in most instances who are Canadian citizens," he said. "A lot of them were born here. A lot of them who were not born here immigrated to Canada with their parents at a very young age." Hooper did not provide any specifics on numbers or their whereabouts. The Royal Canadian Mounted Police Commissioner Giuliano Zaccardelli also told the committee that the Mounties and CSIS were working closely to thwart potential homegrown terrorist threats. The two agencies have been criticized for being at cross-purposes during the lengthy investigation into the 1985 Air India terrorist bombing that claimed 329 lives. Committee chairman, Senator Colin Kenny, said Britain's terrorist experience in 2005 should provide a wake-up call for the problems Canada could encounter with homegrown terrorists. "They'd been born in the country", Kenny said of the men who detonated a series of bombs in London (England), "They had all of the slang and comfort with the culture that you and I have, and yet, boom, here they are committing terrorism acts."[7]

Canadian and European leaders are yet to show in public the same courage, determination and straightforwardness in fighting terrorism as the Australians. Instead, they hide behind suicidal formulas of "multiculturalism" which penetrate their culture unilaterally (namely recognition and acceptance of Islam by the host countries, but rejection of Western culture by the guest Muslims). But the message of existential self-defense for the sake of the survival of Western culture is beginning to make deep inroads into the most liberal societies which for too long have borne in silence their own manipulation and distortion by Muslim immigrants. A case in point has been a lawsuit in Canada where a Muslim Imam is accused of misusing the legal institutions of that liberal country by undermining the very nature of freedom of speech. The Alberta

Human Rights Commission is suing the Canadian political journal *The Western Standard* for "hate speech", on behalf of a radical imam, Syed Soharwardy. This imam initially had attempted to have the editor of *The Western Standard* arrested. Since that wasn't possible, he sought the backing of the Alberta Human Rights Commission. So, the *Western Standard* was sued in a human rights court in the matter of publication of the Danish cartoons. Its editor, Ezra Levant, who was disgusted by the maneuver, remarked that:

"It's been ten years since I've graduated from law school, and I've never seen a more frivolous, vexatious, infantile suit than this. But that's the point - this complaint is not about beating us in the law. Freedom of speech is still in our constitution; we'll win in the end. It's a nuisance suit, designed to grind us down, cost us money, and serve as a warning to other, more timid media. The hand-written scrawl and the spelling errors were what first disgusted me with the suit; but the arguments were what really got me. The complainant, Imam Syed Soharwardy, a former professor at an anti-Semitic university in Saudi Arabia, doesn't just argue that we shouldn't have published the cartoons. He argues that we shouldn't be able to defend our right to publish the cartoons. The bulk of his complaint was that we dared to try to justify it. He argues that advocating a free press should be a thought crime. Here is a letter I sent out to our e-mail list, explaining our legal situation:

"And here is where you can chip in to our legal defense fund if you want to support us. Our lawyers tell me we'll likely win, but it could cost us up to $75,000 to do so - and the case against us is being prosecuted by government employees using tax dollars. We're a small, independent magazine and we don't have deep pockets to fight off nuisance suits, so please chip in if you can. In response to various commentators, unfortunately, even if we are successful in the human rights commission, we will not be compensated for our legal fees. It's not like a real court, where an unsuccessful plaintiff would be ordered to pay a successful defendant's costs. So even if we win, we lose - the process is the penalty. Worse than that, the radical imam who is suing us doesn't have to put up a dime - the commission uses tax dollars to pay lawyers and other inquisitors to go at us directly. Human rights tribunals themselves are illiberal institutions".[8]

In 1991, the Canadian province of Ontario passed what seemed at the time to be an enlightened, multicultural act of legislation. Called the Arbitration Act, it stipulates that if two parties agree to engage a commercial, religious, or other arbitrator to settle a civil dispute, the provincial authorities will then enforce the verdict, so long as it is in accord with Canadian law. A spokesman for the Ontario Attorney General specified that "People can use any arbitrator they want and can use a religious framework if it is mutually acceptable. If the settlement is not compatible with Canadian law, then the court will not enforce it. You can't agree to violate Canadian law". Over the years, Jews, Catholics, Jehovah's Witnesses, Mennonites, and aboriginals, among others, made use of arbitration to settle family law questions without using Ontario's court system. The system worked quietly. "If there have been any problems flowing from any rabbinical court decisions, I'm not aware of them," observed the Ontario region chairman of the Canadian Jewish Congress, Joel Richler. Then, in October 2003 an organization called the Islamic Institute of Civil Justice proposed the creation of Muslim Arbitration Boards. As explained by the institute's founder, Syed Mumtaz Ali, the boards, arbitrating on the basis of Islamic law, the *Shari'a,* would permit a Muslim to live according to Islam's "complete code of life". A first news article on this initiative came out in November 2003; within days, prompted by WorldNetDaily. com ("Canada prepares to enforce Islamic law"), a huge dispute arose . A hitherto obscure Ontario provision prompted a sharp national debate and street rallies in twelve Canadian and European cities. Interestingly, the main opposition came from Muslim women's groups, who feared that ignorant, isolated females would submit to the inescapably misogynistic *Shari'a,* a law code that permits parents to marry off pre-pubescent girls, men to marry multiple women, husbands unilaterally to establish a divorce, fathers automatically to win custody of children over certain ages, and sons to inherit more than daughters. The *anti-Shari'a* campaign succeeded. On September 11, 2005—after almost two years of public debate—the premier of Ontario, Dalton McGuinty, held that religious-based arbitrations "threaten our common ground". He announced that "There will be no *Shari'a* law in Ontario. There will be no religious arbitration in Ontario. There will be one law for all Ontarians." His decision means that faith-based arbitration can continue to operate, as it did long before 1991, but the government will no longer enforce its verdicts.

This summary of the situation was reviewed by the prominent American critic of Islamism, Daniel Pipes,[9] who saw the catch in McGuinty's statement which the jubilant *anti-Shari'a* forces in Canada had missed when they pronounced the statement to be "the best news in five years." Acting on the correct premise that Islam must be treated the same as other religions, he determined that if Muslims cannot enjoy state enforcement of faith-based arbitration, then neither can anyone else. Therefore,

McGuinty said, his government would "as soon as possible" introduce legislation to repeal the Arbitration Act of 1991. This result prompted a pained reaction from those who would lose state enforcement of their arbitration decisions. Some denounced it as a "knee-jerk reaction against the *Shari'a* issue". A Montreal Rabbi added, sadly, "the Ontario government felt compelled to throw the baby out with the bath water". Pipes remarked that Orthodox Jews and others might lose ground to an emerging pattern, whereby efforts to integrate Muslims into the West upset a benign status quo. He cited other recent examples: French nuns for the first time must take off their cowls for identity card or passport pictures because of anti-*hijab* legislation. Likewise, French schoolchildren may not wear crosses or the Star of David to class. Large populations - British underground riders, American airport passengers, Russian theater-goers -must undergo extensive security checks, thanks to Muslim terrorists. Danes marrying foreigners face extensive restrictions to bringing them into Denmark because of immigration abuses (the so-called "human visa" problem) involving Muslims. Santas, Nativity plays, Christmas carols, and Bibles are curtailed in western countries so as not to offend Muslim sensitivities. Unremarked upon by most Westerners, Islam's presence has started to change their way of life. In a recent survey it was found that 63% of Canadians oppose giving any religious community the right to use faith-based arbitration to settle divorce, custody, inheritance and other family disputes. Asked specifically if the Muslim community should be allowed to use faith-based arbitration, the same percentage of Canadians said no, the survey reported. The findings suggest that anti-Muslim sentiment was not behind the loud opposition in Ontario to allowing *Shari'a* courts to arbitrate family law. "It wasn't singling out a particular community. We found that people were generally opposed to do it for any community. So, that kind of explains the opposition to granting the Muslim community that right."[10]

In Canada, like in most European countries, a test was established to systematize the uncontrollable flow of immigrants in general, but specifically to target Muslim immigrants, some of whom are now perceived as threatening Canadian national security. The Canadian test looks at the rights and responsibilities of citizens as well as basic knowledge about the country. Whether the test will stem the immigrant tide remains to be seen, because those details can be easily learned by candidates for the immigration test. Much more important and relevant would be to ensure education for democracy and for mastery of the official languages, allegiance to the State of Canada and a verifiable commitment to renounce terrorism and denounce it to the authorities when it becomes known to any individual. The questions as of now test basic knowledge of Canadian history and the constitution, and are a first hurdle requiring the new incomers to demonstrate their keen interest in their new homeland.[11] In spite of these toughened requirements for immigration into Canada, a permanent fear permeates the authorities, the media and the public about the price their country might have to pay for its excessively lax policies towards Muslim immigrants, its often unfriendly castigations of Israel in order to appease its Muslim population, notwithstanding. It is not that warnings were not given. Many books and articles were published since the 1980s, alerting a complacent West against this upcoming wave of Muslim terror, but western authorities refused to take note. When Steve Emerson in the US pioneered these alerts after his comprehensive *Jihad in America* was put on film, he was ridiculed and maligned, even after the first attempt on the Twin Towers in 1993. It was already known then that the tentacles of Muslim terrorism were expanding worldwide. The book *Islamikaze: Manifestations of Islamic Martyrology,* published in London in 2003, made five separate references to Canada[12], and many more precise ones to London (England) and Birmingham where cells of Muslim terror were being erected. But who paid attention to them? Even when disaster struck in London in July 2005, the stunned British leaders spoke of a bunch of unruly "criminals" who had wreaked havoc on the subway system, as if those perpetrators stood to gain anything from their "crime", the way regular criminals do. The British authorities refused to read the reality that it was homegrown Muslim terrorism, carried out for no other reason than ideological commitment, for which the culprits incurred heavy risks and no gain. Then, on the 3rd of June 2006, as if the sinister prediction of the British Chief of Police came true (see the Introduction), it was announced in Toronto that twelve would-be terrorists were arrested before they could mount a string of terror attacks on an enormous scale, after they had stored explosives and weapons in order to carry out their scheme. Like in England, the Ontario Police did not dare to utter the word "Muslim" to characterize the suspects, leaving their public in the dark, though its illustrious Mounted Police, the equivalent of the American FBI, knew what it was all about. The Police simply refused to acknowledge the fact that no Christian , Hindi, Sikh or Jewish groups have ever launched such a frightening and sustained terrorist campaign against the West, and yet they somehow still feared that by spelling out that simple fact which was suspected by all, they would thereby "stain" all Muslims. The fact is that no one can hide the unfortunate empirical finding that most terrorists from all over the world, from the Philippines to Canada and from Indonesia to East Africa, are Muslim, Islam-driven, Islam-financed, Islam-indoctrinated, Islam-trained and Islam-dispatched. Some argue that they do not represent "true Islam", but then, what is "true Islam"? In any case, that does not excuse the terror carried out in Islam's name.

A charismatic British imam who has been accused of publicly vilifying Hindus, Jews and liberal Muslims made a return visit to Toronto in June 2006 at the invitation of a Scarborough (Canada) mosque. Sheikh Riyadh ul Haq was slated to be keynote speaker at a youth conference - a visit already protested by at least one group and by individuals who accused him of lifting passages from the Qur'an and altering them to suit his often controversial conclusions. Federal Immigration Minister Monte Solberg was urged to deny him entry. Ul Haq, a prominent cleric in England, had mostly passed unnoticed during at least four previous appearances in Canada. The arrests of 17 Greater Toronto Area residents on terrorism-related charges, however, provoked questions about just who is preaching to Canada's Muslim youth - and led to concerns about ul Haq's presence at the Youth *Tarbiyah* (culture) conference. In Toronto, he was to address an audience of 2,000 on current issues facing Muslim youth, according to Mohammad Alam, president of the Islamic Foundation of Toronto, the event organizer. "Whoever is objecting should make their own judgment and come hear him speak. He is a very learned scholar in Europe, or at least that's my understanding", said Alam. But some Muslim scholars say ul Haq often quotes the Qur'an out of context, and also refers to events out of historical context. For instance, in a speech posted on an Islamic website he quotes a Qur'an passage that states, "Of the whole of mankind, you shall find the most intense in their hatred and enmity towards the believers, *al-Yahood* (Jews) and the *mushrikeen* (the idolaters)". Then he paraphrases, saying that the ones who are bitterest in their enmity towards Muslims, the most unrelenting, unforgiving, are the Jews and the *mushri-keen* (idolaters) in all their forms. To avoid accusations of anti-Semitism, he added: "Allah, the creator of the Semites, says that, and in any case, the chief idolaters today are the Hindus."[13]

In fact, says Muslim scholar Shabir Ally, the passage refers only to the coalition of the Jews and the pagan Arabs who were together attacking the Muslims in Mohammed's time, in the seventh century. Thus, ul-Haq ignores the historical context in which it was mentioned. If it says "Jews" in the verse, he takes it to be all Jews for all times and all places, says Ally, president of the Islamic Information and *Da'wah*

Centre International in Toronto. He points out that ul Haq omitted the Qur'anic verse that states—again in Mohammed's era—that a Christian is a Muslim's friend. He just focuses on the part he needs because he wants to show that the world is against Muslims, says Ally. Earlier, reacting to the terrorism-related arrests, Munir El-Kassem sermonized, "We should be more careful in controlling the youth in the public domain—not everybody should be allowed to talk or lead the youth. They are the most vulnerable. He will also speak at the Toronto conference." El-Kassem had heard ul Haq speak twice: "It is purely religious and there is nothing I could call controversial.... He is a powerful speaker; his style is both compelling and motivational." Ul Haq spoke to an audience of 15,000 at the Reviving the Islamic Spirit Conference at the Rogers Centre late 2005, alongside controversial Americans such as Imam Zaid Shakir and Sheikh Hamza Yusuf. He also frequently travels to the United States as a speaker. But Tarek Fatah, of the secular Muslim Canadian Congress, has said that "those who invite ul Haq here should take ownership of hate…. We don't want this man to come to Canada unless he is willing to debate us in public", says Fatah. Born in 1971 in Gujarat, India, ul Haq, also known as Shaykh Abu Yusuf Riyadh, moved to the United Kingdom at age three to join his father, an imam at a Leicester mosque. At 13, he enrolled in an Islamic seminary in Bury, UK, the *Darul Uloom al Arabiyyah al Islamiyyah* (The Institute of Arabic and Islamic Studies), where he met Sheikh Husain Patel, currently imam at the Islamic Foundation. "He is honest, he has integrity and he is a very good speaker. He is well liked by the Muslim youth," says Patel. "He sometimes is critical of certain segments of the society and people. He has been critical of the British government and the British prime minister and their participation and invasion of Iraq and the Gulf War, and very rightly so."[14]

Ul Haq is the author of two books and was an imam at the Birmingham Central Mosque until 2003, the year he was arrested but not charged in a drive-by shooting incident that left two men critically injured. British police later said the shooting involved two groups targeting each other. Ul Haq now runs the *Al Kawthar* (Abundance, also a river in Paradise) *Academy,* a website packed with his lectures and excerpts from his books. There are people who are taking his quotes out of context and just recycling them, says Patel. Basically ul Haq has hundreds and hundreds of tapes, that's what he does. He gives lectures and speeches all around the world. In a sermon on his own website, ul Haq says of Europeans that they have made it clear that they will not tolerate a Muslim force or power in Europe: "If it means massacring Muslims, if it means genocide, if it means a holocaust in Europe again, so be it, but this time the target is Muslims". He also accuses the West of being people with hearts of stone, concerned only about stones, alluding to the furor over the *Taliban* destruction of the famed Buddhist statues at Bamiyan in 2001; these he deemed as idols, an abhorrence to Islam, and therefore an affront to the concept of *Tawhid* (Unity of Allah). And he castigates moderate Muslims who in their weakness say: "Well, Muslims should be careful, we shouldn't rebel, we shouldn't stand up against these powers." "Where in his speeches are the good things that are happening to Muslims? Of Muslims who live in his own neighborhood?" wonders Shabir Ally, of the information center. "He is piecing together, by his interpretation, motivation for people to reach certain conclusions. It is not good for youthful minds." Alia Hogben, president of the Canadian Council of Muslim Women, is also concerned about how ul Haq might influence young Muslim minds in Canada. The issue is the fine line between allowing someone to have freedom of speech and the danger of inflaming others to hate and anger, says Hogben. "If his comments, as in this speech, are repeated - they are racist, intolerant, with an unreasonable vilification of the West - then his entry needs to be assessed carefully, especially in light of the recent events; or close watch needs to be maintained when he does speak here". A federal immigration ministry spokesperson said that although UK citizens may enter Canada without a visa, those who incite hatred might well be prosecuted. The Canadian Coalition for Democracies, an Ottawa-based lobby group, is calling on the authorities to refuse entry on security grounds. "He has preached hatred of Hindus and Jews while glorifying martyrdom and *jihad"* said coalition director David Ouellette. Ul Haq was also scheduled to speak at a Montreal conference in July, 2006 while a seminar at McMaster University, based on his book *Causes of Disunity,* was cancelled - officially because of a time-table conflict.[15]

Reported in the US, the matter of the 17 terrorists looked and sounded more urgent. The *Washington Post* emphasized that on June 3, 2006 Canadian police and intelligence agents foiled a "series of terrorist attacks" by a group that had obtained three tons of explosive fertilizer - more than the amount used in the Oklahoma City bombings - to attack targets in Ontario. Twelve men - described as "mainly Canadian citizens" - and five juveniles were arrested in a series of raids at locations in the outlying suburbs of Toronto in enclaves for immigrant groups in Canada. The men, all with Arabic names, were mostly in their twenties. Police say they seized weapons, walkie-talkies, and a large quantity of ammonium nitrate. Police refused to identify the targets of the alleged bomb plot or discuss details of the plan. Reports in the Canadian press said the investigators moved because the bombing was evidently in the first stages of planning, and targets included large public buildings. Authorities said it was the biggest sweep conducted under Canada's anti-terrorism laws, passed after the September 11, 2001 attacks. Mike McDonell, an assistant commissioner of the Royal Canadian Mounted Police, gave notice at a press conference that the arrested men were "planning to commit a series of terrorist attacks against solely-Canadian targets in southern Ontario". They had acquired all the components of the bomb, he said. "This group posed a real and serious intent. They had the capacity and intent to carry out an attack". He explained that the group had trained together, and the arrests show that "Canada is susceptible to criminal terrorist activities as much as any [other] country." The investigation, which McDonell said involved more than 400 persons, included the Canadian Security Intelligence Service (CSIS). Luc Portelance, the CSIS assistant director of operations, said the arrested men "are Canadian residents from a variety of backgrounds. For various reasons, they appear to become adherents of a virulent ideology inspired by al-Qa'ida". But McDonell later suggested investigators had found no direct connection with al-Qa'ida. The men, dubbed "home-grown terrorists" by the Canadian media, were scheduled to appear in court to hear terrorism-related charges. The subjects were held at a police station in Pickering, 18 miles west of downtown Toronto, with heavy security posted outside the building. Police said they were not permitted to give any information about the five juveniles. Canadian reports said the raids were the consequence of the arrests by the FBI of two Georgia men in April. At the time, the FBI had announced that the two men had met with others in Toronto to plan attacks.[16]

The *Weekly Standard* offers another perspective which sees the Toronto plot as part of an international web, because such a cell cannot be "an island on its own". Initially, many media reports said nothing about the arrested suspects - and two other individuals already in custody - beyond the fact that all were Canadian residents and most were Canadian citizens. Yet it soon emerged that the twelve adults and five teenagers were Muslims of Somali, Egyptian, Jamaican, and Trinidadian origin. Media reports named the Peace Tower in the Canadian Parliament, the CN Tower complex, and the Toronto Stock Exchange as possible targets for the plot, but what is reasonably clear is that the participants intended to inflict mass casualties. Although, as stated by Luc Portelance (CSIS), the suspects had "become adherents to a violent ideology inspired by al Qa'ida," and despite all the uncertainties, a number of media outlets and terrorism analysts, taking a cue from McDonell (RCMP), rushed to declare the entire affair the work of homegrown terrorists operating independently of any broader network or organization. Typical of this interpretation were the comments of former White House counter-terrorism czar Richard Clarke, who told ABC News following the arrests, "This is leaderless terrorism, . . . cells that are not connected to anything…. There's nothing in their communications that would indicate this is terrorist communication. The calls are domestic. They're not going back to Afghanistan. And what's probably being said is the equivalent of, 'Let's all get together at Joe's house'". Yet there are good reasons to doubt this view. According to the *Los Angeles Times,* the Canadian arrests are "part of a continuing, multinational inquiry into suspected terrorist cells in at least seven countries". Far from having completed their investigation, the *Times* reported, "authorities were combing through evidence seized during raids in Canada … to look for possible connections between the 17 suspects arrested and at least 18 other Islamist militants who had been arrested in locations including the United States, Bangladesh, Bosnia-Herzegovina, Britain, Denmark, and Sweden." *CanWest News* Service reported that "the six-month RCMP" [Royal Canadian Mounted Police] investigation, called "Project Osage", is one of several overlapping probes that includes an FBI case called Operation Northern Exposure and a British probe known as Operation Mazhar. Further, the newswire noted, "the intricate web of connections between Toronto, London, Atlanta, Sarajevo, Dhaka, and elsewhere illustrates the challenge confronting coun-terterrorism investigators almost five years after 9/11". According to *CanWest,* "linking the international probes are online communications, phone calls and in particular videotapes that authorities allege show some of the targets the young extremists considered blowing up." While none of this proves an international dimension to the plot, it strongly suggests it. [17]

And there are other hints of international connections. Canadian journalist and columnist Andrew Coyne notes that the father of terror suspect Shareef Abdelhaleen confirmed to the *Canadian Press* that he once posted bail for one Mohamed Mahjoub, who has been held by Canadian intelligence on the basis of secret evidence since June 2000. According to a CBC News article from September 2005, Mahjoub is accused of being a member of the *Vanguards of Conquest* - a faction of Egyptian Islamic *Jihad,* the group led by al Qa'ida second-in-command Ayman al-Zawahiri. While Mahjoub denies any connection to terrorism, he admits that he met bin Laden in Sudan in the 1990s. Perhaps the link between the

Abdelhaleens and Mahjoub is just an amazing coincidence. Another suggestive bit of information is that the Canadian suspects were in contact with Syed Haris Ahmed and Ehsanul Islam Sadequee. These two men, both American citizens from the Atlanta area, are alleged by the US government to have traveled to Canada in March 2005 to discuss "strategic locations in the United States suitable for a terrorist strike" with three individuals subsequently identified in media reports as being among the Canadian suspects now in custody. According to the FBI affidavit against Ahmed and Sadequee, the two discussed traveling to Pakistan to attend a terrorist training camp. *WAGA-TV* reported in April that Ahmed later traveled to Pakistan in an effort to do just that. As for Sadequee, he was arrested in April 2006 in Dhaka, the capital of Bangladesh, and turned over to the FBI, who according to the affidavit, found him in possession of a CD-ROM with encrypted files and a map of the Washington area. The affidavit accuses Sadequee of lying about traveling to Bangladesh to visit his aunt. It should be noted that in 2005-6 Bangladesh was rocked by a wave of violence organized by Islamist groups loyal to the now-incarcerated Sheikh Abdur Rahman, a key signatory of bin Laden's 1998 declaration of war. The nature of the relationship among the Canadian suspects, their Atlanta counterparts, and any additional accomplices is subject to deeper inquiry, as is the nature of any relationship between the younger Abdelhaleen and Mahjoub. And so also is the fact that two of the Canadian suspects, Mohammed Dirie and Yasim Abdi Mohamed, attempted to smuggle weapons and ammunition from the United States to Canada in August 2005 before being arrested by Canadian border police at Fort Erie, near Buffalo. According to the *Toronto Sun,* documents from the Canadian National Parole Board show that Dirie told Canadian officials he had gone to Buffalo "frequently, over a few months", as well as to Ohio, where he claimed that he needed to purchase a gun because a friend had been robbed. The Canadian parole board didn't buy that claim, but neither did it offer any comment on Dirie's account of his travels to the United States. Was Dirie's story true? If so, who did he meet with during these travels and why?[18]

With so many questions remaining unanswered, it is far too soon to rule out connections between the Canadian conspiracy and terrorists abroad. Certainly, much evidence has come to light challenging the view that homegrown terrorism is an entirely insular phenomenon. Unfortunately, the desire to ignore or downplay international connections between individual terrorist suspects on the one hand and terrorist networks on the other has become increasingly prevalent in public analysis since September 11, and particularly since the rise of the Iraqi insurgency. Today, even a careful observer could easily get the mistaken impression that terror cells are produced by something like spontaneous combustion. Even more misleading are attempts to nail down a pseudo-legalistic "six degrees of separation" between terrorist organizations and specific attacks carried out by their followers. Thus, many analysts and reporters assert that no connection exists between al Qa'ida and either the March 2004 train explosions in Spain or the July 2005 bombings in London. But that is far from incontrovertible. On the contrary, multiple investigations into these attacks by the Spanish and British governments have drawn clear connections between their perpetrators and al Qa'ida or its associate groups. Commentators who deny these connections often claim to be correcting a widespread misconception that all acts of Islamist terrorism are personally ordered by Osama bin Laden. Instead, they seek to highlight the role of extremist ideology in the shadowy world of international terrorism. But while Islamist ideology is indeed a powerful motive for terrorism, it is simply not the case that terrorist cells spring into existence altogether independently. Al Qa'ida and allied organizations still play a role in providing strategy and direction as well as funding, training, and propaganda to prospective *jihadists*. With regard to the Canadian plotters, if indeed they took their "inspiration" from al Qa'ida, we do not yet know how this occurred. Did they read strategy documents posted on the Internet? Did they respond to calls by al Qa'ida leaders to carry out attacks against Canada and Canadian nationals? Did they receive paramilitary training that some of the suspects appear to have conducted in Washago, Ontario, according to Canadian media reports? Such local training was encouraged by al Qa'ida strategist Mustafa Setmariam Nasar prior to his capture in 2005. No serious examination of the Canadian plot should minimize the potential foreign connections out of blind adherence to a convenient analytical model. Like all other leads, the considerable evidence suggesting foreign connections should be vigorously pursued, as some media suggested.[19]

Characteristic of Muslim terrorists worldwide is that their kin will always deny and then justify, in the aftermath, every one of their acts of horror. After September 11 and London 7/7, the first reactions of the Muslim community was that "things like that could not be done by Muslims", or that "they were good boys who would be incapable of inflicting death", therefore the atrocities were attributed to Israel, the Mossad, the Jews or a conspiracy of the CIA. After Bin Laden took the responsibility, justifications began to appear, such as "frustration", "anger", an "ambition to blunt American / British arrogance", "punishment for Afghanistan and Iraq", or "to avenge the atrocities against the Palestinians, the Iraqis, the Somalis etc."[20] Even following the most horrific plot to blow up ten aircraft over the Atlantic in August 2006, denials of that sort were voiced. The arrests are systematically condemned by the Muslims as "police abuse", because those middle-class and home-grown boys who came from respectable backgrounds "could not possibly be associated with terrorism". Now, after the arrests and the evidence, Canadian Muslims want us to believe that their kinsmen indulge in terrorism because the poor darlings "have too much time on their hands."[21] So it is Canada's fault that they are bored. At least the youth of the "decadent" West indulge in sex and drugs when they are bored, and do not seek the thrill of a kill. And it ill behoves the Muslim Canadian MP to speak of "disenfranchisement" as a spur for terrorism. "Disenfranchisement" takes place in Muslim countries, not western ones. Let us look at the details as they appeared in the *Globe and Mail*.[22] Prime Minister Stephen Harper issued a ringing defense of cultural diversity, rejecting calls for Canada to be less open to immigration as a way of curbing terrorism. "I believe, actually, the opposite is true," Mr. Harper told the opening session of the United Nations' World Urban Forum in Toronto, "Canada's diversity, properly nurtured, is our greatest strength." Mr Harper made it clear to the thousands of delegates who crowded into the city's convention centre that his pointed remarks were a direct result of the alleged terrorist plot uncovered in Toronto. But reversing himself he stated that though Canada has so far been "spared the horror visited on London, New York and Madrid", the arrest of 17 suspected terrorists "reminded us that the potential for hate-fuelled violence in Canada is very real."

The threat of terrorism, said Harper, is "sadly, the most serious challenge" modern policy-makers face: "It casts a shadow over cities in the world." Some commentators have blamed Canada's open, multicultural society for spawning the alleged terrorist network, Mr Harper added. "They have said it makes us a more vulnerable target for terrorist activity." But rather than shutting out those from other countries with different ethnic backgrounds and religions, Canada should maintain its longstanding, open-door policy, he proclaimed. "It is true that somewhere, in some communities, we will find ... apostles of terror, who use the symbols of culture and faith to justify crimes of violence ... They hate open, diverse, democratic societies like ours, because they want the exact opposite," Mr Harper declared. " [They want] societies that are closed, homogeneous and dogmatic." Yet the terrorists and their vision will be rejected "by men and women of good will and generosity in all communities," Mr Harper affirmed to loud applause. "And they will be rejected most strongly by those men and women living in the very communities that the terrorists claim to represent, as we have already seen in Canada since those arrests." He indicated that his confidence stemmed from the openness of the ethnic communities established by immigrants to Canada. "We've largely avoided ghettoization . . . and the impoverished, crime-ridden, ethnically polarized no-go zones." Underscoring his commitment to a multicultural Canada, Mr Harper pledged that his government would do all it could to ensure terrorism finds no comfort in Canada. And it would do so by "preserving and strengthening the cultural diversity that makes us strong". At other times in his speech, however, Mr Harper seemed to strike an oddly discordant note to the serious urban issues facing the UN conference. He said the recent budget provides $50 million to communities for programs aimed at giving young people "alternatives to guns, gang and violence",[23] (albeit that he knew that much of it is perpetrated by Muslims). At the same time, some "Muslim experts" were more apologetic for Muslims, as is their custom, by deflecting blame from Muslim perpetrators, whom they represent as victims of outside forces. "Canadians must understand that an alleged plan to launch a terrorist attack in Ontario wasn't engineered by Muslims, but instead was a plot by people who happened to be Muslim", experts, politicians and community leaders said. The government and other authorities said it would be a mistake for people to draw rash conclusions about the possible failures of Canadian multiculturalism or to seek radical societal changes until after more was learned about the 17 suspects arrested under the federal Anti-Terrorism Act. "Canadians who believe Muslims are cheering the actions of the accused need to have a better understanding of their fellow residents", said Mohammad Alam, president of the Islamic Foundation of Toronto. "No religion will permit any terrorism, and every religion will teach us to love and care for each other.... We appeal to (worried) Canadians that we are Canadians ourselves.... If (the suspects) are convicted, we believe they should be punished according to the law. If there's a terrorist in any community we should root him out." Professor Wesley Wark of the University of Toronto's Munk Centre for International Studies alerted that some critics may soon push to clamp down on immigration or strengthen anti-terrorism laws. But Wark hopes those calls would be held in check by more reasonable opinion. "Neither Canadian society nor the Muslim community want terrorism to take root here", he said. "I don't think there's much (support) for terrorist thinking among the

Muslim community or other ethnic communities…. That doesn't mean that occasionally small numbers of individuals might decide to go down that path, encouraged by visiting *jihadist* websites, encouraged by the general propaganda that swirls out of al Qa'ida," Wark stated. But he did not say how anyone can be caught up in Bin Laden's propaganda or in *jihadi* rhetoric unless he is Muslim. "But I think there's little likelihood of much broad-based support for terrorist activity among ethnic groups in Canada." But who speaks about "ethnic groups", and who has ever suspected any non-Muslim group? That is the issue. He continues: "The terrorist threat has the potential to unite Muslims and the rest of the Canadian public, much like what happened after the London bombings last summer". Wark was maybe unaware that in London (England) itself, the act of terrors created, on the contrary, much controversy, division and fear in the Muslim community. He erroneously added: "What you have seen in the United Kingdom is a bringing together of mainstream Muslim thought to try to reject the idea of tolerating extremist preaching in mosques." If he was right, where did the conspiracy of blowing up airliners in flight come from?[24]

Liberal Omar Alghabra, one of Canada's four Muslim MPs, has made clear that community leaders have to take responsibility to shut the door on any opportunity for radicalization: "We need to make sure those people who are bent on radical ideologies don't recruit and seduce our youth…. Ultimately, the goal is to offer venues and opportunities to youth and community members to be empowered and to be engaged rather than being seduced by any form of radicalization that may be the outcome of marginalization". Muhammed Alam, President of the Toronto Islamic Foundation, also stressed that it was not difficult to live in Canada as a Muslim and it shouldn't be difficult for Muslims to fully integrate into society. However, he added, "there could definitely be more funding for youth programs that would help prevent disillusioned youth from being swayed by radical groups. There's a lack of activities. When people have too much time on their hands, they're doing things they're not supposed to be doing," Alam said. But interestingly enough, no other "bored" group but Muslims, even not the delinquents among them who raise the crime statistics, do engage in terrorism and plot mass murder. So maybe the problem is not with idle youth but with Muslim youth? Besides, who has prevented the Muslim leadership and parents from educating their children and filling their free time with something educational and fulfilling? The problem is precisely that: Muslim youths go in their spare time to the mosques where they fall prey to radical imams, but if someone should suggest that Muslim youth should be diverted from mosques to sports or other educational activities, he would be accused of racism and Islamophobia - Catch 22. Another Liberal MP Wajid Khan said, "the problems of Muslim youth aren't very different than the troubles of young people across Canada". If so, why is it that only Muslims are suspected of terrorism, in Canada and elsewhere, and no other youth from any other origin or conviction? Khan continued: "When we talk about youth being brainwashed we can look at it in a broader sense…. If you look at all the gun violence, the drugs and prostitution (across Canada), how do you think that happens? I'm sure it's all disenfranchisement to some extent." But are only Muslims "disenfranchised"? And who disenfranchised them? How can he, just like Tony Blair after 7/7, compare regular crime to ideological crime that is spawned by radical Islam? "Still, Canada isn't facing a growing crisis in its ethnic communities and to think so would be a huge over-reaction", proclaimed Joseph Heath, associate professor of philosophy at the University of Toronto. "It would be a mistake to draw general lessons about the success or failure of Canadian multiculturalism by looking at the behavior of such a small number of individuals", he emphasized, adding that there's no comparison between the ethnic clashes in Canada versus those that have occurred in Europe. "The situation you've had in the United Kingdom, or Holland, or in France, with highly concentrated ethnic ghettos, with serious structural unemployment, none of that exists in Canada along the same scale". But one should fear that if Canada continues to ignore the Muslim problem, by comparing itself favorably to Europe, it will not be long before terror catches up with it.[25]

It would seem paradoxical that Muslim lay leaders who are involved in national politics should find fault with the system of which they are part, while Muslim clerical leaders who spend their lives in their Muslim enclaves, should sound more responsive to the authorities out of their concern to eliminate biases against Muslims in the community. Indeed, Muslim religious leaders promised to report any suspicious behavior on the part of their followers to authorities and abide by a zero-tolerance policy against preaching hatred, in the wake of the terror arrests.[26] In fact, leaders representing more than 30 mosques and Muslim organizations throughout Canada gathered in Toronto after the June 2006 arrests to deliver the message - and also to remind Canadians not to discriminate against Muslims. The leaders admitted that there are pockets of radical fundamentalists within their community who believe in violence, but said co-operation by the Muslim community led to the arrests of the 17 terror suspects. The alleged bombing plot in southern Ontario was a wakeup call to Muslims, leaders stated. "They were sleeping and didn't realize it was a real issue", said Ahmed Amiruddin, who taught at a Mississauga mosque where some of the accused men worshipped. "They would sometimes appear in the mosque with military fatigues, and there's more than one witness for this. Many people have seen them", he said. "The only thing that concerned me is that they tried to shut themselves out to anything we tried to preach to them", added Asad Dean of the Canadian Council of *Ahl al-Sunnah wal Jamaah*. "Canadian youth of Muslim faith have been unduly influenced by radical thought", explained Yasmin Ratansi, a Liberal MP. The alleged ringleader, 43-year-old Qayyum Abdul Jamal, hardly a youth himself, was a role model for teenagers at the Al-Rahman Islamic Centre in Mississauga, which was also attended by six of the other terror suspects. "Let's make sure that we take a second look at who we are allowing to come and preach, what books are allowed into our centers", he said. "We will have to become more vigilant as well in the Muslim community, that if we see any signs of this, we immediately pay attention and take action to address this issue". The Council of *Ahl al-Sunna wal Jamaah* (CCAS) blamed the Toronto terror plot, as well as the terror attacks in London and Madrid, on a small minority of Muslims who subscribe to a "vile doctrine of literalistic ideology". If they were indeed emphatic in their condemnation, time will tell whether they can confront the position of the majority, and explain the jubilation of the masses of Muslims everywhere when a terror attack is carried out. The group stressed that the "vast majority" of Canadian Muslims follow a moderate form of Islam. But the problem here is that there is no moderate doctrine of Islam which can challenge the orthodox one, though there are certainly many moderate Muslims. We have seen above that the confrontations between the literalists and the reformers have invariably left the latter in the minority. "The (CCAS) is convinced that the time has come for Muslim Canadians to adopt a different approach in view of the reality it now finds itself in," said spokesman Akbar Khan. Liberal MP Wajid Khan has made clear that he is tired of hearing Muslim speakers emphasizing that Islam is not to blame for the arrests. "Nobody is saying it is (Islam)," he said. "Why are we talking about these 17 people based on faith? Let's not take the temperature up so high…. There is an issue and we have to address it as a nation".[27] But when he refers to a "nation" is he referring to the Muslim *Ummah* only, or to Canadians in general?

The rhetoric of calm and self-reckoning among Canadian Muslims notwithstanding, the Canadian Security Intelligence Service has issued this warning: There is an increasing threat from what Canada's CIA calls "home-grown terrorists" living in communities across Canada. And presumably awaiting orders. The warning came from Jack Hooper, CSIS deputy director of operations, in his May 29, 2006 testimony before a Canadian Senate defense committee. He told the committee that, since 2001, some 20,000 immigrants from the Afghanistan/Pakistan region have entered Canada. And, said Hooper, in what passes for a Canadian understatement: "We're in a position to vet one-tenth of those. That may be inadequate." What that means for the United States is obvious. Its northern border must be guarded more closely than ever before in history. Indeed, it has been, for a century, an unarmed, unpoliced border. Hooper said, according to CBC News, that young Canadians with immigrant backgrounds are: (1) becoming radicalized through the Internet and (2) seeking targets within Canada itself, not abroad. "They are virtually indistinguishable from other youth", said Hooper. "They blend in very well to our society, they speak our language and they appear to be - to all intents and purposes - well assimilated. They look to Canada to execute their targeting". Hooper pointed out that the men responsible for the London 2005 subway bombings were from immigrant families. He testified ominously: "I can tell you that all of the circumstances that led to the London transit bombings, to take one example, are resident here and now in Canada".[28] As the co-conspirators were brought to justice, their targets were revealed to the public and caused a shudder to run down their spines. The 17 Muslim suspects who appeared in a Canadian court were charged with allegedly planning to attack the Peace Tower at the centre of the parliamentary complex in Ottawa, which commemorates Canada's First World War dead. The tower stands at the front of the main neo-Gothic parliament building, which also contains the House of Commons, the Senate and the office of the prime minister, Stephen Harper. Law enforcement officers made a string of arrests, including not only the 17 Canadians (12 adults, and five under-18s) but also two Americans who had contact with the suspects. *The Toronto Star* reported that the police had followed the alleged conspiracy as it was hatched in internet chat rooms.[29]

Newly aware of the international networks of Muslim terrorists which may be targeting it, Canada has decided to fund monitoring organizations that track terrorism. The proposed international organization that would track funding to terrorist groups will be headquartered in Toronto, the country's finance minister announced. Finance Minister Jim Flaherty said Toronto will house the headquarters of the Egmont Group - an organization which represents more than 100 financial investigation units. The government will contribute C$5 million (US$4.5 million) over the next five years to help establish the group, which will analyze, investigate and prosecute terrorist financing and share financial intelligence on money laundering. Flaherty says Canada is taking an international leadership role to combat terrorist financing. His announcement is part of a series of measures the Conservative government plans to announce to fight the funding of terrorists.[30] The international tenor of the Toronto cell has certainly strengthened the Canadians in their efforts to monitor terrorism at its source. It turned out that many of the arrested were of Middle Eastern or Somali background, while at least two are converts to Islam. Some have jobs and some don't, while others are high school or university students. The father of one of the accused works for Atomic Energy of Canada, while the father of another is a doctor, not exactly from a background of deprivation as has been reputedly attached to terrorists. Two are related by marriage. They live in nice suburban houses or in city apartments, sometimes close to each other. Moreover, one Toronto newspaper reported that the AEG contract employee had once posted bail for an Islamist currently being held in an Ontario jail on a security certificate, awaiting a deportation order. The group's members, according to security officials, had met through radical Islamist internet sites, now one of the chief means of recruiting *jihadists* in the West. But CSIS officials say it was their surveillance of these fundamentalist websites in 2004 that first attracted the intelligence community's attention to the group. It was also CSIS who had arranged the sale of the fertilizer to the alleged terrorists in a sting operation, arresting them shortly thereafter. An earlier visit to Toronto by two Islamists from Georgia, now in American custody, may also be connected with the investigation. It was reported that one of the two had attended high school in Toronto.[31]

Security officials state that this group is part of the new wave of homegrown Muslim terrorists appearing in the West. Like the British subway bombers, these second- and third-generation Muslims have never lived in an Islamic country, at least for any length of time, and have never attended an al Qa'ida training camp, but are inspired by Osama Bin Laden's hatred for the West. Their motive, they claim, for plotting to kill their neighbors and for attacking the countries that have opened their doors to them and their families, is the West's supposed persecution of Muslims in such places as Iraq, Afghanistan and Chechnya, and their support of the United States in the war on terror. Despite al Qa'ida having mentioned Canada twice as a potential terrorist target and a top al Qa'ida official demanding that Canada get its troops out of Afghanistan, Canadians were shocked by the arrests. Up until now, terrorists, some of them Canadian citizens, have mostly used Canada to raise money, find recruits and plan attacks in other countries. The most noteworthy example was Ahmed Ressam, an Algerian living in Montreal, who had intended to blow up the Los Angeles airport as part of the Millennium Plot. American officials arrested him at Washington State's Canadian-American border with a car-load of explosives en route to Los Angeles. But the arrest in 2004 of a Canadian-born Muslim indicated that Canada had a homegrown terrorism problem. Mohammad Momin Khawaja, whose father is Pakistani, was arrested in Ottawa for his involvement in a terrorist bomb plot that was to unfold in London. A large problem in Canada's fight against terrorism at home was the previous Liberal government, which was voted out of power earlier in 2006, after twelve years of rule. The Liberals are Canada's party of multi-culturalism. As a result, the Liberal government hesitated to crack down hard on terrorist groups, enforce deportation orders (such as the one against Ahmed Ressam) or tighten lax immigration and asylum laws for fear of alienating the urban ethnic vote that forms a large part of their constituency. Former Liberal Prime Minister Jean Chretien once even had the temerity to say that there were no terrorist groups in Canada, causing CSIS to go to the Canadian public via the media to contradict him, saying there were at least 50 terrorist organizations operating on Canadian soil. A vindictive Chretien then cut CSIS's budget. So is it any wonder that Canada's only court-recognized expert on *jihadism*, Tom Quiggen, recently told a Canadian national newspaper that "some of the world's most infamous terrorists have operated in Canada almost unhindered for years".[32]

Meanwhile, Canadian Islamic groups have reacted differently to the Toronto arrests. While one Muslim leader sensibly said that Muslims themselves must fight against this extremism in their community, another predictably blamed the federal government for not giving Muslim groups enough money to study why young Muslims are turning to fundamentalist ideologies. Families and friends of those arrested, also predictably, have said that those charged are good people who have been wrongly accused despite the fact that two of them are already in jail serving a two-year sentence for smuggling weapons into Canada. In the eye of the Muslim beholder, Muslims can never be wrong. But Joe Warmington, who was present in the courtroom for the shackled suspects' bail hearing, termed some of the alleged terrorists' behavior "bizarre", saying they were smiling and laughing, as they waved to family members, some of whom were clad in *burkas*. That is also characteristic of Muslim terrorists, for whom being seized, tried and jailed is for their families, friends, cell members and other Believers of their kin the best proof that they fulfilled their *jihadi* obligation without fail. "You could see that they were proud of themselves," said Warmington. And with the police still searching for two suspicious men who were filming the Toronto subway system the week before, their twisted sense of pride may not yet be misplaced.[33] On the reasons why Canada is growing its own terrorists - and they were not looking for "Afghanistan reasons", Jack Hooper, the CSIS Deputy Director of Operations, testified that these young Canadian Muslims have somehow become radicalized while growing up in Canada, namely they are "homegrown". In other words, they have emerged from within Canada, rather than infiltrating it from abroad. They are insiders, not outsiders like Millennium Bomber Ahmed Ressam, who was behind Canada's last major terrorism scare in 1999. "Increasingly, we are learning of more and more extremists that are homegrown," says a declassified CSIS report obtained by the *National Post*. "The implications of this shift are important". Across the Atlantic, the term "European *Jihad*" is now used to describe the new generation of young Muslim extremists who not only live in Europe, but also consider it a legitimate terrorist target. A "Canadian *Jihad*" is apparently underway as well. Canada's top national security problem used to be the homeland terrorism that occurs when foreigners bring to Canada the violent causes of their countries of origin. Other people's wars have been seeping into Canada for decades as a result of what intelligence officials call "the spillover effect", which is what happened when Sikh terrorists in British Columbia bombed two Air-India planes in 1985. Homeland terrorists such as the Tamil Tigers remain a security problem for Canada, but they are no longer the country's only major threat. Of equal concern to counterterrorism investigators is homegrown Muslim terrorism.[34]

"We have a bifurcated threat at this point", Mr. Hooper testified. "The threat that comes to Canada from the outside, as well as a homegrown threat.... We must be vigilant on two fronts", he added, "that which is coming to us from the outside environment and, increasingly, that which is growing up in our communities". In Europe, the United States and Australia, intelligence agencies have been reporting the same trend: loose homegrown youth networks (some of them virtual networks that exist only in cyberspace) inspired by al-Qa'ida but that operate locally and autonomously. The suicide bombings in London on July 7, 2005 that killed 52, for example, were the work of three British-born Muslims and a Jamaican-born immigrant who had converted to Islam. "The attacks showed very clearly that terrorism is a 'homegrown' problem", had said a British parliamentary committee's report on the bombings. Western *jihadist* youth counterculture is the next phase in the evolution of global terrorism. Since becoming a credible threat in the late 1980s, but after its defeat and the elimination of the *Taliban* regime in 2001-2, al Qa'ida decentralized and spread from its origins in Pakistan and Afghanistan to such an extent that a "high percentage" of the extremists on the CSIS radar screen are now Canadian-born. "These individuals are part of Western society, and their 'Canadian-ness' makes detection more difficult", a "secret" CSIS report notes. This *jihadi* generation encompasses a variety of ethnic backgrounds, and includes Africans and South Asians as well as converts to Islam. Some are educated and computer-literate, while others have criminal records and more closely fit the profile of street-gang culture. But they share a devotion to puritanical Islam, contempt for non-Muslims (and other Muslims deemed not sufficiently Muslim), and a seething anger at what they see as the worldwide oppression of Muslims. On top of that, they believe that terrorist violence is a justified response to the "war on Islam" which they are convinced the West is waging in such places as Afghanistan and Iraq, as well as within Western countries such as Canada, where Muslims have been arrested for terrorism. While they look to Osama Bin Laden for inspiration, they are not formal members of al-Qa'ida. They often have no apparent connection to any terrorist groups. Most have never been to a terrorist training camp (although some have been trained in Canada, abroad or online).[35]

Rather than taking orders from overseas bosses, these *jihadis* plan and execute their activities locally, "without input from masterminds abroad," states one CSIS report. The Internet provides all the indoctrination and instruction they need. But what truly distinguishes them from the old guard is that whereas homeland terrorists tended to go overseas (Afghanistan and Chechnya, for example) to fulfill their violent fantasies, homegrown terrorists want to fight their *jihad* right in the West. They see Canada and Europe as another battlefield. This new generation of young radicals is "a significant threat to national security" and "a clear and present danger to Canada and its allies", according to de-classified CSIS reports. "A small number of Islamic extremists in Canada advocate violent *jihad* in pursuit of their political or religious aims", states another intelligence report written in the days after the London bombings. "The reasons for this radicalization are varied and include a general sense of anger at what is seen as oppression of Muslims throughout the world

[and] parental influence." Intelligence agencies have been struggling to explain the "*jihadization*" of Western Muslim youths and are posing the question: what is driving some of them to embrace extremist violence against their own countries? The Dutch General Intelligence and Security Service, dealing with many of the same problems as CSIS, stated in a report released in May 2006 that radicalization is a result of the struggle among young Muslims to reconcile Islam with an increasingly modern, global and secular world. The report also states that although Muslims worldwide are faced with globalization and modernization, young Muslims growing up in secular Western societies, in which Islam is just one more religious and cultural movement, are much more acutely confronted with problems of existential and religious orientation. These youths may turn to the Qur'an for guidance, but lacking strong Muslim cultural roots and sometimes ignorant of true Islamic teachings, they can fall into the trap of believing that to be "good Muslims" they must adhere to extremist interpretations of the faith. "With the help of radical web sites and chat sessions, they compile a radical 'cut-and-paste' version of Islam from Qur'an quotations which they reshape into a revolutionary pamphlet of global violent *jihad*", the Dutch security service has reported.[36]

Tom Quiggin, a former RCMP expert on *jihadism* who now works in Singapore, has said that homegrown terrorists tend to become serious about religion in their late teens and twenties. "Their so-called 'religious education' is usually nothing but cherry-picked Qur'anic statements heavily laced with poisonous *jihadist* messages that bear little resemblance to the actual message of Islam". The Intelligence Assessments Branch of CSIS acknowledges that, "There does not appear to be a single process that leads to extremism: the transformation is highly individual". But CSIS has singled out some of the factors that it says are leading Canadian youths down the path to terror. One of the most common is family ties. Fathers with extremist Islamic beliefs are raising their children to be extremist believers. One example is Ahmed Khadr, the Canadian who sent his sons to training camps in Afghanistan and encouraged one of them to become an Islamikaze ("suicide bomber"). Many homegrown terrorists are also radicalized as a result of a spiritual leader who guides them to extremism. This was the case with Mohammed Jabarah, who joined al-Qa'ida after graduating from high school in St. Catharines, Ontario. His guide was a Kuwaiti cleric named Sulayman Abu Gaith, who recruited several young boys, many of them now dead or in prison. Another factor is religious conversion. CSIS reports that Islamic terrorists are actively seeking out Western converts, who are "highly-prized by terrorist groups for their familiarity with the West and relative ease at moving through Western society". "As newcomers to the Islamic faith, converts can be prone to recruitment into extremism because they are unfamiliar with true Islamic teachings and are therefore vulnerable to manipulation.... The issue of radicalized converts will grow over the next few decades", explains a CSIS report. And from the federal government's Integrated Threat Assessment Centre: "Much like the attraction of extreme ideologies of past decades, radical Islam will continue to appeal to the disenfranchised and those struggling with a personal or spiritual crisis". The Internet is cited by CSIS as well. The Internet has been described as the engine propelling the global *jihadi* movement. It serves as a virtual training camp, where everything from recruitment literature to explosives recipes are available for downloading by youths sitting in their living rooms. "Once hooked into these webs of information, susceptibility to recruitment increases", according to the CSIS. One of the challenges with homegrown terrorism is how to respond. Traditionally, CSIS has used a three-tiered approach to fighting terrorists: prevent known terrorists from coming to Canada; if that fails, intercept them at the border or airport; and as a last resort, investigate and deport them. None of those measures apply to homegrown terrorists. "When we talk about the homegrown terrorist phenomenon, in most instances, these are people who are Canadian citizens. You cannot remove them anywhere", Mr. Hooper testified. "We have two options", he added. "We can work in collaboration with law enforcement to prosecute them or we can work to disrupt their activities".[37]

"Having a *jihadist* father like Ahmed Said Khadr, to cite but one example, often leads to an atmosphere of extremism where the children are raised to see the justification of using violence to attain political goals," states a Canadian intelligence report. In 1998, a World Islamic Front letter was sent to police advising that a biological and chemical weapons attack would be launched in the Montreal subway system. A group of Algerians was arrested and deported. "In the summer of 1999, Samir Ait Mohamed and Ahmed Ressam discussed placing explosives in the Outremont suburb of Montreal because it was a predominantly Jewish neighborhood", the FBI reported. In 2001 a "special file" was constituted for Abu Bakr al-Albani on the nature of his mission: "to gather information on ... the possibility of obtaining explosive devices inside Canada...." In August 2001 an e-mail was found on an al-Qa'ida computer in Kabul. In the lead-up and immediate aftermath to 9/11, there was a conspiracy of eight individuals who had designs to execute an act of serious violence in the

Toronto area. In 2002 an Osama Bin Laden audiotaped speech, "As you kill, you will be killed" was released that threatened Canada. In 2004, *Al Battar,* an al-Qa'ida training manual, instructed: "Human Targets: We must target and kill the Jews and the Christians ... The grades of importance are as follows: Americans, British, Spaniards, Australians, Canadians, Italians". And in 2005, stating "And now you will get news of what hurts you" *a jihadist* video production, posted on the Internet, repeated Bin Laden's 2002 threat to Canada. As Mr Hooper warned in 2006,: "We have a bifurcated threat at this point - the threat that comes to Canada from the outside as well as a homegrown threat, and the homegrown variant looks to Canada to execute its targeting".[38]

Finally, it is instructive to let the Canadian Islamic Congress introduce its approach to the deep crisis of the Muslim community in Canada following the arrest of the 17. Following a wave of arrests overnight on June 3, 2006, that led to more than a dozen Toronto-area men and teens being held on charges of suspected terrorism, the Canadian Islamic Congress issued a statement saying:

> All suspects involved in the current investigation -those now arrested and any who may yet be charged - must be treated as innocent until proven guilty; If and when any individuals are proven guilty under Canadian anti-terrorism legislation, then they are criminals. Canada's 750,000 Muslims should not be made guilty-by-association, either in the Canadian media or through any public pronouncements; We praise today's statements by CSIS, RCMP and the Mayor of Toronto for putting today's arrests into proper context as criminal activities by suspects; [this is precisely the point, it is not a criminal activity for the purpose of gain, for which only the individuals concerned are to blame, but a no-gain ideological crime which the Muslim community has allowed to grow in its midst. Though not all the Muslims of Canada can be prosecuted for terrorism, they certainly bear part of the responsibility for not having cleansed themselves of the jihadist plague. Instead of shouldering responsibility, they attack the government]. It is irresponsible for our Prime Minster to paint today's arrests as a battle between "us" and "them". Such a statement puts all Canadian Muslims in great danger; Governments, both federal and provincial, must fund legitimate academic research to diagnose this serious social problem and provide scientific solutions to it. The CIC statement elaborated saying: "There is no solid social science research that details why and how imported extremist ideologies are finding their way to some vulnerable Canadian Muslim youth. Zero dollars were spent by governments to investigate and follow up on such disturbing trends." "The Canadian Muslim community is law-abiding and loyal, but we have been up front in recognizing that no group is without problems," the statement continued. "We at CIC have initiated a nation-wide Smart Integration program and need more help from Canadian academic researchers to scientifically diagnose problems and devise solutions. But our governments have refused to share in the cost of research that could benefit all Canadians. They have said, in effect, 'this is your problem, you solve it.' . . . This is a short-sighted attitude. If other social problems, such as the high rate of crime among inner city youth, received millions of dollars in research funding over the past decade, why are proactive Muslim initiatives being ignored?"[39]

The world has become accustomed to the fact that many of the Muslim terrorist acts are rationalized in terms of "American aggression against Islam, or Israel's treatment of the Palestinians, or the hatred to Islam of both". So, why Canada? - a pacific country which excels in absorbing Muslims from all over the world, contributes to peace-keeping all over the globe, dispenses the "right" amounts of anti-American and anti-Israeli rhetoric, and considerable amounts of money to the Palestinians to please the Arabs and the Muslims, has no soldiers in Iraq, and certainly does not discriminate against Muslims at home. It is true that leaders of Islamic terrorist groups are universally agreed that no government is legitimate unless it is Islamic. But there are many other non-Islamic states less friendly to Muslims. So, the drive for an Islamic state is probably not enough of a salient motive to explain why Canada has been included in the list of the targeted Western countries by Islamic terror. Telling young Muslims that their non-Muslim Canadian neighbors are going halfway around the world to Afghanistan to rape Muslim women strikes a raw nerve. Believing that members of the *Ummah* (the world body of Muslims) need to be defended makes someone far more susceptible to messages that violence should be waged in the name of Islam or Allah. How many American, European and Canadian imams are brainwashing their followers with vicious lies about their fellow Americans, Canadians and Europeans? How many Muslims believe that their Jewish and Christian neighbors are the ones responsible for the mass murder of innocent Iraqis, Afghanis and others? How many believe that Israeli soldiers slaughter Palestinian women and children for sport - and that the US openly supports it? The answer to all of the above is: At least some. We know this from public record, particularly information stemming from various terror arrests. Here is a more pertinent question: Who is actually fighting this propaganda? Who is combating the spread of radical Islam? Law enforcement can intervene to thwart planned violence, but what can it do about hate speech? Not much. Even fire-breathing imams enjoy constitutional protections in the West. They don't, however, enjoy freedom from condemnation. Thus the most important question is not how many fiery imams there are in the West, but rather, how many Western Muslims will take a stand against the indoctrination that pushes their offspring in the direction - if not into the arms - of terrorists?[40]

Consider Zaynab Khadr, who was amongst the crowd of relatives gathered at the Toronto-area courthouse waiting for the appearances of the 17 Canadian Muslims unmasked in Toronto. The accused were captured in a terrorist sting that authorities say prevented them from carrying out a plot to blow up various sites around Toronto. The name Zaynab Khadr may not be familiar to many, but it is to terrorism analysts. Ms. Khadr, who appeared at the courthouse to advise and support the families of the accused along with well-known *jihadist* preacher Aly Hindy, is a member of what Daniel Pipes has called "Canada's First Family of Terrorism".[41] Her father, Ahmed Sa'id Khadr, was one of Osama bin Laden's closest lieutenants and a top al-Qa'ida financier who received $325,000 from the Canadian government from 1988 to 1997 for his "charitable work" in Afghanistan. He was also involved in the 1995 bombing of the Egyptian embassy in Pakistan, was arrested by Pakistani authorities, and released only through the intervention of then-Canadian Prime Minister Jean-Paul Chretien. Immediately after his release, he enrolled several of his sons in al-Qa'ida-operated terrorist training camps in Afghanistan. He was killed in a gun battle with Pakistani troops in 2003 near the Afghan border, during which his son (Zaynab's brother), Abdul, was also shot and para- lyzed. Abdul and his mother live in Toronto. But Zaynab shouldn't be judged for the sins of her family; she has her own activities to answer for. When she returned to Canada in 2005, Royal Canadian Mounted Police anti-terrorist officers seized her laptop, cell phone, and other documents which proved to be a rich treasure-trove of al-Qa'ida intelligence. In re- sponse, she vehemently denied that the family had any ties to al-Qa'ida and said that the information found in her possession wasn't hers. At 26, Zaynab Khadr is a twice-divorced single mother. One former suitor was none other than a Sudanese terrorist who purchased one of the trucks used in the 1995 Egyptian embassy bombing in Pakistan. She has been accused by Canadian intelligence authorities of formerly helping her father funnel money for various al-Qa'ida activities and for helping her brother, Abdullah, run an al-Qa'ida training camp. Osama Bin Laden was also amongst the guests at her 1999 wedding. And her family lived in Bin Laden's compound in Afghanistan. All that notwithstanding, Khadr insists that her family does not have any al-Qa'ida ties.[42]

When she isn't assisting the families of terrorism suspects, Khadr spends her time pressuring the Canadian government to obtain the release of her youngest brother, Omar, who currently resides at Guantanamo Bay. At 17 years old, he is the youngest person in US custody related to terrorist activities. When he was 15, he was the sole survivor of a battle between non-Afghan al-Qa'ida fighters and the 19th US Special Forces Group at Ayub Kheyl, Afghanistan. After the battle ended, Sergeant First Class Christopher J. Speer, a Special Forces medic, was attending to the

wounded when Omar jumped up from between two mud-brick buildings, throwing a grenade at Sgt. Speer, killing him. Omar was shot twice
(non-fatally), and was found surrounded by a large cache of grenades,
ammunition, and automatic weapons. After his capture, the *National
Post* (one of Canada's largest circulation papers) wrote a glowing portrait
of Omar, including quotes from his doting sister Zaynab, entitled "The
Good Son". The long ordeal of Canada's accommodation of the Khadr
family perfectly illustrates the utter inability or unwillingness for Canada
to deal with their internal terrorist threat. As recent events have shown,
many Canadians are content to let their potentially fatal immigration
policies and lunatic multiculturalism slowly asphyxiate their society. The
suicidal intentions of Canadians would be all well and good if not also
threatening to facilitate homicidal consequences for the United States,
of America, as well, according to author, Patrick Poole.[43]

When Muslims set out to murder Canadians, and Canadians worry
about showing "sensitivity" to their killers, of course Muslims would
believe they are in the ascendancy, and further encouraged to go on the
jihadi warpath. Before the raids that led to the arrest of the 17 Muslim
suspects, came the sensitivity training: Tactical-squad Mounties learned
how to properly handle copies of the Qur'an prior to arresting the 17
terrorism suspects. And that's not all. The RCMP also made sure there
were clean prayer mats on hand for their suspects when they were sent
to jail cells. Then, after everything was wrapped up, authorities met
with a number of Muslim leaders to impress upon them that officers
were pinpointing specific individuals, and not the community as a
whole. "Our officers need to be respectful", said RCMP spokeswoman
Corporal Michele Paradis. "We want to make sure the investigation
is pristine". Stung by allegations of racial-profiling in the past, the
Mounties made sure this time they would protect themselves against
complaints of racism. The RCMP had to consider all kinds of potential
scenarios, such as, what if a target tries to blow himself up during the
course of an arrest? There is a precedent for this: Al-Qa'ida suspects in
the deadly Madrid train bombings blew themselves up in an apartment
rather than be caught by police. So the RCMP consulted the experts.
"They brought in Spanish police, because of what happened in Madrid,
when the guys blew themselves up and everything", one source said.
"They brought in the Spaniards to sort of get their take on what they
did wrong and what they could have done right".[44] The Spaniards did not
have any compunctions of the sort that seem to torment the Canadians, but
they too will learn from experience that if you spare the guilty you will

end up punishing the innocent. Take, for example, Toronto Police Chief Bill Blair. He arrested Muslims for planning and plotting to subvert the country which he is charged with protecting, but, like Tony Blair refraining from uttering the M (Muslim) word, and he was proud of that, stated: "I would remind you that there was not one single reference made by law enforcement to Muslim or the Muslim community". It is unfortunate that "political correctness" is interpreted as the need to cover up clearly relevant issues such as the identity of perpetrators, or would-be perpetrators. If a crime is for instance a civil crime such as spousal murder, then mention of the identity of the perpetrator whether Muslim or other, is clearly irrelevant, and therefore racist. But with the worldwide phenomenon of counteracting the current ever-expanding *tsunami* of terrorism, it is not only in the public interest, but is in fact an essential element of effective counterterrorist strategy. Christie Blatchford's account below provides a more reasoned perspective.

She explains that she drove back from the news conference at the Islamic Foundation of Toronto in the northeastern part of the city, following that dramatic arrest, where so frequent were the bald reassurances that faith and religion had nothing - nothing, you understand - to do with the alleged homegrown terrorist plot recently disclosed by Canadian police and security forces, that for a few minutes afterward, she wondered if perhaps it was a vile lie of the mainstream press that the 17 accused young men were all, well, Muslims. But no, she has checked. They are all Muslims. Barely two days after the nighttime raids that saw 15 of the accused arrested (the remaining two, in Kingston, had already been arrested on gun charges), "the great Canadian self-delusion machine was up and running at full throttle. Why, it's not those young men - with their three tons of ammonium nitrate and all the little doohickeys of the bomb-making trade - who posed the threat. No sir: They, thank you so much, are innocent until proved otherwise and probably innocent and, if convicted, it's because of the justice system. It's those bastard vandals (probably crazed right-wing conservatives, or maybe the Jews) who broke windows at a west-end mosque who stand before us as the greatest danger to Canadian society", she wrote. As Toronto Police Chief Bill Blair, who came to the building to offer his assurances that Muslims and Muslim institutions will be protected, said at one point: "Hatred in any form and certainly in its expression in violence and damage to property will not be tolerated". It is indeed good to be reassured that windows everywhere in Canada's largest city are safe, especially windows in mosques. The war on windows will be won, whatever the cost. "Such is the state of ignoring the biggest, fattest elephant in the room, in this country, that at one point Chief Blair actually bragged - this in answer to a question from the floor - 'I would remind you that there was not one single reference made by law enforcement to Muslim or Muslim community' at the big post-arrest news conference". Indeed, law-enforcement personnel took enormous pains to say just the opposite: The arrested men are from a diverse variety of backgrounds ("They're students, they're employed, they're unemployed" one official said, which is akin to running the gamut from A to oh, C); they come from all parts of Canadian society.... Even before the writer knew for sure that they were all Muslims, she suspected as much from what she saw on the tube, perhaps because she is a trained observer, or perhaps because she simply has eyes. The accused men are mostly young and mostly bearded in the *Taliban* fashion. They have first names like Mohamed, middle names like Mohamed and last names like Mohamed. "Some of their female relatives at the Brampton courthouse, who were there to support them, wore black head-to-toe *burkas* (now there's a sight to gladden the Canadian female heart: homegrown burka-wearers darting about just as they do in Afghanistan), which is not a getup I have ever seen on anyone but Muslim women."[45]

"And from far outside the courthouse," she adds, "if the Muslim question wasn't settled, there were the likes of Scarborough Imam Aly Hindy telling the *Toronto Star* that: 'Because they are young people and they are Muslims, they are saying it is terrorism'". She emphasized that: of course it is a good thing that Chief Blair, who is a wonderful guy, made the trek out to Scarborough; It's even good that he told local Muslims that their places of worship will get extra patrols, as if their mosques were threatened and not they who threatened the rest of the community; and that if anyone wearing traditional beards or the *hijab* is hassled, the police will investigate and treat it seriously. The chief is right that now, she thought, "as in the aftermath of 9/11, that all of us have to be particularly tolerant of one another. And he is also right that there is a distinction, though in my view it may be a distinction without a difference, between terrorism motivated purely by religious zealotry, and terrorism, as was the alleged case with these 17 mostly young men, motivated by political ideology - even if the ideology seems to have been nothing more than the ideology of rage and a religious ideology fuelled by overseas conflicts". She emphasized that it should go without saying - but it never ever can in Canada, but needs to be constantly emphasized - that this whole business is as at least as distressing to the vast majority of good, peaceable

Canadian Muslims as it is to everyone else. But what became clear at that meeting, which was an odd mix of community venting and news conference, is that many of those people who went to the microphone to ask questions, and some of those who answered them from the podium, were far more concerned about a possible anti-Muslim backlash to the arrests than about allegations that seventeen young Toronto-ites were bent on blowing something up in the city. Those same citizens are generally aggravated about Canadian soldiers involved in military actions in Afghanistan, as are Americans in Iraq. Only one question from the floor, this from a young man, really dared to depart from the convention of deploring the supposed coming anti-Muslim backlash and the idea of Muslim as victim. He asked what the imams were doing to ensure that the sort of violent views that allegedly motivated the homegrown terrorists were not allowed to "become entrenched in our community". Sheikh Husain Patel answered him. "It is important we educate our young brothers", he said. He mentioned a series of conflicts overseas, including Iraq and Palestine, then said: "You cannot justify a legal goal by using illegal means. The politics of overseas should not be addressed in a violent manner in Canada". That did not ring in the author's ears as a renunciation of violence per se, but as a renunciation of violence in Canada. She wondered if the answer had satisfied the young man who asked the question, but she lost him in the crowd afterward. But she concluded that "The war on windows, though - that goes well".[46]

But even Canada has begun to awake. In a press release of the Canadian Coalition for Democracies[47], commenting on the controversy around the voting techniques imposed by Muslims in the country, the organization applauded Prime Minister Harper who intervened against *Shari'a* law practices and in favor of the law of the land. "Prime Minister Harper is right to demand that all voters, regardless of their religion, be equal before the ballot box", said Alastair Gordon, CCD President. "Permitting or accommodating the anonymity of a full Muslim veil or *burka* at a polling station undermines the integrity of our electoral system". On March 25, 2007 Marc Mayrand, Canada's Chief Electoral Officer, met with the Directeur General des Elections du Quebec, then consulted with at least two Muslim groups - the Canadian Arab Federation (CAF) and the Canadian Council on American Islamic Relations (CAIR-CAN) to seek their views on women voting with veils. Following these consultations, Mr. Maynard effectively bowed to *shari'a* standards, and agreed to exempt women with face coverings, including full *burkas,* from the accepted practice of photo identification to which all other voters are, and should be, subjected. "The risk is that once such a principle is accepted, we will face radical demands for its consistent application in other areas of our lives", added Gordon. "Having said that photo ID is not required for one religious group for a transaction as important as voting, the same demand for *shari'a* privileging can be made for driver's licenses, passports, airport security passes, and other accepted mechanisms of personal accountability and public safety.... A bedrock principle of our successful democracy is that people are open and identifiable. That openness has helped create the relatively safe, tolerant, pluralistic society that we enjoy today. Cloaked voting clearly breaches this principle. By agreeing to bend our electoral system to *shari'a* demands, we not only undermine our democratic system, but create a precedent that will have potentially deadly consequences if extended into areas of public safety and national security," added Gordon. The Canadian Coalition for Democracies expressed special concern about reports that some public officials' might favour a "solution" calling for fully-veiled voters to raise their veils exclusively to female electoral officials for identification purposes. Any such approach would constitute a grossly unacceptable enforcement of *shari'a* gender sensibilities and inequalities by government personnel and processes. It would undermine gender equality and electoral integrity, and represent a constitutionally unacceptable affront to the human rights of male officials barred from the performance of their duties on this account.

This topic had a genesis which unfolded in the Canadian press in the preceding months. At first, it was taken for granted that "veiled women will be able to vote in the upcoming Quebec by-elections" - and all future federal contests - without showing their faces, based on the decision of Elections Canada. "It applies throughout the country", said spokesman John Enright. "It applies to all federal elections, including by-elections and referendums". But the announcement was deeply divisive in Quebec, where there is both a sizeable Muslim population and heated opposition to this and other types of accommodation - this latter, a touchy word in the province that refers to concessions it might make to its religious and cultural minorities. Premier Jean Charest called the development a "bad decision" and added that the debate had already happened in his province, which banned the practice. "Every person who comes out to exercise their vote must be clearly identified and in my eyes it's as simple as that", he told the Canadian press in Sherbrooke. Federal Transport Minister Lawrence Cannon, a Quebec MP, also criticized the decision. "We feel that it doesn't make any sense. Political correctness has superseded common sense. These are the kinds of things ordinary people don't understand". Liberal leader Stephane Dion, whose party is struggling to build support in the province, also opposed the move. "We do believe that when they are casting a vote in elections, Canadian citizens have a responsibility to fully reveal their identities," Stephane Dion said. "For this reason, we would ask Elections Canada to reconsider its decision, and to require veiled women to unveil their faces to confirm their identities".

Stemming from a bill to amend the Elections Canada Act that was given royal assent in June 2007, the new stipulations use gender-neutral language and focus on "the identification of electors wearing face coverings for religious practices". Under the new regulations, the voter - presumably a woman wearing a *niqab* or *burka*—will need to present a valid piece of identification with a photo and address as well as a back-up document that meets the standards of an authorized list. "This is a new requirement for all voters", Mr Enright said. "We're not singling out one segment of the votership. If she does not have these two documents, she can have her identity vouched for by another voter in the same polling station. Both parties would have to be voters in the same polling division and would be required to make a sworn statement under oath. If these conditions are not met, she would have to show her face. The rules do not apply to provincial contests, which are not governed by Elections Canada". Many groups have already registered their dismay over the decision. "It's part of a greater threat to undermine democratic institutions", said David Harris, a senior fellow at the multifaith, Ottawa-based Canadian Coalition for Democracies. "At some point some of our ostensible freedoms must have limits".[48] When Elections Quebec introduced a similar proposal in March 2007, it was met with vociferous opposition before chief returning officer Marcel Blanchet was forced to retrench. The province's three parties all oppose the idea; Mr Blanchet received threatening phone calls, brought in two personal bodyguards and assigned security officials to survey the building where he worked. Some Quebecers at the time argued that such a move would send the province down a slippery slope of tolerance and set itself up for some bizarre scenarios. Would, for example, someone in a Darth Vader mask be able to vote without identification? "If someone came in wearing a Halloween mask or a Darth Vader mask, they'd be asked to remove it," Mr Enright said. "If they refused to remove it, they would be asked to leave". When asked if a man could vote while wearing a head covering, Mr Enright responded that he would first be asked to provide identification.[49]

Such are the absurdities to which any democratic system which insists on being overly "liberal" can sink, if the current trends in Canada and other democracies are emulated, and are not guided back into the fold of reason.

5

The Land Shifts in Asia

Globalization in general and especially the global dimensions that Islamic terrorism has assumed, compel one to say something about this onslaught of radical Islam against other parts of the world outside the West. Al-Qa'ida presence in practically all Western, Asian and African countries of importance, with the assumed links between them - ideological, financial, organizational and otherwise - directly affect Islam in Europe. One of the mainstays of fundamentalist presence in the Asian continent is Pakistan where there is a dense network of *madrasas,* counting in the thousands (some say 11,000), each of which has a student body of thousands of young Muslims aged between 8 and 20s (altogether some 1.5 million). These students come from western countries where there is a Muslim minority, from Arab and African countries, and from Asian countries like Malaysia, Thailand, China and Russia. It is in Pakistan that the *Taliban* received their Islamic education and then battled the warlords of Afghanistan, taking over power in 1996. In July 2005, and in response to President Bush's urgings, President Musharraf ordered all the 3,500 foreign students (400 among them Americans) to return to their homes, but many elected to stay, and they continue to receive subsidies from their families in the West to pay for their tuition, room and board. The total budget of the *madrasas* is said to match that of the Ministry of Education in Pakistan, and as more requests are filed with the government, thousands more *madrasas* will open, amounting to a truly formidable radical educational establishment that has no match in any other Islamic country. Since the London July 7, 2005 bombings, President Musharraf has indicated that he wants to reform that system which has become a veritable brainwashing machine and a fertile ground for recruiting jihad fighters for international terrorism.[1]

Islam on the March: The Case of Asia

Much of the torment and turmoil in the contemporary world is connected one way or another with Islamic territory, doctrine or politics. Not that Islam as such is necessarily inherently prone to conflict and strife, but many fundamentalist trends therein, from Hizbullah and Hamas in the Middle East, via Bin Laden and his disciples in Afghanistan and elsewhere, to the Abu Sayyaf group in the southern Philippines, have vowed to force their way of thinking via violence. Thus, we see a mounting wave of Muslim fundamentalist groups sweeping vast swathes of the globe, within Islamdom and in countries to which Muslims lay claim, or, are involved in all manner of armed struggle. Examples abound across the world map, especially in the Middle East and Asia: Muslim-related strife in such countries as Pakistan, Afghanistan, Algeria and Egypt; anti-Christian manifestations in Indonesia, Egypt, the Philippines, Sudan, Black Africa and Israel; regional conflicts in the Middle East, Kashmir and Central Asia; Muslim secessionist movements in Chinese Turkestan, the Caucasus, Thailand, the Philippines, Burma and the Middle East; discontent and subversion among Muslim minorities in Western countries and Israel; Muslim regimes imposing re-Islamization of their societies, often amidst strife, in Iran, Afghanistan and the Sudan; and violent Islamic opposition groups in countries where the regimes in place resist such moves, such as Egypt, Jordan and Algeria. Cause for tension is also provided by local and international Muslim terrorist movements operating in and from the Middle East, and in South, East, Central and Southeastern Asia, or worldwide against American, Western and Israeli interests, as in Saudi Arabia, East Africa, Argentina, on European and American soil, and certainly and most visibly in Israel and its neighbouring countries. Lately, illegal immigration of Muslim refugees from North Africa, Iran, Iraq and the rest of the Arab world, to western countries and Australia, and the consequent spill-over of the Arab-Israeli dispute into the Muslim diasporas in the West, have added fuel to the fire of this universal Muslim unrest.

To map out and analyze these worldwide phenomena, and to find out whether they are all causally or organizationally interconnected, one would have to examine the long list of these events over the past two decades or so, attempting to detect the unifying themes which have evolved over time, and the particular circumstances of each cluster of events as they unfold. But such a task is beyond the purview of this chapter, which will focus mainly on the landmass of Asia, especially the troublespots of the central and southeastern parts of the continent, most particularly as they relate to the worldwide wave of Muslim terrorism that also affects the West. However, to get a measure of the themes that concern those countries, as they are affected by the world Islamic movements, it would be instructive to look into a debate in which Abdul Rahman Wahid figured; he is the most famous pragmatic and moderate Muslim leader of Asia who also served as President of Indonesia, and is the founder and leader of the largest Muslim organization in the world, *Nahdat al-'Ulama'*, which counts tens of millions among its membership.

Westerners may derive comfort from believing that there is "moderation" in Islam, but Muslims are not impressed or influenced by such labels. To them, the utility of such terminology lies in its success in deceiving a gullible West. There is basically only one Islam: it abides by the same doctrine and pillars of the faith *(arkan),* and unless its tenets are rejected or reformed, which is very unlikely, it cannot be considered as "moderate" by any stretch of the imagination. That the West prefers to dabble in semantics in order to assuage the fears of its own people is doubly fortunate for the Islamists, for while they self-confidently persist in the pursuance of their doctrine that recognizes no place for other creeds, naive westerners keep inventing distinctions that are not there, and cultivate a Utopia of a "peaceful" Islam that amounts to no more than wishful thinking. On their part, Muslim moderates like former President Wahid of Indonesia, in their effort to claim that a moderate trend in Islam does exist, misrepresent the tenets of Islam to the West in order to escape its castigation. The following acrimonious debate between a traditionalist Muslim (not a radical or extremist) and a Western specialist-scholar, will illustrate the point. The issue was Abdul Rahman, an Afghani Muslim convert to Christianity, who was threatened with death for apostasy in his country. Wahid's repudiation of that verdict on the one hand, and Robert Spencer's counter arguments which expose the insincerity of Wahid on the other, exemplify how difficult it is to conduct a dialogue even between "moderate" Muslims and Western scholars who are qualified to expose their inconsistencies, as they attempt to please the West at the same time as they defend the reputation of their faith; even more difficult is a dialogue with the radicals, who demand a total submission to their way of thinking. Wahid's arguments were laid out in an article in the *Washington Post.*[2]

1. Abdul Rahman, a Muslim convert to Christianity, narrowly escaped the death penalty for apostasy when the Afghan government - acting under

enormous international pressure - sidestepped the issue by ruling that he was insane and unfit to stand trial. This unsatisfactory ruling left unanswered a question of enormous significance: Does Islam truly require the death penalty for apostasy, and, if not, why is there so little freedom of religion in the so-called Muslim world? The Qur'an and the sayings of the prophet Muhammad do not definitively address this issue. In fact, during the early history of Islam, the Agreement of Hudaibiyah between Muhammad and his rivals stipulated that any Muslim who converted out of Islam would be allowed to depart freely to join the non-Muslim community. Nevertheless, throughout much of Islamic history, Muslim governments have embraced an interpretation of Islamic law that imposes the death penalty for apostasy.

2. It is vital that we differentiate between the Qur'an, from which much of the raw material for producing Islamic law is derived, and the law itself. While its revelatory inspiration is divine, Islamic law is man-made and thus subject to human interpretation and revision. For example, in the course of Islamic history, non-Muslims have been allowed to enter Mecca and Medina. Since the time of the caliphs, however, Islamic law has been interpreted to forbid non-Muslims from entering these holy cities. The prohibition against non-Muslims entering Mecca and Medina is thus politically motivated and has no basis in the Qur'an or Islamic law. In the case of Rahman, two key principles of Islamic jurisprudence come into play. First, that every problem should be addressed in accordance with its purpose, namely if a legal ordinance truly protects citizens, then it is valid and may become law. From this perspective, Rahman did not violate any law, Islamic or otherwise. Indeed, he should be protected under Islamic law, rather than threatened with death or imprisonment. The second key principle is that the law is formulated in accordance with circumstances. Not only can Islamic law be changed - it must be changed due to the ever-shifting circumstances of human life. Rather than take at face value assertions by extremists that their interpretation of Islamic law is eternal and unchanging, Muslims and Westerners must reject these false claims and join in the struggle to support a pluralistic and tolerant understanding of Islam.

3. All of humanity, whether Muslim or non-Muslim, is threatened by the forces of Islamist extremism. It is these extremists, masquerading as traditional Muslims, who angrily call for the death of Abdul Rahman or the beheading of Danish cartoonists. Their objective is raw political power and the eventual radicalization of all 1.3 billion Muslims worldwide. Western involvement in what Muslims call this "struggle for the soul of

Islam" is a matter of self-preservation for the West and is critical given the violent tactics and strength of radical elements in Muslim societies world wide. Muslim theologians must revise their understanding of Islamic law, and recognize that punishment for apostasy is merely the legacy of historical circumstances and political calculations stretching back to the early days of Islam. Such punishments run counter to the clear Qur'anic injunction, "Let there be no compulsion in religion" (2:256).

4. People of goodwill of every faith and nation must unite to ensure the triumph of religious freedom and of the "right" understanding of Islam, to avert global catastrophe and spare millions of others the fate of Sudan's great religious and political leader, Mahmoud Muhammad Taha, who was executed on a false charge of apostasy. The millions of victims of "*jihad-ist*" violence in Sudan - whose numbers continue to rise every day - would have been spared if Taha's vision of Islam had triumphed instead of that of the extremists. The greatest challenge facing the contemporary Muslim world is to bring a limited, human understanding of Islamic law into harmony with its divine spirit - in order to reflect God's mercy and compassion, and to bring the blessings of peace, justice and tolerance to a suffering world.

These wonderful lofty ideas and genuine desire to reform Islam, while they sound attractive to western ears, albeit never practiced by any Muslim regime, raise the questions: why was there no attempt to implement them when Wahid was the President of his country; why was Wahid displaced from the presidency of his country; and why is his moderation not heeded in the Islamic world where radicals like Qaradawi today, and Hassan al-Banna and Sayyid Qut'b yesterday, were far more attractive to Muslim opinion than Wahid? Far more worrying, however, is Wahid's attempt to hide aspects of Islam that he certainly knows very well, while he exposes to western eyes only the "moderate" facets of his faith. This demonstrates once again that while there are moderate Muslims, they are drowned in an environment that does not permit the rise and growth of a reformed, modern and moderate Islam. This is a summary of what Robert Spencer, a Western scholar of Islam, has undertaken to do, by attacking item by item, Wahid's contentions on the pages of *FrontPage Magazine*.[3] He argued that:

1. Despite the enthusiasm that greeted Wahid's piece, it was not in fact the heartening indication of Islamic moderation that many took it to be; for while it is easy to convince Westerners who know nothing of Islam that

Islam is peaceful, it is ultimately a fruitless exercise to do so. Spencer counseled Wahid not to spend his time writing articles in Western media outlets, but convincing the *mujahideen*. His point is that if moderates' moderation won't convince Muslims, what's the point of it? To make non-Muslims feel better?

2. Reform isn't accomplished by deception or self-deception. Reform is accomplished by acknowledging the problem and coming up with ways to deal with it. So Wahid must confront the specific Qur'anic passages, *Hadith* passages, examples from the life of Muhammad, and rulings of the *madhahib* (Schools of law in Sunnite Islam) that the *mujahideen* use to recruit and motivate Muslims to commit violence.

3. The Qur'an and the sayings of the Prophet Muhammad do not exhaustively address this issue. Throughout much of Islamic history, Muslim governments have embraced an interpretation of Islamic law that imposes the death penalty for apostasy. Wahid ignores, of course, evidence that both the Qur'an and Muhammad do address this issue. The Scripture (4:89) states: "They but wish that ye should reject Faith, as they do, and thus be on the same footing (as they): but take not friends from their ranks until they flee in the way of Allah (from what is forbidden). But if they turn renegades, seize them and slay them wherever ye find them; and (in any case) take no friends or helpers from their ranks...."

4. Wahid says that it is vital that we differentiate between the Qu'ran, from which much of the raw material for producing Islamic law is derived, and the law itself, because while its revelatory inspiration is divine, Islamic law is man-made and thus subject to human interpretation and revision. But in practice, it is the text that prevails.

5. According to Wahid, in the case of Rahman, two key principles of Islamic jurisprudence come into play. First, the question of "Every problem should be addressed in accordance with its purpose", namely if a legal ordinance truly protects citizens, then it is valid and may become law. From this perspective, Rahman did not violate any law, Islamic or otherwise. Indeed, he should be protected under Islamic law, rather than threatened with death or imprisonment. The second key principle is "The law is formulated in accordance with circumstances", which means not only can Islamic law be changed - it must be changed due to the ever-shifting circumstances of human life. This is great, says Spence, except that this rule is not absolute, and no Muslim would take it to be so.

Spencer also reproaches Wahid that while he was saying that all of humanity, whether Muslim or non-Muslim, is threatened by the forces of Islamist extremism, it is these very extremists, masquerading as traditional Muslims, who angrily call for the death of Abdul Rahman or the beheading of Danish cartoonists. Again Spencer applauded Wahid but challenged him to prove that traditionalism is indeed a masquerade: "Show us the traditional Islam that rejects their position. Claiming that the Qur'an and Muhammad don't say what they say isn't enough".

Spencer agrees that Muslim theologians must revise their understanding of Islamic law, and recognize that punishment for apostasy is merely the legacy of historical circumstances and political calculations stretching back to the early days of Islam. The greatest challenge facing the contemporary Muslim world was identified by Wahid as "bringing our limited, human understanding of Islamic law into harmony with its divine spirit - in order to reflect God's mercy and compassion, and to bring the blessings of peace, justice and tolerance to a suffering world". But Spencer wondered if that last sentence is a veiled statement of Islamic supremacism. After all, the *mujahideen* are fighting to impose *Shari'a* on the world, a struggle which they envision as bringing peace, justice and tolerance to the world.

The Timeless and Ubiquitous Ideology of Jihad

Earlier chapters have detailed manifestations of Muslim terrorism in Western countries which exemplify the realization of actions of *Jihad* geared to transform those societies and submit them to its rule. All the more so in the land mass of Asia which has come to encompass nearly two-thirds of all world Muslims (almost a billion out of 1.5 billion). Almost half of them are concentrated in the Indian sub-continent (150 million in each of India, Pakistan and Bangladesh, over 20 million in Afghanistan, and also those Muslim minorities of Nepal and Burma). The rest are split between Indonesia, the largest Muslim country with over 200 million, the 25 million Malay Muslims of Malaysia, the Philippines and Thailand, the 30 million of China, the 35 million of Central Asia and the Caucasus, and the 30 million of the Russian Federation.

The present wave of revivalist Islam in Asia is connected to, fed by and in turn feeds into the mood of *jihad* which pervades many Muslim countries and societies worldwide. This *jihad*, manipulated by charismatic and militant clerics such as Sheikh Yassin (the famous, now deceased Hamas leader), Sheikh Nasrallah (Hizbullah) or Osama Bin Laden in Afghanistan, is particularly directed against the United States, as the arch-representative of the West. It vents, in an explosive fashion, an accumulated rage which has its roots not only in the perceived Western domination of the world and the corruptive effect it has had on Muslim youth everywhere by its pop culture, consumerism and permissiveness, but especially by the fact that Muslim societies, unlike the economic giants of Asia, have remained haplessly trailing behind in both political and economic development, while the hated West has been strengthening its hold on the world through globalization. Therefore, the return to Islam by re-Islamization of society and imposition of the *shari'a* where there is a Muslim majority, accompanied by the embracing of Islamic politics of confrontation with the West, have been seen by these circles as the panacea to disengage from their spiral of decay and to chart new paths for modernity-cum-Islam, whether independently of the West, or even in collision with it.

Bin Laden, who has made it his holy duty to eradicate any American presence from all Muslim countries, also wants to replace the corrupt and autocratic regimes in place - those mistakenly deemed as "moderate" by the West - by Muslim radical governments, the likes of which have taken power in Iran, Afghanistan and the Sudan in recent years. For that purpose, Bin Laden and his followers and peers not only subvert the existing regimes throughout Islamdom, but also demand the physical elimination of Americans (civilian and military alike) wherever they can be found. *Newsweek International*[4] reports that a fundamentalist cell in Chechnya has posted on the Internet a map of the world which will become entirely Muslim within a century. Naturally, such an enterprise can be achieved only when victory is won on both the domestic and external fronts.

On their way to victory, the militant groups are cultivated and aided by the three Muslim fundamentalist regimes mentioned above (and Saudi Arabia). The latter provides a living proof that Islamic regimes are feasible and workable in the modern world, and can wield considerable influence in world affairs. Those regimes support Muslim radicals elsewhere to achieve the same: Iran sustains the Hamas, the Hizbullah, the Bosnian Muslims and the Kosovo Liberation Army; Sudan provides training grounds and launching pads for activists against the Egyptian and other African regimes; Saudi Arabia supplies funds to Muslim activists throughout Africa, Asia and Europe; and Afghanistan turns its attention to the former Soviet Central Asia, notably to the Islamists of Tajikistan and Chinese Turkestan. Iran, by far the most powerful and most devoted to the cause of Muslim radicalism, not only often, finances terror activities, but also convenes meetings of the Terrorist International in Tehran in order to strengthen the front which rejects any reconciliation with the

US (and Israel), and which promotes subversion of pro-Western regimes in other Muslim countries.

For these fundamentalists Islam is not just *one* of the revealed religions, but is the only valid faith which must be imposed upon all of Allah's creatures, peacefully through submission if possible, forcefully through *jihad* if necessary. Indeed, in spite of the oft-voiced complaint by other Muslims who do not follow this line of logic, that the militants have been "misusing", "abusing" or "manipulating" *"real"* Islam, the worldwide conflicts in the name of Islam, and the visible successes that the Islamists have registered, make the radicals far more credible in the eyes of the Muslim masses than their quietist adversaries. The fervor of *jihad* is also fueled by the ongoing conflicts within Islamic lands or against them, (Bosnia, Kosovo, Israel, Chechnia, Kashmir, Central Asia, the Philippines, the Moluccas, Chinese Turkestan), where *jihad* is used as a mobilizing and rallying symbol against the perceived non-Muslim occupiers, oppressors and exploiters.

The Spatial Muslim Upheaval in Asia

Many issues deserve to be tackled in the context of the Muslim upheaval in Asia: the question of Islam's encounter with other established religions and the notion of tolerance in a pluralistic society; Muslim-majority states (Pakistan, Afghanistan, Bangladesh, Central Asia and Indonesia) as against Muslim-minorities (in China, Thailand, India, Nepal etc.); the various Islamic groups which have opted for either the violent quick fix of Islam here and now, versus the long haul re-Islamization by consensual means. And what about the link between democratization and Islamization - are they mutually compatible or exclusive? Which raises the questions as to what is the source of political legitimacy: the sovereignty of the people or the rule of Allah and His Scripture? And what about autocratic regimes leaning on the military (Pakistan, Suharto's Indonesia until recently) or Muslim autocracies based on the former Communist regimes in Central Asia. There are even valiant attempts to democratize (in Indonesia and Afghanistan). The great question also imposes itself as to whether all these movements are examples of separate and independent local manifestations of Islam, or whether they are inter-connected. For example, what is the unifying role of the "Afghans", those volunteer Arab veterans of the Afghan war who returned to their home countries radicalized and battle-hardened, where they are now stirring unrest.

In view of the limited purview of this chapter, those major issues have to be left for other publishing opportunities. The focus here is mainly on the Muslim upheaval in the Asian locale, albeit that we shall address some aspects of the questions posed above as we proceed. In the Indian subcontinent it is not only the perennial and much-publicized problem of Kashmir which stands out as an example of Muslim manipulation in a political and military confrontation, but also the equally acute issue of the large Muslim minority in the state of India (close to 150 million), the unrest caused by fundamentalist groups in Pakistan and Bangladesh, and the threatening proximity of Afghanistan.

The Muslim minority in India is doubly marginalized by the fact that it once belonged and was identified with the ruling splendor of the Mughal Empire that is no more, and also by its choice to remain a tolerated population in Hindu India, rather than adopt the decision to move to the newly-established Muslim state of Pakistan when partition became inevitable. Whether they did well to stay in place in their ancestral land and not join the other *Muhajirun* (migrants) who had hurriedly flocked to Pakistan, remains a matter of divided opinion. Be that as it may, an enormous Muslim community of this size, with its kin across a hostile border, cannot but engender contradictory feelings of loyalty to their country and their people. Occasional eruptions of inter-communal and interfaith strife between the Muslims and the predominant host cultures of India exacerbate the precarious balance between the parties.

India's rehabilitation of its relations with the US and its accelerated economic growth, directly reflect on its tenacity on the Kashmir front, especially in light of China's indication that it is willing to cooperate with Delhi about problems of separatist forces and terrorism as in India's Islamic problem, where they often coexist. This policy might shift China's regional balance away from Muslim Pakistan and closer to India's Muslim concerns, in spite of Beijing's assurances to the contrary. For the common fear evinced by India and China from restive Muslim minorities (in Kahsmir and East Turkestan respectively) might plaster over the suspicions entertained heretofore between them as regards their strategic interests and objectives. Both India and China's huge pace of economic development which make them petroleum thirsty, has compelled them to align themselves with radical Iran, one of their biggest prospective suppliers of oil and gas, despite leadership by Tehran of Muslim fundamentalists elsewhere.

At the same time, however, improving economic and strategic relations between India and ASEAN (some of whose members are Muslim), based on their shared suspicion towards China, might tilt the balance towards collaboration with Muslim countries thereby hoping to obtain the silent consent of these countries to any firm Indian policy towards its Muslims, rather than throwing in its lot with the Chinese who outright oppress their rebellious Muslims in Xinjiang. A step in this direction was executed in recent years when Wahid's Indonesia announced its support for India's policies towards religious fundamentalism and secession.

Democratic and economically and strategically emerging India can become more and more attractive to prospective partners in Southeast Asia and even to China, at a time when Pakistan is unstable, subject to military rule, the home and supplier of the radical graduates of its *madrasas,* and viewed as the supporter and sustainer of the trouble-making Muslims of Kashmir. Southeast Asian countries, while edging slowly towards India, are also aware of their commonality of interests with Delhi in containing their domestic Islamic fundamentalism which not only discredits them in the eyes of the West, due to anti-Christian abuses in East Timor, the Moluccas, Irinjaya, Java proper and the southern Philippines (see below), but also, and even more significantly, has had a destabilizing effect on the domestic politics of the Filipino and Indonesian archipelagoes, at a time when Wahid's hold on power seemed fragile and uncertain until his ultimate downfall and replacement by Megawati whose fortunes were not much more enviable, until the more democratized and seemingly stable new regime took power in 2006 and committed itself to the battle against terrorism.

In Central and Eastern Asia, the rampages of the *Taliban* in Afghanistan and the unrest of the Uighurs in Eastern Turkestan are closely watched by their Asian neighbors as potential threats, and even more as this external nationalism reverberates within and impacts upon their own countries. The active support and shelter given to Bin Laden by the Kabul regime, until its own demise, as well as the ideological and training sustenance they lent to the *Islamikaze*[5] groups currently based there, have turned Central Asia into one of the main centers of Islamic violent radicalism in the world. Moreover, the battle going on in Central Asia, between Turkey and Iran, and Iran and the Arabs, for the souls and future orientation of the populations of those former Soviet republics, has produced some odd bed-fellows whose common objective is either to push the entire area to Muslim fundamentalism, Iran and *Taliban* style, or to steer it towards what was the pro-Western Turkish model. The latter has been fostered by the US, Turkey, Israel and the former Communist rulers still in place, and aims at economic development in the erroneous belief that they can thereby scuttle Muslim radicalization. But since 2002, the ruling Islamic party in Ankara has been veering away from the US, and there is no telling what its domestic unrest and constitutional crisis might engender. The early elections declared in the summer of 2007, against the background of the constitutional crisis engendered by the confrontation between the Islamist government backed by Parliament on the one hand, and the secularist alliance of the President and the military on the other, produced a resounding victory for PM Erdogan's party. Moreover, the election of Abdallah Ghul, the second-in-command of the Islamists, as the new President, has tipped the balance in the Islamists' favor, for now.

The emerging paradox is therefore that, like in other areas of the Islamic world, the West and its moderate satellites find themselves supporting oppressive and undemocratic, but seemingly stable regimes for fear that democracy might boomerang and give rise to Muslim fundamentalism, as the Algerian scenario of 1991/2 has clearly demonstrated. Conversely, support for the existing regimes would, it is hoped, generate the kind of economic growth and prosperity, with Western investment in the energy industry, Israeli investment in advanced agriculture, and Turkish overseeing of the return of the Turkic heritage, to ensure a steady development towards the Ankara model of moderate Islam. It is unclear, however, whether and for how long this pattern could be maintained, in view of the resounding collapse of similar pro-Western models in monarchical Iran in 1979, in Western-supported rebellious Afghanistan in 1996, and the current imminent dangers to the same in Egypt, Jordan and elsewhere in the Islamic world.

This Muslim-Turkic unrest extends also into Chinese Turkestan. Indeed since the end of the 1980s, the Chinese regime, under the supreme guidance of Deng Xiaoping, has seemingly relaxed its minority policy so as to make any social unrest unwarranted. However, that policy opened the door to widespread violence in practically all areas of Xinjiang, the northwest and the far west of China. Admittedly, some of the violence was triggered by printed insults of the Muslims, but it escalated after the military intervention of the People's Liberation Army, as in Xining in the Fall of 1993. In some areas, as in Kashgar, *Islamikaze* bombing was perpetrated (October, 1993), and the ominous war cries of *jihad*, associated with a local "Hizbullah" (Party of Allah), were heard.

This whole series of manifestations of Muslim violence began in 1989 with what has come to be known as the "Chinese Rushdie Affair", when multitudes of Muslims, first in Beijing and then elsewhere, went out to the streets to demonstrate against the blasphemous depiction of their faith by Chinese writers. Initially the Beijing demonstrations by representatives of all Muslim "nationalities" were supported and allowed to be reported by the Chinese authorities. These demonstrations later spilled into Turkestan. By 1990, and certainly thereafter, these sentiments which had at the outset just generated demonstrations, were later woven into a powerful fabric of rebellion, supported by cries of "Free East Turkestan!!" by the Muslim minorities who lived there, notably the Uighurs. Unlike the Beijing demonstrations which were a plea to the authorities to deal with the blasphemous writers, this uprising was directed against the Chinese authorities and was aided from the outside, mainly by the *Mujahideen* of Afghanistan and the adjoining Kirghiz, Tajik and Kazakh Republics. These riots were triggered in an atmosphere which viewed Islam as a victor (in adjoining Afghanistan) and godless Communism (namely the Soviet Union) as the routed enemy. Once the Soviet Communist giant had foundered, the other Communist superpower - China - was eyed as the next target.

Today China is waging a propaganda and security battle to guarantee its control over Xinjiang, its name for the vast province, where its nuclear and space industries dwell, and which is rich in minerals and strategic supplies of oil and gas, vital to the expanding Chinese economy. China claims that Al-Qa'ida has trained more than 1,000 members of the (Uighur) East Turkestan Islamic Movement, classified as a terrorist group by America and the United Nations. The group took its name from the short-lived Republic of East Turkestan that was declared in Xinjiang after the Second World War, then crushed by the communist revolution of 1949. China has persuaded Pakistan and Kazakhstan to hand over captured militants for interrogation, secret trials and execution, a policy that may have fuelled the fundamentalist rage now gripping Pakistan. Chinese security services have also created a pervasive apparatus of informers and deployed new units of black-clad anti-terrorist police to patrol around mosques and markets in the cities of Xinjiang. But the iron-fisted security policy has made more enemies than friends. Extensive travel and interviews in Xinjiang by western journalists has unveiled a society segregated by religion and ethnicity, divided by reciprocal distrust, living in separate sections of tightly policed cities. The same human rights abuses that exist across China - forced labor for peasants, children trafficked to slave as beggars, girls lured into sweatshops - deepen political tensions and turn young men to violence. Western intelligence officers have indicated that the Chinese consistently exaggerated Uighur terrorist links with Al-Qa'ida to exploit any opportunity to strike at their homegrown opponents. Chinese information was unreliable and no western intelligence service has handed back Muslim citizens to China, they said.

One of the officers said the real concern was that Chinese repression was creating recruits for terrorism.[6]

Events of early 2007 have afforded proof that 58 years of Chinese military "occupation" have crushed significant opposition but failed to win loyalty. Officials have confiscated the passports of thousands of Muslims in a crackdown to break the growing influence of militant Islam. Police ordered the Muslims to hand in their passports and told them that the documents would be returned only for travel approved by the authorities. The aim is to stop Chinese Muslims slipping away to join militants in Saudi Arabia, Pakistan and Afghanistan. The decision has inflamed resentment among Muslims preparing to go to Mecca for the annual *hajj* in December. "Bin Laden, *hao*" (good) said one angry Muslim, who had been deprived of his passport. "Saddam, *hao*", "Arafat, *hao*". According to this report, the clash of civilisations resounds today loudest in Kashgar, 2,400 miles west of Beijing, a crossroads of religions, commerce and culture. In January 2007, only 48 miles to the southwest, antiterrorist units raided a training camp in the mountains where the old Silk Road winds into Pakistan, and killed 18 men with the loss of one policeman. The clash was hailed by the state media, which called it a blow to the East Turkestan Islamic Movement. But Chinese residents said the operation was bungled, allowing militants to escape. They made a mess of it and those people are still out there. "We know they have many smuggled weapons", said a retired military officer."[7]

All cars traveling south from Kashgar must have an armed escort along a section of the road through the desert, said a local tour operator. China has invested billions of *yuan* to modernize Kashgar, renovating the square in front of its principal mosque and building new hotels to accommodate backpackers and affluent western tourists. It has also imported thousands of ethnic Han Chinese to populate new apartments, a pattern of mass immigration used across Xinjiang. They dwell effectively segregated from the Muslims, who keep to their old quarters of mud-brick houses, mosques and reeking alleys where freshly killed sheep hang up for sale. The "Communist Party does its best to achieve integration through politics". According to the *Kashgar Daily,* 84% of local members are Uighurs. Good relations are only on the surface, said a Chinese businesswoman. In 1949 the Uighurs were 90% of the population of Xinjiang. Today they account for less than half. It is the classic colonialist model, said Nicholas Bequelin of Human Rights Watch, author of a critical report on Xinjiang. In Urumqi, the industrialized capital city of Xinjiang, there was evidence that repression had united Uighurs with other Muslim ethnic groups such as the Hui, who constitute the mainstay of Islam in China proper. Chinese intelligence woke up late to the fact that Hui Muslims were being financed by extremists from the Middle East. Their clerics, influenced by Saudi Arabia's purist *salafi* doctrine, often fulminate against Israel and the West. The Hui are much more radical than the Uighurs, said Bequelin. Such radicalization is fuelled by injustices endured by many Chinese but all the more potent when suffered by an angry minority. South of Kashgar, an almost medieval system of forced labour, known as the *hasha,* continues to exist on plantations, where local Muslims are ordered to pick almonds and fruit for sale to the thriving markets of China.[8]

The price for the remarkable economic development driven by the government, say the Uighurs, is the slow extinction of their identity. Their children take compulsory Chinese lessons. Teaching in Uighur is banned at the main university. Their fabled literature, poetry and music are fading under the assault of *karaoke* culture. Their history is being rewritten. For western tourists, who come to Xinjiang to roam the ruins of the Silk Road, the Chinese have erected a new museum in Urumqi. It portrays the final Chinese conquest of this harsh territory, first claimed by the Han emperors in the era before Christ. While most of the Hui-Muslim minority is widespread over practically all China proper, thus lacking a specific territory it can claim as its own and use as its base (and therefore impotent to demand secession), Qinghai and Xinjiang, which are closer to the Islamic world and have been drawing support from some of it, have advanced such demands, and violence has been resorted to in pursuance of the secession goal. Thus, due to both the lax policy of the Chinese government, which permits links and visits between its Muslims and the Muslim world, and the pressing interests of the radical elements in Islamdom, more and more outbursts of this sort can be anticipated which may culminate, if the circumstances so allow, in concrete demands for outright secession from China, not unlike the process that brought the Soviet Union to its demise. On the other hand, however, in view of the Unitarian concept of government in China, which has never acknowledged the existence of "federated republics" in its midst (unlike in the Soviet Union), nor tolerated secession (for example as in the unfortunate Tibetan example), it is hard to conceive a China that would sit idly by while its borders are permeated by rebellion and chaos.

Southeast Asia has also been subject to a wave of Muslim fundamentalism of late. In the words of one writer, "religious divisions based on Islam have exacerbated ethnic differences, and some religiously-oriented groups are engaging in violent and extreme acts that pose a potentially serious long-term threat to stability in the region".[9] According to Rubenstein and other scholars, the Islamic radicalization that began in the 1980s has migrated from the Middle East to Asia and now poses a challenge to the new leadership of those countries who had theretofore put their emphasis on economic development.

Under the autocratic Suharto regime in Indonesia (the most populous Muslim country in the world - some 220 million), political Islam was discouraged. But in the chaos that reigned since he was removed (1998), fundamentalists continually attempt to gain a position in the new order. In 1990, Minister Habibie had established under Suharto's aegis the Association of Indonesian Muslim Intellectuals (ICMI), in order to contain Muslim intellectual ferment. This "establishment" organization was, however, criticized by Abdurrahman Wahid, the influential Muslim scholar who later became the President of the state. Since 1996, riots took place in rural Indonesia when Muslim crowds began attacking Christian churches, Buddhist temples and property belonging to the Chinese minority. The combination of xenophobia, imported Middle Eastern Muslim radicalism, economic deprivation and the local political autocracy, raised the specter of Muslim fundamentalism as a viable alternative. Indeed, the violent student riots which brought down Suharto in 1998 were regularly dominated by posters invoking the Khomeini revolution in Iran and the success of the *Taliban* in Afghanistan. In effect the general and presidential elections of 1999 were overshadowed by ten different Muslim groups which brandished Muslim symbols such as the *Ka'ba* in Mecca and the Muslim Crescent, though the main struggle for hegemony was waged between the traditional and modern streams of Islam, namely *Nahdatul Ulama* and the *Muhammadiyah* headed respectively by Wahid and Amien Rais. Wahid emerged as the president due to his alliance with Megawatti Sukarno, that was also ultimately supported by Rais. This signaled a moderation in the government of Indonesia, and a more tolerant and pluralistic policy which veered away from Muslim fundamentalism.

However, the Aceh separatists, a fiercely Muslim group in Sumatra who aspire to a Muslim state, and the eruption of Muslim-Christian clashes in the island of Ambon in the Moluccas, have caused thousands of casualties. In addition, militiamen self-styled as *"Jihad* Army, were discovered training around Jakarta, with the intention of joining their co-religionists in Ambon.[10] Some of them made it and further fed unrest in that island, while other Muslim radicals, including Rais, proceeded to criticize Wahid for his policies of reconciliation and his moderate policy of openness towards Israel. It is possible that as Wahid left power, the mounting sounds of Islamic radicalism that he was able to silence may rise again, temporized as they are by the trends of modernization and the vigorous anti-Islamist measures taken by the new democratic government which committed itself to fight terrorism, in an attempt to wipe out the scary memories of the terrorist acts of Bali and Jakarta.

The other major country of the Malay world - Malaysia - was also rocked by both an equally restive Muslim radicalism and an economic crisis that deepened the Muslim sentiment the radicalism instigated and led by the opposition PAS (Islamic Party of Malaysia) which aspires to establish a Muslim state in the country. This movement has its roots in the Malaysian Youth Movement and the *Dakwah* upsurge of the 1970s which raised Muslim consciousness to become a primary element of Malaysian identity. As a result the Mahatir government, especially since the co-optation of the Muslim student leader Anwar Ibrahim in 1982, was forced to adopt a Muslim policy of its own in order not to appear as lagging behind the Muslim opposition. He hosted the Organization of the Muslim Conference in Kuala Lumpur in 2002, where he lambasted Israel and followed up on his virulent anti-Semitic pronouncements. But at the same time, the government banned any manifestations of Muslim radicalism.

The ousting of popular Vice Premier Ibrahim, who had in the meantime risen through the ranks and threatened Mahatir's primacy (his trial took place in 1998), signaled a turning point in the relations between Government and Muslim opposition. The 1999 elections, after Ibrahim's arrest, saw the PAS emerging as the main opposition to Mahatir's government. Mahatir, who stayed in power mainly due to his Chinese partners who are just as scared of Islamists in power, began to crack down on the Muslim radicals whose mounting popularity after Ibrahim's trumped up conviction began to challenge his hold on power. His hand-picked successor, Badawi, presides over the weakened government's capacity to contain the *Dakwah* and the PAS popular support, but the current strong revival of the economy militates for the moment against instability and chaos, which, given the right circumstances, may come dangerously close to Indonesia's Muslim upheaval and Suharto's demise at the end of the 1990s.

The Muslim Rebellions

If the Indonesian and Malaysian governments have been so far holding their ground in their attempt to partly co-opt Islam and partly to clamp down on its most extreme manifestations, in the countries of Southeast Asia where Islam is in the minority the situation is much more complicated and dangerous due to the protracted armed conflicts involved. This is reflected in the decades-long Muslim insurgencies in Burma, Thailand and the Philippines. While the two former are Buddhist countries where minority Islam's use of violence is mitigated by the background of the tradition of tolerance there, the latter, being Christian, invokes the age-old memories of Christian-Muslim enmity since medieval times until today. Furthermore, while in the Muslim-majority countries, such as Indonesia and Malaysia, the struggle is mainly about the nature of the regime and the souls of the population, in the Muslim-minority countries Muslim secession threatens to break away large swaths of territory from the host-countries and wreak havoc on the concept of national sovereignty as it is currently understood and manifested there.

Invariably, the Muslim rebellions in Burma, Thailand and the Philippines erupted in close proximity to Muslim-majority states (Bangladesh, Malaysia) which have served since the onset of these conflagrations as the foci of indoctrination and assistance, and sometimes as launching pads and countries of refuge. The result is that the Muslim minorities in these restive provinces of non-Muslim countries sometimes entertain irredentist claims in order to connect with the mother countries they aspire to join. It is also noteworthy that since these rebellions are led in well-defined territories where the Muslims predominate, it is relatively easier for them to claim autonomy, independence or secession than if they were spread out and diluted within the majority host-countries, as in the case of the Chinese Hui Muslims. Due to their minority status (4-6% in these cases), they cannot entertain any hope of attaining their goal by direct and open military confrontation, hence their resorting to guerilla warfare.

However, while the Moros of the southern Philippines and the Patani Muslims in southern Thailand have been able to connect to the outside Muslim world and elicit support, the Arakan Muslims of Burma have been much less capable of doing so. The reason lies in the fact that the former are Malay, and through Malaysia and Indonesia, which are relatively prosperous and high profile, they can get their voices heard in ASEAN, the Islamic Conference and other international forums, while the relatively quiescent and low-profile Bangladesh can hardly speak for itself, let alone for the Arakan Muslims. Hence also perhaps the differences between the high aspirations of the former for independence/secession and the latter's resignation to autonomy, if that. These differences have also had an impact on the intensity of warfare: the Moros' battle, and to a lesser extent the Patanis', has sometimes attained the height of a full-fledged war while the Arakans have confined themselves to much lesser activities.[11]

Another facet which affects the different levels of intensity of these respective rebellions is the internal divisions within the rebels' ranks and leaderships, which not only tend to blunt the acuity of their messages but also to generate confusion as to their ultimate goals, and to weaken their causes in consequence. In the Philippines it is the Moro Islamic Liberation Front (MILF) and the Abu Sayyaf (ominously meaning the "Father of the Sword") group which are locked in a bitter armed struggle against the government. The older Moro National Liberation Front (MNLF), led by Nur Misuari, had previously signed a peace agreement with Manila (September, 1996) which was squarely rejected by the other more militant organizations.[12] These latter groups, who have also indulged in plain terrorism, kidnappings and hostage-taking of foreigners, are aided by such militant regimes as Kabul's in terms of weapons, funds, training, and moral and doctrinal support. Both militant groups speak in terms of *jihad* with a view to establishing a fully independent *Shari'a* state over Moro lands. The Abu Sayyaf group, though much smaller than the MILF, also espouses the use of violence against the Christians of Mindanao in order to intimidate them and extirpate them from their domain, this, with the express purpose of bringing about universal Islamic hegemony.

In Thailand, the Malay-Muslim population of the south has been creating chaos since the 1960s in that border area under various names, titles, leaderships and organizations, but all aspiring to a Muslim state around Patani, with or without ultimate attachment to neighboring Malaysia. Contrary to the Philippines, where moderate concessions by the government at least pacified the Misuari faction while incensing the others to more extremism, all political moves of the Thai government towards reconciliation have failed to date to erode the secessionist import of the rebellion, right into the twenty-first century and the new millennium. In the late 1990s the Mahatir government in Malaysia, itself threatened by fundamentalist fervor at home, collaborated in arresting Patani leaders who sought refuge there, and that seemed to allay the Thai government's fears about the persistence of the crisis. The Thai authorities, however, like other governments who suffer from Muslim insurgency, also miscalculated by assuming that economic development might lure the rebels away from warfare. This same logic, which has been voiced in many Western *milieus,* and has wrongly equated Muslim fundamentalism with poverty and under-development, not only has proven wrong in practice (Iran and Saudi Arabia are rich and fundamentalist at the same time), but it is also deemed patronizing and is therefore rejected by the Islamists. It is refuted because it erroneously predicates that for a handful of dollars Muslim radicals would forego their ideological fervor and their warring commitment. In any case the Thai government, like the Egyptian and Jordanian authorities, have stepped up their large-scale campaign of repression, which has shown some promising signs of pacifying the insurgency and violence, but it is not clear for how long.

The rebellion in Burmese Arakan has adopted the much more modest goal of simply attaining freedom of worship in spite of the oppressive regimes that have led Burma since the death of U Nu in the 1960s. The Rohingya Muslims therefore never reached the levels of violence attained by the Moros or the Patanis. To be sure, the Arakan *Mujahideen* at first put the Burmese authorities to the test by engaging in rebellion, but after they were ruthlessly quelled, they retreated into petty border skirmishes on the Bangladesh boundary area, or resorted to faint diplomatic moves seeking to enlist the favors of the international community or the bargaining positions of the Muslim world. Some of the rebels have surrendered in exchange for land or cash grants, or copies of the Qur'an, but those acts do not seem to have made a significant dent in the zeal of the rebellious mainstream.

Consequences

Contrary to what some experts in the West thought, or are still maintaining, the Islamic fundamentalist wave which has swept the world, including Asia, while it may have peaked is far from showing signs of recession. Naturally, each individual Muslim rebellion or discontent may show temporary signs of retreat due to exhaustion, lack of funds, isolation, resolute oppression, or disregard by the outside world, but the general trend is yet to peter out. As against the partial settlement between the Filipino government and the Moros's of Misuari, for example, Abu Sayyaf has emerged, perhaps as a sign of despair, but also as a sure manifestation of more violence, extremism, zeal and cruelty. Similarly, the fast growing Muslim demography in Asia, manifested by both relative and absolute numbers within their majority countries, or as minorities within other host cultures, can only generate more and more confrontations in the years to come, between those minorities who are vying for independence, autonomy or secession, and their authorities who dread such prospects.

Asian Islam has been traditionally much more quiescent than in the core area of the Middle East, not only in the countries where it constitutes the minority but also in the areas where its hundreds of millions have long ago shifted the demographic center of gravity of Islam from the Middle East eastwards. Naturally, eruptions of militant Islam have plagued modern Asian history, as seen in nineteenth-century India and China and in other rebellions in southeast Asia. But those were all local or regional manifestations of unrest that were dealt with on a case by case basis, and were brought to their end by oppression (China) or partition (India), or continue to fester (Kashmir and Xinjiang, Thailand and the Philippines). What characterizes the contemporary eruptions of Muslim fundamentalism in Asia and elsewhere is not only their virulence and seemingly uncompromising platforms, but mainly their instant worldwide reverberations and the international involvement in their cultivation or *denouement.* This is due to the internationalization of the Muslim rebellions themselves either through the direct imprint of countries such as Iran and Afghanistan which lend assistance to them, or the context of terrorism (like hostage taking, the drug trade, or violence against Western interests) which dramatizes and raises international interest as the events unfold.

Whether Asian Muslims can or will revert to their traditional stand of moderation and preference for economic pursuit, or will be further drawn down the abyss of unflinching radicalism, Hizbullah-style, only time will tell. There are indications both ways. Against former President Wahid's inclusive and tolerant style of responsible leadership in Indonesia, which did not hold for long, there are more militant groups that watch for opportunities to overturn his successors, and many of these groups may cause upheaval now that he was removed from power and replaced by a democratically-elected government. Similarly, as against the virulent Muslim separatist movements in Chinese Turkestan, the Philippines and Thailand that emulate the models of Central Asia and the Caucasus, there is the overwhelming presence of those respective national states which will not allow secession to tear them apart and set precedents for further national disintegration.

It remains doubtful, however, that this current wave of radical Islam in Asia can be laid to rest before the ripples of the much more significant fundamentalist current of the core lands of Islam can be quieted and dissipated. Even though the oft-cited *hadith* "seek learning even unto China" has been abused by far-fetched commentaries and pure speculation, it still demarcates, nevertheless, the farthest limits of Muslim expansion. Today, with a Muslim population of over 25 million, divided almost evenly between the Hui, namely the ethnically Sinified Muslims of China Proper, and the Turks (mainly Uighurs, but also tiny Kazakh, Kirghiz and other minorities) in the Chinese northwest and Tibet, Chinese Islam, or Islam in China as some would have it, constitutes the core of Muslim presence in East Asia. The other countries of East Asia, to wit Japan and Korea, have been home to Muslim minorities only in recent decades, and most of them are not native or converted Muslims but rather members of foreign Muslim communities of diplomats and traders who have settled or, more often, have been posted provisionally there. For those who count Taiwan as a separate entity, one may also take notice of the small, (a few tens of thousands) but thriving Muslim community, which derives from Mainland Islam, immigrating to the Island in 1949 together with military forces and populations accompanying Chiang Kai shek and his retinue into exile.

Today, due to the unrest by the Uighurs of Xinjiang, aided by their exiled kin in the West or in the adjoining former Soviet Muslim republics of Central Asia, Islam in those far-flung confines of the world has taken center-stage, not only for its own sake and because of the challenge it poses to the jealously Unitarian Chinese state, but also when viewed in the context of the Muslim fundamentalist wave that has rocked much of Asia. Indeed, the terms *Jihad* and *Hizbullah* (Party of God), and occasional acts of terror which have been resorted to in northwest China of late, are too reminiscent of Middle Eastern violence, of the Bin Laden activities in Southern and Central Asia, and elsewhere, or of the Abu Sayyaf "exploits" in the Philippines, and the rampages of some Muslim radical groups in the Malay world of Southeast Asia which are generally ignored or glossed over.

In view of the basic demand of Islam that its followers should live under Muslim regimes, difficult problems are posed by the very idea of any Muslim minority living in non-Muslim lands, as is certainly the case with China (unlike the Muslims of South, Southeast and Central Asia who constitute majorities in their respective countries). We are not only talking about majority-minority and host culture-guest culture relationships, but also about some basic requirements short of which a Muslim minority may rebel against the ruling government and even try to secede from it. This issue, which has repeatedly recurred in the history of Muslim minorities throughout the world, not least of which were the bloody secessionist rebellions in nineteenth-century China, acquires more acuity in China at the present time due to the extraordinary convergence of several major factors:

1. Chinese society and culture, which has a long tradition of assimilating foreign cultures, had to contend in this case with a self-confident guest culture which, with a vast hinterland of Islam outside the confines of China, hardly lends itself to ready acculturation;

2. Chinese Communism, which has until recently been strictly anti-religious, has been moderating of late, creating a more accommodating environment for religious, if not yet political, pluralism;

3. The growing interest of the Islamic core in the minorities of the periphery, partly due to the current revival of Islam, has raised the feasibility of Islamic renewal in the remote fringes of the Islamic world;

4. The proximity to Chinese territory of the newly independent former Soviet Muslim republics, some of whose kin (e.g. Kazakhs and Kirghiz) live in China, has made the latter permeable to ethnic-nationalist influences from the outside; and

5. The universal Muslim turmoil leaves its traces everywhere Islam is found, even in an Islamic minority, for perceived successes in one part of the globe are bound to inspire others to try their luck too. In this regard, the achievements of the Muslim minorities in the West are bound to be copied by other Muslim minorities in Asia, especially given that some of the leaders of this Muslim upheaval are located nearby in Pakistan and Afghanistan.

Summary
Muslim Rewriting of the Past and Charting of the Future

Amazingly for a culture that systematically aggrandizes itself and denigrates its rivals, denying any wrongdoing and imputing all evil of the world to the West in general and America and Israel in particular, open admission of its own violence, conquests and forceful spreading of Islam is something quite novel in the modern world where it has consistently tried to pose as the eternal victim of others. In this culture, where the victorious future of Islam is a matter of course, it is the past that is given to being rewritten and readjusted to fit the changing image that Islam has of its rivals. A prominent Saudi cleric, Sheikh Ahmed al Qubeisi, who was interviewed on the new Saudi Channel *al-Risalah* (the Message), which purported to promote moderation and project a positive image of Islamic "tolerance", accused the US of destroying, killing, occupying, plundering and colonizing the world in order to spread its ideas of democracy. But his stunning statement followed:

> The West's conflict with Islam and the Muslims is eternal, a pre-ordained destiny that cannot be avoided until the Day of Judgment.... The means used by America to spread democracy.... *are the same used by Islam* (my emphasis) when it spread monotheism..., at the time when idols and people were worshipped. It is one and the same. What was said there is said here. If that was correct, then this is correct. If that was a mistake then this is a mistake. In Islam jihad is conducted to spread its principles, justice and views. This is exactly what America is doing today when it spreads democracy.... The terms violence or jihad, or you would call it aggression or colonialism, mean that you take control of the resources of others, out of economic or political greed. On the other hand, Islam does this (my emphasis), to bring people to worship Allah and to establish justice among all people.[1]

It is hard to know from the text whether the venerable Sheikh sought to justify Islam's past and present deeds in terms of what America does, or the other way round. One thing is clear, however, namely that what America does, or is perceived as doing, will certainly serve as a precedent and model for what Islam might do in the future. As far as proselytizing by Islam in the modern world, especially in Europe where it has taken the most far-reaching *elan* this poses the ideological basis for further proselytism. The foundation is not only moral, that is to spread the word of Allah and to rally as many people as possible to its Call *(da'wa),* but anything done to that end is *a priori* justified both by the Muslim historical precedent which has had a sweeping success and by the counterexample offered by America today. For Muslims, it is obviously a much more worthy cause to convert people to Islam and to spread the word of Islam among Unbelievers, in comparison with what the Americans do to promulgate democracy - this latter, being the antithesis of Islam inasmuch as it subtracts sovereignty from Allah and accords it to humans. We have seen that in the attempt to calm the mood following the Cartoon rift between Islam and the West, representatives of Arab and Danish student organizations met in a "dialogue", which was covered live by *al-Jazeera,* an indication of the Arab public interest in the debate. While the Danes were apologizing and clearly on the defensive for an offense they did not commit, the Arab students aggressively and shamelessly endeavored to rewrite history, state "facts" that have no substance and assert their "right" to be "understood" even in the face of their actual violence, all the while playing on the unjustified sense of guilt that the hapless Danes brought to the debate. The end result was that far from cleansing the air and opening new avenues of dialogue, it became evident that dialogue could not profitably continue as the Muslims commandeered the moral high-ground, distorting their history to appear benevolent. Instead of mending fences with the West and apologizing for the abuses against freedom of speech and the violence used against Western institutions during the cartoon controversy, they unequivocally claimed victimhood, heaping blame on the US in an attempt to drive a wedge within the Western alliance and alienate the Europeans from America.

The Arab Students Union Chair, Ahmed al-Shater, started off by denying the link between Islam and terrorism, notwithstanding the fact that most acts of terrorism today are Muslim-perpetrated or Muslim related, and accusing "Imperialism and Zionism" of smearing Islam with such allegations. He claimed that even in times of war it is "forbidden to uproot a tree, to kill a woman, to kill a child, destroy wells…. It is forbidden to harm human life, to destroy a church, to attack a religious belief. He also asserted that America was the "leader of international terrorism", together with Zionism and Imperialism, because they "kill children in Palestine and Iraq, destroy schools, churches and mosques, violate our honor, rape women and slit open the stomachs of pregnant women"[2]….

These words of blanket propaganda, which do not consider evidence as necessary to back facts or claims, are repeated throughout the Islamic world, with no solid basis in reality, much less in history. It is instructive to read Muslim theologians who sanction *jihad* and prescribe how enemy women and children are to be taken prisoner and enslaved and the men massacred.[3] Indeed, it is high time that Muslims acknowledge the multitudes of women and children murdered on September 11 in New York, in Bali, Indonesia, in Iraq and in Palestine by Muslims who act against other Muslims, and against westerners in London, Madrid and the streets of Israel. The problem is that even when students follow the news, they deny what they see and conveniently forget about the countless churches that are being burned every day in Nigeria, Indonesia, Kosovo and Egypt. This is hardly a sign of "respect for other religions" that they so vehemently claim for themselves. Conversely, when al-Shater (ironically meaning "the smart one") speaks about "slitting the stomachs of pregnant women", he does not produce one single evidence of one single case anywhere done by non-Muslims to Muslim women in modern times, while the record is full of such atrocities occurring daily in Iraq, Algeria and other places where Muslims are involved in conflict. The conclusion is three-fold: one, that Muslims rewrite their history at their ease, as needed to serve their domestic and international propaganda, while abnegating all concern for intellectual integrity; secondly, when the Muslims hurl unfounded accusations at their opponents, they thereby reveal their own moral standards insofar as they imagine what their enemy must be doing, based on what they would themselves do in such situations; and thirdly, they have learned that repetition of horror stories turns their own public into firm believers in its veracity and provokes their uninformed western interlocutors to feel an uneasiness which translates into guilt regarding their perceived "sins of omission" towards these "victimized" groups, all of this accompanied by a more empathic "understanding" towards the story tellers.

Muslim Lessons and Blueprint for the Future

In view of their understanding of the present state of affairs, Muslim fundamentalists have drawn several lessons, and prepared a blueprint for the confrontation with the West, which in its gradually emerging details has proven quite popular with the masses of Muslims in general, who are in no mood for compromise or "understanding". The feeling of Allah's blessing on their venture has been so deeply rooted in their hearts that they sense no fatigue, fear or recoil from implementing their plan, even if, or precisely because, there seem to be difficulties and obstacles. For

Allah had tested in the past many of His followers, and he ultimately ensured their victory, as one of His many names (al-Nasser, the Victorious) indicates. Victory is sought, and nothing less. Those Muslims who wish to confront the West are equipped with the requisite faith, zeal and enthusiasm as the acronym of *Hamas* (The Islamic Resistance Movement) indicates; are boundlessly devoted to Allah, as their various Hizbullah (Party of God) groups profess; are determined to pursue their *da'wa* (Mission, Call) the world over, this mission lending its name to many of their organizations; are intent to wage a merciless *jihad* (Holy War) if their "peaceful" message demanding surrender is not heeded by their enemies as evidenced by their recurrent attacks against America and Israel, and as the names of many of their associations ("Islamic *Jihad*") remind us; and lastly many of them are coordinated by the main base (= *al-Qa'ida*), physical and spiritual, that trains candidates for *Islamikaze*, finances their operations, plans their schemes and initiates the time and place of their spectacular strikes. The main components of this blueprint can be summarized as follows:

1. The West must be defeated, or at least weakened, frightened and put on the defensive. For not only does the West corrupt the Muslim world with its debauchery, innate corruption, alliances with certain Muslim countries and its value-less societies, but by its posing a luring alternative to young Muslims; with its permissive way of dress, co-ed schools, music, pornography, mixed dancing and frolicking, alcohol, technology and Western movies, it threatens the future generation of Muslims. Naturally, the fundamentalists, with the acquiescent silent support of many conservative Muslims, dread the prospect of their societies slipping from under their grip and supervision; therefore they enlist for their endeavor any Allah-fearing Muslim, who though not necessarily of their affiliation, is concerned, like them, about the rapid drift of the young towards modernity and the West.

2. A first step towards the goal of defeating the West is to cultivate the rift between pro-Arab, pro-Muslim Europe, on the one hand, and "Zionist-controlled America", on the other. Thus, while both belong to the evil West, it is imperative to go easy on Europe at this time, due to its assistance, both directly to the Muslim world, and indirectly by diminishing America's power and somehow keeping it in check. This policy has proven a success for the time being, inasmuch as the European Council has been openly favoring the Palestinians over the Israelis in spite of US misgivings, while the Muslims have succeeded in enlisting the Europeans to their side

in the Balkans (Bosnia, then Kosovo, then Macedonia). The Muslims have even managed to engage the US and its forces in implementing jointly with NATO the European-Muslim design in the Balkans (Bosnia, Kosovo and Macedonia).

3. Europe's turn will come after America is driven out of its hegemonic status in the world and Israel is eliminated. Muslim fundamentalists speak about their own *reconquista* in Europe, first of the territories that used to be under Muslim rule in the Iberian Peninsula (what they call Andalusia), southern France and Sicily and then the rest of the continent. The first signs of those ambitions have already begun to emerge in speech and in writing, as demonstrated earlier in this book. A special awareness of this turn of events has been evident among North-African immigrants into Europe, legal and illegal, who are aware of the historical reversal that is under way. Already in the 1980s, former Gaullist French Prime Minister, Michel Debre, who was made aware of the school curricula in Algeria, decried across a first page of a Parisian daily: "The Danger Comes From the South", with little response or concern evinced by his fellow French or Europeans. Indications of such schemes, indeed a foretaste of them, dawned on the Europeans on the morrow of 11 September, after which several major Islamic terrorist strikes were foiled in Paris, Strasbourg and Brussels. Al-Qa'ida bases and undercover lodges exist in practically all European capitals, and in due course they will be activated. Part and parcel of preparing for the showdown in Europe has been both testing the grounds in public opinion for the Muslim *reconquista,* first of the Spanish vestiges of their colonial rule in North-Africa (Ceuta and Melilla) and some disputed islands in the Mediterranean; and increasing the numbers of Muslims who migrate to Europe - legally if possible, and illegally if necessary, in order to hasten their taking up political rights individually, and then begin to claim cultural and political group rights. The upward of 30 million Muslims of Europe today, varying from 5 to over 10% of the population of each country, have already made an impact in domestic politics in their countries of shelter, both due to their continuing immigration, and even more importantly by reason of their high birth rate, which drives up the proportionate numbers of Muslim children, this all reinforced by the family "re-unification" schemes which bring entire clans in the wake of the "refugees".

4. Jews, and by inference Israel and Zionism, have to be eliminated - as Bin Laden, Iran, the Hamas and the Hizbullah have vowed. They are accused of having invaded the lands of the Muslims in Palestine and established their hated Zionist state, which in effect tore off a valuable piece of

Dar al-Islam (The House of Islam) and turned it into *Dar-al-Harb* (The House of War), which requires *jihad* for retrieval. The Jews constitute a Western salient in the midst of Islamic society which they intend to corrupt and undermine from within. The Jews stand accused of "desecrating" the holy places of Islam in Jerusalem with a view to insulting even moderate Muslims. And, most dangerous of all, they act as the American agent in the Middle East, hence their close links to Washington, to an extent that makes it hard to determine who is subservient to whom. For all these reasons Jews are targets not only in their state - Israel - but worldwide, as the frequent attacks against them, throughout their world diasporas, since October 2000, have demonstrated.

5. And above all the United States of America, which by its military and economic power not only dominates the West and leads it, but also attempts to battle Islam into submission, protects Israel and serves its purposes, and produces and disseminates the decadent sub-culture that arouses the wrath of Islam. The United States is deemed to be the first model of imitation for youth all over the world, including Muslims, and this circumstance is purported to be the reason for the ills of the world. If America, the Great Satan, as another fundamentalist, Khomeini, called it, cannot be reduced to submission, at least it can be battered, threatened, humiliated and weakened, to the extent that it will no longer be able to protect its citizens and its interests around the world. The rationale and purpose behind this outlook is so that its many allies, primarily Israel, Europe and the illegitimate Muslim rulers it sustains, would no longer trust the US and depend on it. America is also singled out by the Islamists for being the only power that can, and is willing, to block effectively the fulfillment of their schemes. Hence the hatred of America, first and foremost, that is decried by the slogans and propaganda statements of the fundamentalists, and also by the massive acts of terror against the United States.

6. And finally, pending the anticipated Muslim victory, much long-term groundwork is required, which the Muslim radicals wholeheartedly support and initiate, and even push Muslim governments and individuals to help finance. The list is long: recruiting new converts in the West; lending financial support to families of the *Islamikaze* martyrs; raising money, either from "charitable organizations" in the West itself, to be used against it, or from donor states and individuals (Saudi Arabia and Bin Laden, for example); erecting mosques, Islamic Centers and *madrasas,* in Washington, Paris, Stockholm, and London, and elsewhere in those unsuspecting countries, ostensibly for the Muslim populations of the West,

but diverting their use to conversion programs, indoctrination and the diffusion of hate propaganda, and recruitment of trainees for *Islamikaze* purposes; strengthening Islamic education in already Muslim countries in the periphery, such as Indonesia, South and Central Asia, and raising Muslim consciousness among the Muslim minorities in Nepal, Thailand, Israel, India, Europe and America. It is the fruit of such endeavors which ripened the *Taliban* in the *madrasas* of Pakistan, Shi'ite fanatics in the religious schools of Qum in Iran, the Hizbullah in the Lebanese fields of opium, the *Islamikaze* terrorists in Afghanistan, and the mosques of Europe and America, from whence emerged the planners and executors of 11 September.

Given this blueprint - all of which has been set out in speech and document by radical Muslims - the West is in disarray as to what steps should be taken to counteract these inherent threats. However, some clear minds are beginning to speak up about the need for the West to unite and change the rules internationally. John Reid, the former British Defense Secretary, has called for sweeping changes to international law, including the Geneva Convention, to counter the threat of global terrorism. He has stated that the legal grounds for conducting pre-emptive strikes is inadequate in the "current climate of suicidal terrorists", as are the laws to prevent genocide and internal repression. He expressed his fears that unless changes to international law are made, countries would be hamstrung in countering terrorist threats that are intent on killing on a huge scale utilizing weapons of mass destruction. He suggested that the Geneva Conventions dealing with the treatment of prisoners of war ought to be revised, because when those rules were agreed upon in the nineteenth century it could not be envisaged that they would not apply in the world of the twenty-first century war against terrorism - a war which is not conventional warfare between states but an asymetric war against terrorists who do not recognize rules or conventions. He emphasized that while the West felt constrained by those civilized rules, the barbaric terrorists do not recognize them, and when weapons of mass destruction fall into their hands they will have no compunction or restriction in using them.[4]

Brendan Bernhard, who reviewed Oriana Fallaci's book on Islam in Europe, *The Force of Reason* asks, following Fallaci, whether Muslim immigration to Europe and the West was not part of a conspiracy to undermine Christian culture there in the first place, in view of the stunning fact that 20 million (now more than 30 million in the meantime) Muslims converged on Europe in a mere three-decade period? How did it grow from a position of an insignificant number of guest immigrants, to that of threatening the entire continent? How could the most popular name for a baby boy in Brussels be Muhammed? Is it true that Muslims plan to build in London a mammoth mosque that can accommodate 40,000 Muslim worshippers? (That project which was earmarked to rise on the site of the London 2012 Olympics has in the meantime been scuttled.) Who is to take responsibility for the fact that Amsterdam and Rotterdam are approaching a Muslim majority population? How is it, asked Fallaci, that in Europe, which was saved twice by the Americans, and the Bosnian Muslims who were saved once again in 1999, Muslims "learn" that one is sent to Heaven if one hates America and to hell if one hates Muslims? Bernhard summarizes Fallaci's book with several insightful points worth mentioning which are partly descriptive of the way she sees history, partly castigatory towards the Western intelligentsia who fail to see what is developing before their eyes, and partly admonishing fellow Westerners to wake up before it is too late:

> Fallaci recalls that already in 1972 the Palestinian terrorist leader George Habash told her that the aims of the Arabs went much farther than Israel: they intended to "wage war against America and Europe" and to ensure that henceforth there would be no peace for the West. He revealed to her that the Arabs would advance gradually, step by step, along years and decades until they expand across the entire planet. While at first she thought that he was only referring to terrorism, she later realized that he also meant a cultural war, a demographic war and a religious war, all geared to take over Europe from its citizens via the devices of immigration, fertility and high birth, and thereafter the multiculturalism that generates Islamization. When one observes today the tremendous effort deployed by Muslim nations to precipitate that process on the one hand, and the soft responses of the West in the face of that onslaught, one has to wonder whether we are witness to the Muslim future being realized before our eyes.[5]

History is not re-written only by Muslims. Some Europeans have initiated the re-writing of history books for their school children with a view of the extirpation of "American influence" and its link to the universal fight against Muslim terrorism, this, at a time when France and its likes (at least until the ascendance of Nicolas Sarkozy to power in May 2007) have wished to distance themselves, and proclaim their desire to accommodate Muslims (thus ignorantly, or in excessive denial, inadvertently supporting their invasion of the European continent). Given historical experience, it might have been expected that Europe would cooperate fully with America in their common fight against the same radical Muslim enemy. While that position certainly holds true for Great Britain (at least until the ascendance of Gordon Brown to power in August 2007), which continues to be America's staunch ally, other countries, notably

France when under Chirac, and to a lesser extent Merkel's Germany, Prodi's Italy and Zapatero's Spain, would rather perpetuate their multilateralism and blame the US for the problems of Europe of today, while ignoring the role of the US in rescuing them on two occasions from the yoke of totalitarianism. This is relevant to the situation set out in the chapters above inasmuch as a distant Europe that criticizes the US for its courageous single-handed stand against Muslim terrorism, instead of collaborating with it, will also inevitably fail to counter the Muslim menace against its very European and Judeo-Christian character and will eventually succumb to Muslim attacks on its shores.

A school textbook designed to give pupils in France and Germany a common vision of postwar history is coloured by anti-Americanism, according to one of the historians who wrote it. Guillaume Le Quintrec said that the book, *Histoire / Geschichte,* contained "unashamedly pro-European ideology" and an underlying distrust of the United States. But he noted that German historians had fought to prevent their French counterparts from introducing an even harder anti-American line into the book. "They got us to tone it down", said M. Le Quintrec, who led the French team of historians that was hand-picked under the Chirac government. "Otherwise, it would have been even worse from a British point of view". The Franco-German textbook, now published, was ordered in 2003 by President Chirac of France and Gerhard Schroder, then the German Chancellor. They wanted to strengthen ties by eliminating differences in the perception of history. "The patriotic cult of victory has given way to a universal demand to remember the victims of the war", the work states. The US and the USSR are presented as broadly equivalent in moral terms during the Cold War. Both were engaged in an arms race described as "the balance of terror" and both sought to "impose themselves by an omnipresent propaganda" that involved "gross exaggerations and simplifications". It is interesting to speculate how those authors would have tackled the issue of "exaggeration and simplification" had the US let the Communists march through Germany, France and the rest of Europe and not counter-balanced their threat in the continent.[6]

The debate is raging in Europe as to how to approach the new Islamic phenomenon in the West, and country by country pragmatic solutions are being sought. Countries of the Muslim periphery - like Canada and Australia, where Muslim presence is still limited - are only beginning to experience the many incongruities between their established cultures and the cultural ethos of immigrants from Muslim countries. Give or take certain individual criminals, who will always infiltrate within the masses of decent immigrants, most of the massive human transfers to Canada and Australia over the past fifty or more years have been crowned with success, and the newcomers have become part of the multifarious social and cultural fiber which enrich those countries. Koreans, Chinese, Vietnamese, Jews to cite only a few, have experienced resounding successes for deprived and penniless refugees who integrated into society and managed to make a living, to improve their standard of living, and raise educated families whose members became useful and loyal citizens. Within almost none of them, except for the Muslims, did their previous faith or customs stand in contradiction to the local culture and almost none of them has resorted to massive violence to register those differences. By contrast, Muslim immigrant communities not only usually refrain from committing themselves to adapt to the new country, but in many cases they openly claim their aspiration to alter their countries of shelter to their tune and submit the public square to their mercy. To achieve that they are prepared not only to demonstrate, which is legitimate, but also to resort to violence, as in 2000-1 in Australia and in the revealed plots against both Canada and Australia. These are the new rules of the game that no country of immigration can accept, and this is what is likely to poison the relations between the host and guest cultures, unless stringent measures are taken to arrest present trends.

Notes

Introduction: The European and British Perspectives

1. Tony Blair, for example, who had been the champion of multiculturalism during the decade of his rule, reversed himself in his last speech in Parliament before he resigned and spoke of the need for a prevalent British culture to help assimilate Muslim immigrants.

2. For Abu Hamza's background, see *al-Ayyam* (Yemen), August 8, 1999; the *Christian Science Monitor,* September 27, 2001. Both cited by MEMRI, No. 72, October 16, 2001.

3. For this term, the combination of Islam and Kamikaze see Raphael Israeli, *Islamikaze: Manifestations of Islamic Martyrology* (London: Frank Cass, 2003).

4. For the description of those camps, see Raphael Israeli, "Islamikaze and their Significance", *Terrorism and Political Violence* 9:3 (1997), pp. 96-121.

5. <*www.al-bab.com/yemen/hamza/hamza.htm*>.

6. *Ibid.*

7. *Online Journalism, Review,* November 15, 1999.

8. *Al-Ayyam* (Yemen), August 11, 1999.

9. *Christian Science Monitor,* January 13, 1999.

10. *Daily Telegraph,* October 5, 2001.

11. *French News Agency (AFP),* February 28, 1999.

12. <*http://dsc.discovery.com/news/briefs/20010910/abroad.html*>.

13. *Middle East Times,* Issue 13, 1999. *MEMRI* 72, October 16, 2001.

14. *Al Quds al-Arabi* (London), July 21, 2001.

15. *Ibid.*

16. *Ibid.*

17. *Ibid.*, and *The Radical,* September 13, 2001. Both in MEMRI 72, October 16, 2001.

18. Terminology is evasive and ambiguous for a reason. The original *Muhajirun* are those who migrated with the Prophet Muhammed from Mecca to Medina in AD 622. In modern times it has come to signify those Muslims who emigrate from what they term as "Unbelieving societies", including their own Muslim countries that are ruled by tyrants who do not respect the *Shari'a* laws. Exactly like the Prophet and his Companions who had migrated from heretic Mecca to establish a society of Believers in Medina, present-day *Muhajirun* equate their act with his, which lends an aura of sanctity to their migration from an ostensibly Islamic land to the land of the Unbelievers. In the London context, the move might signify that the Muslim immigrants are clustering there like the Prophet in Medina in order to build a base and use it to launch an attack on their home countries. The Muslims who left India upon its partition in 1947

to find refuge in the newly created-Muslim country of Pakistan were also dubbed *Muhajirun*. This variety of possible interpretations lends multiple meanings to the term.

19. *The Observer,* August 13, 1995; and *Intelligence Newsletter,* No. 295, September 19, 1996. Both cited by *MEMRI* No. 73, October 24, 2001.
20. *Daily Mirrror,* September 7, 1996.
21. *Al-Ahram Weekly,* October 1, 2001.
22. *Executive Intelligence Review, September 4,* 1998.
23. *Al-Ahram Weekly,* October 1, 2001.
24. *Mail on Sunday,* November 12, 1995.
25. *<http://artsweb.bham.ac.uk/bmms/sampleissue>*, January, 2001, cited by *MEMRI* 73, October 24, 2001.
26. *AFP*, cited by *Al-Hayat al-Jadida* (Palestinian Authority), October 10, 2001.
27. See website cited in *MEMRI* 73, October 24, 2001.
28. *Ibid*. Incidentally, the details remind one of the camps in Afghanistan described in Israeli, "Islamikaze and their Significance".
29. *Ibid.*
30. *CNSNews.com*, May 24, 2000.
31. *Middle East Intelligence Bulletin,* November 2000, citing Milan's *// Giornale,* October 14, 2000.
32. Irfan Hussein, "The Battle for Hearts and Minds", *Dawn Weekly,* October 6, 2001.
33. *Periscope Daily Defense News Capsules,* September 4, 1996.
34. *Roz al-Yussuf* (Egypt), September 13, 1999.
35. *Al-Ahram Weekly,* November 19, 1999.
36. *CNSNews.com*, May 24, 2000.
37. *Al-Ahram Weekly,* November 19, 1999.
38. *La Republica,* Italy, August 24, 1998.
39. *<www.terrorism.com/_trectforum5/000004b5.htm>*.
40. *Los Angeles Times,* October 14, 2001.
41. *<http// artsweb.bham.ac.uk/bmms/sampleissuejanuary2001.asp>*.
42. *Ibid.*
43. *BBC News,* October 14, 2000.
44. For those fiery speeches and the reactions to them by unsuspecting Britons, see *The Times,* September 9, 1996; and *The Guardian,* September 9, 1996.
45. Of course, the Five Pillars of Islam *(arkan)* are slightly different (Statement of Faith, Prayer, Fast, Alms and Pilgrimage), but in the parlance of fundamen talist Muslims *tawhid* and *da'wa* often take precedence.
46. *<www.almuhajiroun.com/islamictopics/islamicissues/jihad.htlm>*.
47. *The Mercury,* cited in *<http://artsweb.bham.ac.uk/bmms/sampleissues>*, January 2002.
48. *Le Monde,* September 9, 1998.
49. *The Jerusalem Post,* May 30, 2000.
50. *AFP*, September 14, 2001.
51. *<www.almuhajiroun.com/press_releases/index.html>*.
52. *<www.obm.clara/net/shariacourt/fatwa/fa5.html>*.
53. Michael Binyon, "Prince pitches for religious tolerance", *The Times,* May 5, 2006.
54. "The clash of civilisations is currently on hold", *Copenhagen Post Online,* April 20, 2006, *<http://www.cphpost.dk/get/95174.html>*.
55. *Ibid.*

56. *Ibid.*
57. "In a new biography, Denmark's Queen Margrethe II says Islam should be challenged", *Copenhagen Post Online,* 14 April2005, <*http://www.cphpost.dk/get/87253.html*>.
58. Nicola Woolcock and Sean O'Neill, " Once a friendly Christian, he now backs the bombers : Two faces, two converts - two Muslim extremists in Britain", *The Times,* April 24, 2006.
59. *Ibid.*
60. *Ibid.*
61. Nicola Woolcock and Dominic Kennedy, "What the neo-Nazi fanatic did next: switched to Islam, Two faces, two converts - two Muslim extremists in Britain", *The Times,* April 24, 2006.
62. *Ibid.*
63. *Ibid.*
64. Kevin Sullivan, "British Slow to Recognize Threat of Terrorism: London Bombings Couldn't Have Been Prevented, Report Says", *Washington Post,* May 11, 2006.
65. *Ibid.*
66. *Ibid.*
67. "French prisons are teeming with Muslims", was a headline reported on *IslamOnline.net* (Paris, June 19, 2005). Iranian-French researcher Farhad Khosrokhavar said in his recently published book *Islam in Prisons* that Muslims make up some 70 percent of a total of 60,775 prisoners in France. As ethnicity-based censuses are banned in France, he said, complexion, names and religious traditions like prohibition of pork indicate that Muslims constitute an overwhelming majority in prisons. Khosrokhavar also noted that Islam has become a sought-after religion in prisons with a Christian prisoner asking prison authorities to provide him with halal meat almost on a weekly basis.
68. Raphael Israeli, "Anti-Semitism Revived: The Impact of the Intifada on Muslim Immigrant Groups in Western Democracies", *Jerusalem Viewpoints,* The Jerusalem Center for Public Affairs, No. 455, June 2001, pp. 1-8.
69. Multiple examples of those happenings in October-December 2000, see *ibid.*
70. See Daniel Pipes, "Fighting Militant Islam, Without Bias", *City Journal,* Autumn 2001, <*http://www.city-journal.org/htm/41/fightingmilitant.html*>.
71. For a basic survey of the Muslims in Europe, see the now outdated work of Gilles Keppel, *La Revanche de Dieu.*
72. *Wall Street Journal, Europe,* November 15, 2001. See also the article by Jocelyne Cesari, in *MSANews,* June 6, 2000, who drew a wide background of the situation of the Muslims in Western Europe.
73. *Associated Press,* cited by *Ha'aretz,* June 20, 2002.
74. Bernard Lewis, "The Roots of Muslim Rage", *Atlantic Monthly,* September 1990.
75. Sharon Sadeh, "The London Bridge is Collapsing", *Ha'aretz,* September 30, 2005.
76. *Ibid.*
77. *Ibid.*
78. *The Spectator,* March, 2002.
79. Jamie Glazov, *FrontPageMagazine, 1* March, 2006. Significantly, not only the participants in this debate were referring to what in their eyes had become a major problem in the West, but this can also be related to the out-of-proportion growth of crime among the Muslim immigrants in Europe and Australia.

80. Incidentally, the Hamas Charter speaks in its Articles 17-18 about the role it assigned to Muslim women, consisting primarily of "manufacturing men" for the next generation of *jihad* fighters. See "The Charter of Allah: the Platform of the Islamic Resistance Movement (Hamas)", in Raphael Israeli, *Fundamentalist Islam and Israel* (The University Press of America), 1993, pp. 144-5.

81. See 78.

82. For *dhimmi* (the "protected people" under Islam, with their subservient legal, economic, political and cultural status) and especially for the *dhimmi* state of mind which obliges individuals and nations to submit to their persecutors, see Bat Ye'or's, *The Dhimmi* and *Islam and Dhimmitude.*

83. See 78.

84. *Ibid.*

85. Jamie Glazov, *FrontPageMagazine,* March 7, 2006.

86. Dr Fatihi, *al-Ahram al-Arabi,* Cairo, October 20, 2001.

87. Brendan Bernhard, "White Muslim: How to Become a Muslim, From LA to New York, to *jihad*?", *LA Weekly*, December 2, 2004.

88. Brendan Bernhard, "White Muslim: How to Become a Muslim, From LA to New York, to Jihad?", *LA Weekly,* December 2, 2004.

89. George Weigel, "Europe's Two Culture Wars", *Commentary,* May 2006. *Ibid.*

90. *Ibid.*

91. *Ibid.*

92. *Ibid.*

93. *Ibid.*

94. George Weigel, "Europe's Two Culture Wars", see 89.

1. Subversive Terminology and Lethal Rhetoric

1. See video clip in <*www.pbs.org/frontlineworld/stories/iran/vid22001.html*>. An edited version of the programme was broadcast on PBS in America, in early 2005 which deleted the gruesome bits. An interview was given by Kokan in the *Washington Post.*

2. Anne Nivat, "Voyage au Pays des Fous d'Allah", *Le Point 1727,* October 20, 2005, p. 30.

3. *Le Point,* 1727, October 20, 2005, p. 37.

4. Raphael Israeli, "Anti-Semitism Revived: The Impact of the Intifada on Muslim Immigrant Groups in Western Democracies", *Jerusalem Viewpoints,* The Jerusalem Center for Public Affairs, No. 455, June 2001, pp. 1-8.

5. Interview of Sheikh Qaradawi, "Homosexuals Should Be Punished Like Fornicators But Their Harm Is Less When Not Done in Public", *Al-Jazeera,* June 5, 2005. Interview taped on video by *MEMRI*, No. 1170, June 5, 2006.

6. *Ibid.*

7. Citations collected by Christophe Deloire, "La France, Terre de Djihad", *Le Point* 1727, October 20, 2005, p. 37.

8. *Ibid.* p. 38.

9. *Ibid.* p. 38.

10. *Ibid.*

11. Muhamed Yacine Kassab, *Les Divisions Musulmanes face a l'Hegemonie Occidental* (Paris: Editions Lanterne, February 2005).

12. *Le Point*, October 20, 2005, p. 38.

13. Shaykh Muhammed Hisham Kabbani, *The Globalization of Jihad: From Islamist Resistance to War agaisnt the West* (The Islamic Supreme Council of America, 2006).

14. "Moderate Muslims afraid to speak out", *Copenhagen Post Online,* November 16, 2004. <*http://www.cphpost.dk/get/83602.html*>.
15. "Moderate Muslims afraid to speak out", *Copenhagen Post Online,* November 16, 2004. *http://www.cphpost.dk/get/83602.html.*
16. "Moderate Muslims meet PM", *Copenhagen Post Online,* February 16, 2006 <*http://www.cphpost.dk/get/93958.html*>.
17. "Muslim MP speaks out against fundamentalists", *Copenhagen Post Online,* February 2, 2006. <http://www.cphpost.dk/get/93729.html>.
18. Andrew Norfolk, "Our followers 'must live in peace until strong enough to wage jihad'", *The Times,* September 8, 2007.
19. Craig Whitlock, "Architect of New War on the West: Writings Lay Out Post-9/1 1 Strategy of Isolated Cells Joined in Jihad" *Washington Post,* May 23, 2006.
20. *Ibid.*
21. *Ibid.*
22. *Ibid.*
23. James Arlandson, "Six million African Muslims leave Islam per year", *The American Thinker* - May 5, 2006. <*http://americanthinker.com/comments. php?comments_id=5044*>.
24. *Ibid.*
25. *Ibid.* This whole web-based conversation is fascinating, although the numbers are exaggerated. Though the scroll bar indicates that it is a long dialogue, much of the file includes threads or comments at the bottom.
26. Laurent Murawiec, "Deterring those who are already dead?", a talk at BESA, the Center of Strategic Studies at Bar-Ilan University, Israel, May 25, 2006.
27. Laurent Murawiec, "Deterring those who are already dead?", a talk at BESA, the Center of Strategic Studies at Bar-Ilan University in Israel, May 25, 2006.
28. *Ibid.*
29. Surya Bhattacharya and Christopher Maughan, "They skipped class to visit prayer hall: Views upset other Muslim classmates", *Toronto Star,* June 6, 2006.
30. *Ibid.*
31. *Ibid.*
32. Isabel Teotonio and Jessica Leeder, "Islamic volunteer preached to youth", *Toronto Star,* June 5, 2006. <*http://www.thestar.com/NASApp/ cs/ ContentServer?pagename=thestar/Layout/Article_Type1&call_pageid=9713 58637177&c=Article&cid=l 149460818243*>.
33. Martin Bright, "Let's shed more light on Islam", *The Observer,* August 28, 2005.

2. Muslim Ambivalence Regarding World Terrorism

1. *Al-Quds al-'Arabi,* London, February 9, 2002, in *MEMRI* 344, February 10, 2002.
2. See Bat Ye'or's classic books on this theme: *Islam and Dhimmitude: Where Civilizations Collide* (Fairleigh Dickinson University Press, Madison 2002); *The Decline of Eastern Christianity Under Islam, (* Fairleigh Dickinson University Press, Madison, 1996); and *Eurabia* (Fairleigh Dickinson University Press, Madison, 2005).
3. *Ibid.*
4. Raphael Israeli, "From Bosnia to Kosovo: the Re-Islamization of the Balkans", Ariel Center for Policy Research, No. 109, November 2000, pp. 1-33.

5.   Martin Bright, "Observer Liberty Watch campaign", *Observer,* July 21, 2002.
6.   *Ibid.*
7.   *Ibid.*
8.   Paul Lashmar and Chris Blackhurst, *The Independent,* September 16, 2001.
9.   *Ibid.*
10. *Ibid.*
11. Martin Bright, *The Observer,* August 14, 2000.
12. Rod Liddle, "Muslims at Alton Towers", *Spectator,* 8 July 2006.
13. *Ibid.*
14. Martin Bright, *ibid.*
15. *Ibid.*
16. *Ibid.*
17. An account from visitors to the IslamExpo is present at <http://anglolibyan.blogspot.com/2006_07_01_archive.html>.
18. *Al-Sharq al-Awsat* (London), 19 July, 2003.
19. Gabriela Keller, *Spiegel Online,* June 30, 2006 in Damascus. *<http://service.spiegel.de/cache/internationaVO,1518,424505,00.html>.*
20. Yaakov Lappin, "UK Islamists: Make Jihad on Israel: British Jihad group declares 'Israel is cancer, Islam is answer', calls on followers to carry out holy war", *Ynetnews.com.* July 2, 2006.
21. Elsa McLaren, "Muslim protestor guilty of soliciting murder", *Times Online,* January 5, 2007.
22. "Cartoon protester guilty of race hate", *Daily Telegraph,* February 1, 2007.
23. Ian Evans, "Cartoon protest Muslim is guilty of soliciting murder", *The Times,* March 8, 2007.
24. *Arab News* (Saudi Arabia), and *Saudi Gazette,* March 7, 2006. Both cited by *MEMRI* 1118, March 19, 2006.
25. "Under the Veil", *The Times,* June 15, 2006.
26. *Ibid.*
27. Michael Binyon and Philip Webster, "Leaders' forum against violence", *The Times,* July 5, 2006.
28. Alexandra Frean and Rajeev Syal, "Muslims in Britain - a story of mutual fear and suspicion", *The Times* - July 5, 2006.
29. *Ibid.*

3. Down Under: The Land of the Fair Go

1.   *The Australian,* January 24, 2002.
2.   *Ibid.*
3.   Sharon Lapkin, "Infiltrating Australian Academe", *FrontPageMagazine,* April 4, 2004.
4.   *Ibid.*
5.   *Ibid.*
6.   "Sydney Bomb Plot Link to Race Riots", *<http://news.ninemsn.com.au/article.aspx?id=92998>,* March 27, 2006.
7.   David King, "Terror suspect bought electricity grid map", *The Australian,* May 2, 2006, *<http://www.news.com.au/story/0,10117,18993062-421,00.html>.*
8.   Ultimately, Faheem Khalid Lodhi, also known as Abu Hamza, was convicted by the NSW Supreme Court Jury in June, 2006 to 20 years in prison for three out of four charges of terrorism, with a 15 year no-parole time and minimum 15 years to be served. That was the first conviction under a new set of stricter anti-terrorism laws enacted by Australia in 2005. The three charges he was convicted for were:

a. Preparation for terrorist attack, by seeking information for the purpose of constructing explosive devices - carrying a maximum sentence of life in jail.

b. Seeking information and collecting maps of the Sydney electricity supply system and possessing 38 aerial photos of military installations, in preparation for terrorist attacks, maximum sentence 15 years in jail.

c. Possessing terrorist manuals detailing how to manufacture poisons detonators, explosives and incendiary devices - maximum sentence 15 years in jail.

9.   Simon Freeman, "Architect plotted terror strike on Australia", *Times Online,* June 19, 2006.

10. Martin Chulov, "I'd chop up PM, claims 'terrorist'", *The Australian,* April 28, 2006, <*http://www.theaustralian.news.com.au/story/0,20867,18954200-2702,00.html*>.

11. *Ibid.*

12. David King, "Rebuke for Terror Suspects", *The Australian,* June 1, 2007.

13. *Ibid.*

14. Richard Kerbaj, "Muslim groups lash new peak council", *The Australian,* May 5, 2006, <*http://www.theaustralian.news.com.au/story/0,20867,19030946-2702,00.html*>.

15. Richard Kerbaj, "Muslim groups lash new peak council", *The Australian* - May 5, 2006 <*http://www.theaustralian.news.com.au/story/ 0,20867,19030946-2702,00.html*>.

16. Linda Morris "Pell challenges Islam - o ye, of little tolerant faith", *Sydney Morning Herald,* May 5, 2006, <*http://www.smh.com.au/news/national/pell-challenges-islam-o-ye-of-little-tolerantfaith/2006/05/04/l 146335872951.htm*>.

17. *Ibid.*

18. Lowell Ponte, "Islamists Down *Under",* *FrontPageMagazine.com,* April 24, 2006.

19. Miranda Devine, "Wolves in sheep's clothing on an extremist Islamic mission", April 23, 2006, <*http://www.smh.com.au/news/miranda-devine/wolves-in-sheeps-clothing-on-an-extremist-islamic-mission/2006/04/22/114S344316019.html*>.

20. *Ibid.*

21. *Ibid.*

22. *Ibid.*

23. *Ibid.*

24. *Ibid.*

25. *Ibid.*

26. *Ibid.*

27. See Ponte, cited above.

28. See the cover of Raphael Israeli, *Islamikaze: Manifestations of Islamic Martyrology* (London: Frank Cass, 2003).

29. Lowell Ponte co-hosts a national radio talk show Monday through Friday 6-8 PM Eastern Time (3-5 PM Pacific Time) on the Genesis Communications Network. Internet Audio worldwide is at *GCNlive.com.* The show's live call-in number is 1-800-259-9231. A professional speaker, he is a former Roving Editor for *Reader's Digest.* See also note 19.

30. *Australia/Israel Review (AIR),* Vol. 31, No. 6, June 2006, pp. 4, 40.

31. Khalid Hasan, "French Al Qa'ida man tells all to interrogator", *Daily Times* (Pakistan), October 21, 2004, <*http://www.dailytimes.com.pk/default.asp?page=story_21-10-2004_pg7_44*>.

32. *Ibid.*
33. Mark Chipperfield, "Put Cook back on curriculum, Canberra tells schools", *Daily Telegraph,* July 6, 2006.
34. Audrey Hudson, "New Zealand ousts 9/11 hijacker's pal", *The Washington Times,* June 26, 2006.
35. Geoff Gumming, "Pilot with 9/11 links found in NZ", *New Zealand Herald,* June 10, 2006.
36. *Ibid.*
37. *Ibid.*
38. Richard Kerbaj," Radical Islamic conference at uni", *The Australian,* 29 June 2006.
39. *Herald Sun,* May 18, 2007.
40. Ben Packham, "Muslims slam 'divisive' test", *Font size,* May 19, 2007.
41. Matthew Schulz, "Radicals can't be stopped", *Herald Sun,* January 9, 2007.
42. Sally Neighbour, "Islamic cleric preaching 'hate'", *The Australian,* October 2, 2007.
43. *Ibid.*
44. *Ibid.*
45. Richard Kerbaj, "Young Somalis lured home by al-Qu'ida", *The Australian,* 2 October, 2007.

4. Under The US Shadow: The Canadian Case

1. "Teacher witnessed transformation of some bomb-plot suspects", *Canadian Broadcasting Corporation,* June 8, 2006.
2. Gregory Bonnell, "Court victory for Khadr: Ottawa wrong to deny passport, but can revoke it once it's granted", *The Canadian Press,* June 10, 2006.
3. Sandro Contenta, "Web used to lure terror suspects: Notorious hacker inspired extremists", *Toronto Star,* June 17, 2006.
4. *Ibid.*
5. *Ibid.*
6. Surya Bhattachariya, Nasreen Ghulamhussein and Heba Aly, "The ties that bind 17 suspects: 'They represent the broad strata of our community,' the RCMP says", *Toronto Star,* June 4, 2006.
7. "Potential terrorists hiding in Canada", *Jerusalem Post* (citing *Associated Press),* May 30, 2006.
8. Posted by Ezra Levant on the website of his journal on March 29, 2006.
9. Daniel Pipes, "Enforce Islamic Law in Canada?", *New York Sun,* September 27, 2005.
10. *Ibid.*
11. "Geography and Identity: Canadian Citizenship Test", *Spiegel Online,* May 9, 2006, <*http://service.spiegel.de/cache/intemational/0,1518,415238,00. html*>.
12. Raphael Israeli, *Islamikaze: Manifestations of Islamic Martyrology* (London: Frank Cass, 2003), esp. pp. 336, 377-8, 382.
13. Surya Bhattacharya, Heba Aly and Graham Eraser, "Imam's visit raises concerns", *Toronto Star,* June 24, 2006.
14. *Ibid.*
15. *Ibid.*
16. Doug Struck, "17 Suspected Terrorists Arrested in Canada", *Washington Post,*

June 3, 2006.

17. Dan Darling, "The international connections of the Canadian cell", The *Weekly Standard,* June 19, 2006, issue 38.
18. *Ibid.*
19. *Ibid.*
20. See Chapter One of Raphael Israeli, *Islamikaze.*
21. *Globe and Mail,* June 20, 2006.
22. Rod Mickleburgh, "Harper defends Canadian diversity: PM rejects calls to curb immigration, calls open society 'our greatest strength'", *Globe and Mail,* June 20, 2006. <*http://www.theglobeandmail.com/servlet/story/RTGAM. 20060620.wxharper20/BNStory/National*>.
23. *Ibid.*
24. "Muslim experts warn about drawing conclusions", *CTV - Canadian Press,* June 5, 2006, <*http://www.ctv.ca/servlet/ArticleNews/story/CTVNews/ 20060605/experts_terrorism_060506/20060605?hub=Canada*>.
25. *Ibid.*
26. "Muslim experts warn about drawing conclusions", *CTV - Canadian Press,* June 5, 2006.
27. "Muslim leaders want 'radical elements' removed", *CTV.ca News,* June 10, 2006.
28. Arnold Beichman, "Is Canada Next? Time to look at the northern border", *Weekly Standard,* June 3, 2006.
29. Francis Harris, "Canada bomb charges", *Daily Telegraph,* June 6, 2006.
30. "Canada to fund global anti-terror finance tracking group HQ", *Ha'aretz* (citing AP), July 8, 2006.
31. Stephen Brown, "Terror in Toronto" *FrontPageMagazine.com,* June 5, 2006.
32. *Ibid.*
33. *Ibid.*
34. Stewart Bell, "Nevermind foreign terrorists, why is Canada growing its own extremists?", *National Post,* June 3, 2006.
35. *Ibid.*
36. *Ibid.*
37. *Ibid.*
38. *Ibid.*
39. "Islamic Congress Criticizes Government For Not Funding Research on 'Home Grown Effects of Imported Extremism'" *Media Communique,* Canadian Islamic Congress, June 3, 2006.
40. Joel Mowbray, "Why Strike Canada?", *Washington Times,* June 13, 2006.
41. Daniel Pipes, "The Khadrs: Canada's First Family of Terrorism", *New York Sun,* March 16, 2004.
42. Patrick Poole, "Canadian Blindness to Terror" *FrontPageMagazine.com,* June 6, 2006.
43. *Ibid.*
44. Colin Freeze, "Raid officers learned about Muslim traditions", *Globe and Mail,* June 6, 2006.
45. Christie Blatchford, "Ignoring the biggest elephant in the room", *Globe and Mail,* June 5, 2006.
46. *Ibid.*
47. Press Release by The Canadian Coalition for Democracies, Ottawa, 10 September, 2007.
48. Craig Offman, "Canadians with faces veiled can vote. Masks are a no go;

Elections Canada Ruling Senseless, Politicians Say", *NationalPost,* September 8, 2007.

49.   *Ibid.*

5. The Land Shifts in Asia

1.   Olivier Weber, "Madrasas: les Fabriques d'Islamistes", *Le Point* 1727, October 20, 2005.

2.   Kyai Haji Abdurrahman Wahid, "Extremism Isn't Islamic Law", *Washington Post,* May 25, 2006. The author serves as senior adviser and board member to *LibFor All Foundation,* an Indonesian- and US-based nonprofit organization that works to reduce religious extremism and terrorism.

3.   Robert Spencer, *FrontPageMagazine.com* May 26, 2006.

4.   *Newsweek International,* 20 February, 2001.

5.   This term was coined by the author in his article "Islamikaze and their signif icance", *Journal of Terrorism and Political Violence* (January 1997), signifying that the so-called "suicide bombers" developed by Muslim fundamentalists are not really bent on self-immolation as a suicidal type, but on the elimina tion of the enemy amidst self-sacrifice if necessary - an action that brings them typologically close to the Japanese *Kamikaze* of the World War II Pacific War.

6.   Michael Sheridan, "War on terror hides brutal crackdown on Muslims", *The Sunday Times,* July 22, 2007. *<http://www.timesonline.co.uk/tol/news/world/asia/china/article2116123 .ece>.*

7.   *Ibid.*

8.   *Ibid.*

9.   Colin Rubenstein, JCPA Jerusalem Letter No. 436, 15 August, 2000.

10.   Rubenstein, op. cit.

11.   See M. Yegar, *Between Integration and Secession* (Maryland: Lexington Books, 2004).

12.   *Ibid.*

Summary: Muslim Rewriting of the Past and Charting of the Future

1.   *Arab News* and *The Saudi Gazette,* March 7, 2006. Both cited by *MEMRI* No. 1118, March 20, 2006.

2.   *<www.memri.org/bin/opener_latest.cgi?ID=SD113506>.* Reported by MEMRI 1135, April, 6, 2006.

3.   See for a selection of these texts, Andrew Bostom (ed.), *The Legacy of Jihad: Islamic Holy War and the Fate of Non-Muslims* (New York: Prometheus Books, 2005), especially Part III.

4.   John Reid, "21st Century Warfare, 20th Century Rules", at the Royal United Service Institute think-tank in London, *Daily Telegraph*, April 4, 2006.

5.   Brendan Bernhard, "Oriana Fallaci asks: Is Muslim Immigration to Europe a Conspiracy?", *LA Weekly,* March 15, 2006.

6.   Adam Sage, "Overmighty, overfed and over here: a Gallic textbook view of the Americans", *The Times,* May 4, 2006.

Bibliography

Newspapers, News Agencies, Websites and Magazines

Al Ahram al-Arabi
Al-Ahram Weekly
*Al-Ayyam (*Yemen)
*Al-Hayat al-Jadida (*Palestinian Authority*)*
Al –Jazeera
*Al-Quds al-Arabi (*London)
*Al-Sharq al-Awsat (*London)
(The) The American Thinker
*Arab News (*Saudi Arabia)
Associated Press (AP)
(The) Australian
Australia-Israeli Review
BBC News
Canadian Broadcasting Corporation (CBC)
(The) Canadian Press
Christian Science Monitor
City Journal
CNSNews.com
Commentary
Copenhagen Post Online
Daily Mirror
Daily Telegraph
*Daily Times (*Pakistan)
Dawn Weekly
Executive Intelligence Review
Font Size
French News Agency (AFP)
FrontPageMagazine
*(Il) Giornale (*Italy)
*Globe and Mail (*Toronto)
(The) Guardian
*Ha'aretz (*Tel Aviv)
Herald Sun
http://artsweb.bham.ac.uk/bmms/sampleissue

http://dsc.discovery.com/news/briefs/20010910/abroad.htlm
http://news.ninemsn.com.au/article.aspx?id=92998
http://www.smh.com.au/news/miranda-devine/wolves-in-sheepsclothing-on-an-
    extremist-islamic-mission/2006/04/22/114s344316019.html
(The) Independent
Intelligence Newsletter
IslamOnline.net (Paris)
(The) Jerusalem Post
*Jerusalem Letter (*Jerusalem Center for Public Affairs)
Jerusalem Viewpoints
(Le) Monde
MSANews
LA Weekly
Le Point
Los Angeles Times
Mail on Sunday
*MEMRI (*Middle East Media Research Institute)
(The) Mercury
Middle East Intelligence Bulletin
Middle East Times
MSANews
National Post
New York Times
New York Sun
New Zealand Herald
Newsweek International
(The) Observer
Online Journalism
Periscope Daily Defense News
(The) Radical
(La)Republica (Italy*)*
*Roz al-Yussuf (*Egypt)
Saudi Gazette
(The) Spectator
Spiegel Online
(The) Sunday Times
Sydney Morning Herald
(The) Times
Times Online
Toronto Star
Wall Street Journal
Washington Post
The Washington Times
www.al-bab.com/yemen/hamza/hamza.htm
www.almuhajiroun.com/islamictopics/islamic issues/jihad.html
www.almuhajiroun.com/pressreleases/index.html
www.pbs.org/frontlineworld/stories/iran/vid22001.html

www.obmclara/net/shari'acourt/fatwas/fa5.html
www.terrorism.com/rectforum5/000004b5.html
(The) Weekly Standard
*Western Standard (*Alberta),
Ynetnews.com

Books

Bat Ye'or, *The Dhimmi,* Fairleigh Dickinson University Press, Madison, NJ.

Bat Ye'or, *Islam and Dhimmitude: Where Civilizations Collide,* Fairleigh Dickinson University Press, Madison, NJ, 2002.

Bat Ye'or, *The Decline of Eastern Christianity Under Islam,* Fairleigh Dickinson University Press, Madison, NJ, 1996.

Bat Ye'or, *Eurabia,* Fairleigh Dickinson University Press, Madison, 2005.

Bostom, Andrew (ed), *The Legacy of Jihad: Islamic Holy War and the Fate of the Non-Muslims,* Prometheus Books, New York, 2005.

Cesari, Jocelyne , "Muslims in Europe", *MSANews,* 6 June, 2000.

Israeli, Raphael, *Fundamentalist Islam and Israel,* University Press of America, 1993.

Israeli, Raphael, *Islamikaze: Manifestations of Islamic Martyrology,* London: Frank Cass, 2003.

Israeli, Raphael, *The Islamic Challenge in Europe,* Transaction Publishers, New Brunswick, NJ, 2008.

Kabbani, Sheikh Muhammed Hisham, *The Globalization of Jihad: From Islamist Resistance to War Against the West,* The Islamic Supreme Council of America, 2006.

Kassab, Muhammed Yacine, *Les Divisions Musulmanes Face a l'Hegemonie Occidentale,* Paris, Editions Lanterne, 2005.

Keppel, Gilles, *La Revanche de Dieu, Paris.*

Khosrokavar, Farhad, *Islam in Prisons,* Paris, 2006.

Yegar, Moshe, *Between Integration and Secession,* Lexington Books, Maryland, 2004.

Articles

Arlandson, James, "Six Million African Muslims Leave Islam per Year", *The American Thinker,* 5 May, 2006.

Beichman, Arnold, "Is Canada Next? Time to Look at the Northern Border", *Weekly Standard,* 3 June, 2006.

Bell, Stewart, "Nevermind Foreign Terrorists, why is Canada Growing its own Extremists?", *National Post* , 3 June, 2006.

Bernhard, Brendan, "White Muslim: How to become a Muslim, From LA to NY, to Jihad?" *LA Weekly,* 2 December, 2004.

Bernhard, Brendan, "Oriana Fallaci askes: Is Muslim Immigration to Europe a Conspiracy?", *LA Weekly,* 15 March, 2006.

Bhattacharya, Surya and Christopher Maughan, "They Skipped Class to Visit Prayer Hall: Views Upset Other Muslim Classmates", *Toronto Star,* 6 June, 2006.

Bhattacharya, Surya, Nasreen Ghulamhussein and Heba Aly, ""The Ties that Bind 17 Suspects: they Represent the Broad Strata of our Society, the RCMP says", *Toronto Star*, 4 June, 2006.

Bhattacharya, Surya, Heba Aly, and Graham Eraser, "Imam's Visit Raises Concerns", *Toronto Star*, 24 June, 2006.

Binyon, Michael, "Princes Pitches for Religious Tolerance", *The Times*, 5 May, 2006.

Binyon, Michael and Philip Webster, "Leaders' Forum Against Violence", *The Times*, 5 July, 2006.

Blatchford, Christie, "Ignoring the Biggest Elephant in the Room", *Globe and Mail*, 5 June, 2005.

Bonnell, Gregory, "Court Victory for Khadr: Ottawa Wrong to Deny Passport, but Can Revoke it Once it is Granted", *The Canadian Press*, 10 June, 2006.

Bright, Martin, "Observer Liberty Watch Campaign", *The Observer*, 21 July, 2002.

Bright, Martin, "Let's Shed More Light on Islam", *The Observer*, 28 August, 2005.

Brown, Stephen, "Terror in Toronto", *FrontPageMagazine.com*, 5 June, 2006.

"Canada to Fund Global anti-Terror Finance Tracking Group HQ", *Ha'aretz*, 8 July, 2006.

"Cartoon Protester Guilty of Race Hate", *Daily Telegraph*, 1 February, 2007.

Chipperfield, Mark, "Put Cook Back on Curriculum, Canberra Tells Schools", *Daily Telegraph*, 6 July, 2006.

Chulov, Martin, "I'd Chop up PM, claims terrorist", *The Australian*, 28 April, 2006.

Contenta, Sandro, "Web Used to Lure Terror Suspects: Notorious Hacker Inspired Extremists", *Toronto Star*, 17 June, 2006.

Darling, Dan, "The International Connections of the Canadian Cell", *The Weekly Standard*, 19 June, 2006.

Deloire, Christophe, "La France, Terre de Jihad", *Le Point*, 20 October, 2005.

Devine, Miranda, "Wolves in Sheep's Clothing on an Extremist Islamic Mission", 23 April, 2006, *http://www.smh.com.au/news/miranda-devine/wolves-in-sheepsclothing-on-an-extremist-islamic-mission/2006/04/22/114s344316019.html*.

Evans, Ian, "Cartoon Protest Muslim is Guilty of Soliciting Murder", *The Times*, 8 March, 2007.

Fatihi, Dr, *Al Ahram al-Arabi*, 20 October, 2001.

Frean, Alexandra and Syal Rajeev, "Muslims in Britain—a Story of Mutual Fear and Suspicion", *The Times*, 5 July, 2006.

Freeze, Colin, "Raid Officers Learned about Muslim Traditions", *Globe and Mail*, 6 June, 2006.

Freeman, Simon, "Architect Plotted Terror Strike on Australia" *Times Online*, 19 June, 2006.

"Geography and Identity: Canadian Citizenship Test", *Spiegel Online, 9 May, 2006*.

Glazov, Jamie, *FrontPageMagazine*, 7 March, 2006.

Gumming, Geoff, "Pilot with 9/11 Links Found in NZ", *New Zealand Herald,* 10 June, 2006.

Harris, Francis, "Canada Bomb Charges", *Daily Telegraph,* 6 June, 2006.

Hasan, Khalid , "French al-Qa'ida Man Tells All to Interrogator", *Daily Times,* 21 October, 2004.

Hudson, Audrey, "New Zealand Ousts 9/11 Hijacker Pal", *The Washington Times,* 26 June, 2006.

Hussein, Irfan, "The Battle for Hearts and Minds", *Dawn Weekly,* 6 October, 2001.

"Islamic Congress Criticizes Government for not Funding Research on Home Grown Effects of Imported Extremism", Media Communique by the Canadian Islamic Congress, 3 June, 2006.

Israeli, Raphael, "The Charter of Allah: The Platform of the Islamic Resistance Movement", in Israeli, Raphael, *Fundamentalist Islam and Israel,* University Press of America, 1993.

Israeli, Raphael, "Islamikaze and their Significance", *Terrorism and Political Violence,* 9:3, 1997, pp. 96-121.

Israeli, Raphael, "Anti-Semitism Revived: The Impact of the Intifadah on Muslim-Immigrant Groups in Western Democracies", *Jerusalem Viewpoints,* The Jerusalem Center for Public Affairs. No 455, June 2001.

Israeli, Raphael, "From Bosnia to Kosovo: The Re-Islamization of the Balkans", in *The Islamic Challenge in Europe,* Transaction Publishers, New Brunswick, NJ, 2008.

Keller, Gabriela, "In Damascus", *Spiegel Online,* 30 June, 2006.

Kerbaj, Richard, "Muslim Groups Lash New Peak Council", *The Australian,* 5 May, 2006.

Kerbaj, Richard, "Radical Islamic Conference at University", *The Australian,* 29 June, 2006.

Kerbaj, Richard, "Young Somalians Lured Home by al-Qa'ida", *The Australian,* 2 October, 2007.

King, David, "Terror Suspect Bought Electricity Grid Map", *The Australian,* 2 May, 2006.

King, David, "Rebuke for Terror Suspects", *The Australian,* 1 June, 2007.

Lapkin, Sharon, "Infiltrating Australian Academe", *FrontPage Magazine,* 4 April, 2004.

Lappin, Yaakov, "UK Islamists: Make Jihad on Israel, British Jihad Group Declares: Israel is Cancer, Islam is Answer, Calls of Followers to Carry out Holy War", *Ynetnews.com ,* 2 July 2006.

Lashmar, Paul and Chris Balckhurst, *The Independent,* 6 September, 2001.

Levant, Ezra, on the Website of his journal, *Western Standard (*Alberta), 29 March, 2006.

Lewis, Bernard, "The Roots of Muslim Rage", *Atlantic Monthly,* September 1990.

Liddle, Rod, "Muslims at Alton Towers", *Spectator,* 8 July, 2006.

McLaren, Elsa, "Muslim Protestor Guilty of Soliciting Murder", *Times Online,* 5 January, 2007.

Mickleburgh, Rod, "Harper Defends Canadian Diversity: PM Rejects Calls to Curb Immigration, Calls Open Society Our Greatest Strength", *Globe and Mail, 20 June, 2006.*

"Moderate Muslims Afraid to Speak out", *Copenhagen Post Online,* 16 November, 2004.

"Moderate Muslims Meet the Prime Minister", *Copenhagen Post Online,* 16 November, 2004.

Morris, Linda, "Pell Challenges Islam- O Ye, of Little Tolerant Faith", *Sydney Morning Herald,* 5 May, 2006.

Mowbray, Joel, "Why Strike Canada?", *Washington Times,* 13 June, 2006.

Murawiec, Laurent, "Deterring Those who are Already Dead?", a talk at the Center for Strategic Studies of Bar Ilan University, Israel (BESA), 25 May, 2006.

"Muslim Experts Warn about Drawing Conclusions", *Canadian Press,* 5 June, 2006.

"Muslim Leaders Want Radical Elements Removed", *CTV News*, 10 June, 2006.

"Muslim MP Speaks out Against Fundamentalists", *Copenhagen Post Online,* 2 February, 2006.

Neighbour, Sally, "Islamic Cleric Preaching Hate", *The Australian,* 2 October, 2007

Nivat, Anne, "Voyage au Pays des Fous d'Allah", *Le Point,* 1727, 20 October, 2005.

Norfolk, Andrew, "Our Followers Must Live in Peace Until Strong Enough to Wage Jihad", *The Times*, 8 September, 2007.

Offman, Craig, "Canadians with Faces Veiled can Vote; Masks Are a No Go; Elections Canada Ruling Senseless, Politicians say", *National Post ,* 8 September, 2007.

Packham, Ben, "Muslims Slam Divisive Test", *Font Size,* 19 May, 2007.

Pipes, Daniel, "Fighting Militant Islam, Without Bias", *City Journal,* Autumn, 2001.

Pipes, Daniel, "Enforce Islamic Law in Canada?", *New York Sun,* 27 September, 2005.

Pipes, Daniel, "The Khadr's: Canada's First Family of Terrorism", *New York Sun,* 16 March, 2004.

Ponte, Lowel, "Islamists Down Under", *FrontPageMagazine*, 24 April, 2006.

Poole, Patrick, "Canadian Blindness to Terror", *FrontPageMagazine.com,* 6 June, 2006.

"Potential Terrorists Hiding in Canada", *Jerusalem Post,* 30 May, 2006.

Qaradawi, Sheikh Yussuf, "Homosexuals Should be Punished like Fornicators, but Their Harm is Less when not Done in Public", *Al –Jazeera,* June 5, 2005.

Reid, John, "21st Century Warfare, 20th Century Rules", lecture at the Royal United Service Institute Think-tank in London, *The Daily Telegraph,* 4 April, 2006.

Rubinstein, Colin, *Jerusalem Letter,* No 436, Jerusalem Center for Public Affairs, 15 August, 2000.

Sage, Adam, "Overmighty, Overfed and Over Here: A Gallic Textbook View of the Americans", *The Times,* 4 May, 2006.

Sullivan, Kevin, "British Slow to Recognize Threat of Terrorism: London Bombings Couldn't Have been Prevented, Report Says", *Washington Post, 11* May, 2006.

"Sydney Bomb Plot Link to Race Riots", 27 March, 2006 *http://news.ninemsn. com.au/article.aspx?id=92998.*

Sadeh, Sharon, "The London Bridge is Collapsing", *Ha'aretz,* 30 September, 2005.

Schultz, Matthew, "Radicals Can't be Stopped", *Herald Sun,* 9 January, 2007.

Sheridan, Michael, "War on Terror Hides Brutal Crackdown on Muslims", *The Sunday Times,* 22 July, 2007.

Spencer, Robert, *FrontPageMagazine.com,* 26 May, 2006.

Struck, Doug, "17 Suspected Terrorists Arrested in Canada", *Washington Post,* 3 June, 2006.

"Teacher Witnessed Transformation of some Bomb-plot Suspects", *Canadian Broadcasting Corporation (CBC),* 8 June, 2006.

Teotonio, Isabel and Jessica Leeder, "Islamic Volunteer Preached to Youth", *Toronto Star,* 5 June, 2006.

"The Clash of Civilizations Is Currently on Hold", *Copenhagen Post Online,* 20 April, 2006.

"Under the Veil", *The Times,* 15 June, 2006.

Wahid, Abdurrahman, "Extremism Is not Islamic Law", *Washington Post,* 25 May, 2006.

Weber, Olivier, "Madrasas: Les Fabriques d'Islamistes", *Le Point ,* 20 October, 2005.

Weigel, George, "Europe's Two Culture Wars", *Commentary,* May, 2006.

Whitlock, Craig, "Architect of New War on the West: Writings Lay Out Post 9/11 Strategy of Isolated Cells Joined in Jihad", *Washington Post,* 23 May, 2006.

Woolcock, Nicolas and Dominic Kennedy, "What the Neo-Nazi Fanatic did next: Switched to Islam, Two Faces, Two Converts—Two Muslim Extremists in Britain", *The Times*, 24 April, 2004.

Index

For Product Safety Concerns and Information please contact our EU
representative GPSR@taylorandfrancis.com Taylor & Francis Verlag GmbH,
Kaufingerstraße 24, 80331 München, Germany

Batch number: 08153776

Printed by Printforce, the Netherlands